ULURU AND THE STAR PEOPLE

Valérie J Barrow and Alcheringa

First Published in Australia by Aurora House
www.aurorahouse.com.au

This edition published 2022
Copyright © Valérie J Barrow and Alcheringa 2022

Typesetting and e-book design: Prepress Plus | www.prepressplus.in
Cover design: Donika Mishineva | www.artofdonika.com

The right of Valérie J Barrow and Alcheringa to be identified as Author of the Work has been asserted in accordance with the Copyright, Designs and Patents Act 1988.

ISBN number: 978-1-922697-42-4 (Paperback)

All rights reserved. No part of this publication may be reproduced, stored in a retrieval system, or transmitted, in any form or by any means without the prior written permission of the publisher, nor be otherwise circulated in any form of binding or cover other than that in which it is published and without a similar condition being imposed on the subsequent purchaser.

 A catalogue record for this book is available from the National Library of Australia

Distributed by:
Ingram Content: www.ingramcontent.com
Australia: phone +613 9765 4800 |
email lsiaustralia@ingramcontent.com
Milton Keynes UK: phone +44 (0)845 121 4567 |
email enquiries@ingramcontent.com
La Vergne, TN USA: phone +1 800 509 4156 |
email inquiry@lightningsource.com

Dedication

We dedicate this work to the Clever Fellas, men, and women from the Australian Indigenous tribes, who have carefully shared their knowledge of the Creation Stories given to them through their DREAMING.

We acknowledge their cleverness, intelligence, and commitment to holding the Creation Dreaming stories without embellishment, through our past, present, and future.

Acknowledgements

A big thank you is given to my husband John, for his support and contribution to this work, and to all others mentioned in our story.

We also are truly appreciative of the professional work given by the team from Aurora House, namely Linda Lycett, Marion Lucy Thomas, Donika Mishineva, and Meredith Anderson.

Contents

Acknowledgements — v
Foreword — xi
Introduction — xv

PART ONE – METAPHYSICS AND SCIENCE — 1

One.	The Story of Uluru	3
Two.	The Start of My Mission	7
Three.	Kariong/Gosford	19
Four.	The Sacred Alcheringa Stone	29
Five.	The Reunion at Canyonleigh	37
Six.	Alcheringa and Andromeda Val	43
Seven.	Reflections After Channelling	55
Eight.	The Beginning	61
Nine.	Uluru from a Scientific Point of View	63
Ten.	Interview with John Barrow	77
Eleven.	Giants of Earth	85
Twelve.	History of Humans on Earth	95
Thirteen.	Another Challenge for the Scientists	101
Fourteen.	DNA	107

PART TWO – THE MYSTERY SCHOOL — 115

Fifteen.	The Mystery Schools	117
Sixteen.	Before the Fall of Atlantis	121
Seventeen.	The Golden Age	131
Eighteen.	Junk DNA	139
Nineteen.	The Fifth Dimension	147

Twenty.	Venus	155
Twenty-One.	The Hathors—Gods of Egypt	159
Twenty-Two.	Star People from Mars	165
Twenty-Three.	The Annunaki	169
Twenty-Four.	Lemuria	175
Twenty-Five.	Pre-Atlantis Wars	181
Twenty-Six.	Asteroid Belt	191
Twenty-Seven.	Star People Experiencing Family Life	197
Twenty-Eight.	Moldavite	203
Twenty-Nine.	Your Thoughts and Your World	209
Thirty.	666	219
Thirty-One.	Creation and the Journey	223
Thirty-Two.	World Peace and Planetary Healing	227
Thirty-Three.	History and Karma	233
Thirty-Four.	End of the Dinosaurs and Coming of the Moon	239
Thirty-Five.	The Journey of Souls	243
Thirty-Six.	Consciousness	251
Thirty-Seven.	Roles of the Sea and Land Creatures	257
Thirty-Eight.	Sacred Geometry	261
Thirty-Nine.	The Extinct Vanara	267
Forty.	Good Living, Food, and Common Sense	275
Forty-One.	Names and Forms	279
Forty-Two.	The Dark-haired, Dark-eyed Peoples	283
Forty-Three.	Sacred Dance	289
Forty-Four.	The Role of Trees	293
Forty-Five.	The Phoenix	299
Forty-Six.	Hanuman	303
Forty-Seven.	Yowies	307
Forty-Eight.	Frustrations and Knowing your Purpose	313
Forty-Nine.	Sister Planets	317
Fifty.	The Opening of Star Gates	321
Fifty-One.	What World Will We Create?	325
Fifty-Two.	The Earth Mother as a Live Being	331
Fifty-Three.	Atlantean and Light Societies	335
Fifty-Four.	Ice Ages	339
Fifty-Five.	Sanat Kumara and the 144,000	341
Fifty-Six.	The Dingo	345

| Fifty-Seven. | Pyramids | 351 |
| Fifty-Eight. | The Journey of the Foetus | 355 |

PART THREE – LEADING TO A NEW WORLD ... AND THE STAR PEOPLE WHO WANT TO HELP US — 359

Fifty-Nine.	Summary	361
Sixty.	Visiting Sai Baba	371
Sixty-One.	The Event	379
Sixty-Two.	Personal News for Me from Alcheringa	391

| Clairvoyant reading for Valérie Barrow | 397 |
| About Valérie Barrow (the Medium) | 403 |

Foreword

by Dino Parisotto – HydroGeologist – Managing director of Earth2Water

Having a hot cuppa and warm discussion about Star People and distant galaxies with Valérie and John Barrow seems like a familiar scene out of a popular science fiction movie. We have just a small snip of Earth's history in our texts, whilst the ancient history covering the planet's formation and Dreamtime stories seems to be embedded in our Aboriginal culture and those gifted with psychic regression skills. Aboriginal stories handed down over many generations about the ancestors, connection to country, location of food and water sources, and lifechanging events such as drought, floods, food scarcity, and even asteroid impacts provide the backdrop for survival.

Valérie seeks to bridge the gap between science and metaphysics. I believe they are also two sides of the one coin and working together seems to be the key to resolve apparent differences. The famous quote by Nicola Tesla, 'everything is energy, frequency, and vibration,' sounds very familiar when listening to Aboriginal elders discussing artwork and the energy in nature. Valérie reminds us that our soul consciousness is not bound by time and space constraints, and all rests within the universal oneness.

Our living Earth is interconnected like a spider's web, from an individual raindrop to its circulation in the hydrosphere, to the journey around the sun and Milky Way galaxy, each in an inter-relationship with another. Likewise, Valérie courageously brings to the table her insightful messages of our inseparable connection to the Earth, and our broader cosmic origins.

As a scientist, the concept that the earth is the only planet with intelligent life seems a very limited viewpoint, given the billions of stars and even more planets and as many other galaxies. Most people on this planet believe in intelligent beings from other star systems like the Pleiades, whilst Aborigine Dreamtime stories and legends involve the adventures and complexities of star beings. Valérie's story of the Rexegena and the star beings that volunteered to help the Earth offers a bigger perspective and a history with a cosmic plan overseen by an advanced neighbouring intergalactic family.

Everything that exists on Earth comes from somewhere else, whether it is from the remains of stars or microorganisms on interstellar ice or rocky asteroids that hit our earth.

As a scientist, I feel we will make significant advancements when unseen influences are just as important as the visible. For example, the recent advances in analytical laboratory technics can peer into the nature of a tiny water molecule, and come to understand the multitude of dissolved chemicals, pollutants, and isotopic fingerprints that indicate the evolution of water, its origins, interactions, and even age, over eons. Water is constantly recycled and purified in nature, and within the universe, like our essence, it is never destroyed but transformed.

As a practicing environmental scientist for almost thirty years, my understanding of Earth, nature, pollution impacts and, in particular, water science, is deepening but is still just the tip of the iceberg. Science does play an important role in our environmental stewardship and handing over a healthy planet to our children. We need to tread lightly on this earth. Our connection to our spirit and soul consciousness is an important part of the healing and protection of the planet from which we all depend upon for survival. The elements in our bodies and food sources come from the elements on our earth. We need to protect and clean our earth to enable greater health and wellbeing for all life forms, including the plants, animals, and our great ocean, which supports all.

Valérie mentions the catastrophic historical events where Star People have used asteroids to wipe out the dinosaurs. Evidence of asteroid impacts have been studied by geologists in Australia and all around the planet. Valérie's spirit guide informs us that Uluru comes from the stars (an asteroid that hit the ancient Euromanga sea approximately 65 MA), which caused the unique evolution of local plants, animals, and the landscape in Australia. The arrow of time in our scientific world moves forward in straight lines; however, we can peer into the past to interpret past events such as continental drift, climate change, or species evolution with our sophisticated technology and analytical laboratories, which provide insights into the microscopic nature of our environment.

From the microscale, such as the tiny molecules in a drop of water, to the macroscale and detection of distant galaxies, there is constant movement and energy of astronomical proportions. Our earth is part of a solar system and spiral galaxy that is connected to other galaxies. Scientists are expanding their consciousness with modern technologies. Similarly, a new consciousness is emerging from separateness to oneness and interconnectedness of all things. Our human bodies are connected to the earth and the universe, just like a young child is dependent upon its mother for survival and nourishment.

We are not separate from our environment, and what is out there eventually becomes inside. Consciousness has also evolved as we understand the bigger picture and our journey through time and space on this earth. We are spiritual beings in earth bodies, anchored to the earth as it orbits the sun and the galaxy and phenomenal speeds.

Valérie's efforts to bring harmony and healing back to the earth and to the human race is a blessing. A message of oneness and balance is a wonderful gift in this time of great change.

Valérie's story of Alcheringa highlights the bridge between science and metaphysics.

Introduction

My name is Valérie Judith Barrow and I have been asked by the Ancient Creator Ancestor Spirit, Alcheringa, to write a continued story about the monolith in the centre of Australia—known by the ancient indigenous people as Uluru.

Uluru was named Ayers Rock when white people came to settle on this ancient land.

Alcheringa tells us he has resided on this earth from its creation. Now it's time for him to tell us about the Star People and how they were appointed to restore this beautiful earth to its original creation.

Please note that the Star People, including myself and my husband John, deeply respect the talent and knowledge that the Indigenous people of Australia have. The Star People confirm they are the first created humans, meaning Light men, and they are the oldest living race on Earth.

I have been initiated many times in my life, enabling an understanding of important creation stories of the Australian Indigenous people and their Dreaming. My knowledge of Uluru comes from the 'Alcheringa Sacred Stone' (wrapped in paperbark and tied with string belonging to the Indigenous people). I shared my sacred stone work with my Aboriginal friend, Gerry Bostock, who helped me, over many years, to understand the Indigenous customs and cultures. He confirmed their Ancient Dreaming Story of Uluru coming from the stars. Gerry was an elder, healer, filmmaker, and storyteller/writer and gave lectures at university.

And so, as a Star Person, I hope that the existence of Uluru and its Magic, such as how it came from the stars, can be understood by everyone. The Indigenous people know and tell the stories I'm about to tell but in different ways. I now want to explain in a scientific way. But it is still the same information.

John and Valérie Barrow

Two soulmates walking through time, from history to the future and back.

EVERYTHING IS HAPPENING AT ONCE. WE LIVE IN A HOLOGRAM, AS QUANTUM PHYSICS WILL EXPLAIN—IT IS JUST A MATTER OF CONSCIOUSNESS WHERE YOUR INTENT AND FOCUS ARE, AND WHERE TIME AND DISTANCE DO NOT EXIST.

I experienced my future self, from 6,000 years in the future, one night beside my bed, surrounded by a hologram of light. She looked the same as humans, although about seven feet tall. She was very happy and pleased to show herself, and said her name was Andromeda Val, although names are not important to them; it is the feel of the energy that is important. All beings from the Star worlds communicate telepathically, or mind to mind. That is why my role is to receive messages the first Tuesday of the month, when agreement is allowed for my voice box 'to be borrowed' by the Star People.

I am a channeler.

PART ONE

METAPHYSICS AND SCIENCE

One

The Story of Uluru

This information was given to me by Alcheringa, dating back to 1994 when he introduced himself to me and I was temporarily gifted a sacred Alcheringa Stone, which belongs to the original people of Australia. The Australian Indigenous People were the first humans on Earth—that is another story to come later.

Uluru, as an asteroid, was sent to destroy the dinosaurs on earth by the Star People; they were destroying the atmosphere and had to be eliminated.

The surrounding geological areas were affected by the aftermath of the Fall of Atlantis at a much later time. A message from the Star person known as St. Germaine gives an extraordinary message of what happened on Earth. Plato spoke of the same event happening in 'One Day and One Night of Misfortune'. It is at the end of this book.

The Ancient Australian Indigenous people have dreaming stories that tell of Earth's creation and evolution. Now the Star People want to give more detail. They are coming from the place of Angelic Realm (pronounced Ongelic Realm) and wish it to be known that the Earth planet was created by them to replace a previous planet that existed in the same place in our solar system. Maldek had been attacked and destroyed and was now part of the asteroid belt within our solar system. The Angelic Realm/Hierarchy came from Andromeda Galaxy M31.

This image of an iceberg is given to show that when Uluru landed in the Eromanga Sea it was buried and later covered with silt and mud once the sea dried out. The image gives an idea of how much of the rock is showing above the earth and how much is hidden.

The monolith came as a fiery ball. It had been 'charged' by the Star People, giving it extra strength, so that it would not break when it landed. Other large rocks, as bombs, were strategically placed around the planet to catastrophically change the planet's atmosphere and earth.

It was the end of the era of giants upon this earth.

The 'charged' bombs caused the end of the giants' era, but the charged rocks (which were part of destroyed planets within the solar system) had been blessed with raised energy and went on to hold the new energy coming onto earth, leading gradually to the fifth dimension frequency and vibration, which led to the Golden Age.

They were virtually recognised as healing rocks. The Indigenous people of the new human race came to understand that and honour the rocks.

Alcheringa tells us He resides at Uluru and has done so ever since our planet was created.

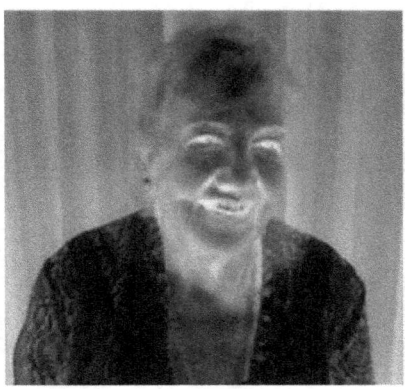

Image for the Cosmic Consciousness Conference held at Uluru 11, 12, and 13 January 2020

Alcheringa posted his image on my computer overnight. He used my image and then added the male image with dark skin, long beard, and light shining from inside the body, suggesting androgyny. He gave a long channelling through me on stage, which you will find at:
https://www.valeriebarrow.com/?p=5241

Cosmic Consciousness Conference – 13 January 2020

Now he is saying there is much more to his story...

The Star People were advised by the Hierarchy/Angelic Realm that the dinosaurs had been illegally created by genetic engineering without permission from the Source of all Creation on Earth and had to be destroyed. They were wrecking the atmosphere by eating too much of the foliage and their dead bodies were slow to die back into ash within the soil. Thus, the atmosphere, which had been so carefully created by the Hierarchy from Andromedan Galaxy, was being wrecked. Planet Earth had to be changed back to its original form.

In the Star Worlds there exists a Leonine race, within the Canis Major Constellation, who were called upon to assist. My husband, John, experienced a spontaneous memory of the warrior Cat people. He was in charge of a mission that came from Sirius. The reptilians, Dinoids and Draco had created the dinosaurs with illegal genetic engineering and believed they owned the planet. They fought back. The Cat people were the 'cosmic cops' and used meteors like artillery and laser beams that could petrify creatures into fossil instantly; some of the artillery used were planetoids, from the asteroid belt, so big it could shatter a planet.

Our book *Starlady*, part two, has much more detail about when Valérie was holding the Sacred Alcheringa Stone, wrapped in paperbark, and tied with string; the Stone belonged to the Indigenous people, and they say it came from the stars. It was first published as *The Book of Love, by a Medium*. The story of the Cat people is included in our book, *Alcheringa, When the First Ancestors were Created*.

Leonine Race, Image drawn by Simon Weir

artist unknown

Valérie has been advised by Andromeda Val that all the animal, birds, etc. on Andromeda, within the Adonis Race, are white, and they are all friendly. The people also have white hair and respect one another. Consensus exists and there is never a weapon raised to sort out a problem.

Their place of living is not unlike Earth itself with hills, mountains, valleys, lakes, rivers, flowers, trees, and fruit trees. The colours are beautiful.

Two

The Start of My Mission

I had been learning from my unseen mentor, White Eagle, from the stars, and then my mission began when Whitley Strieber came to Sydney, Australia in the late 1980s. Harry Miller promoted Whitley to speak on television, and had one metre square posters pasted on all the walls of the square garbage bins in the Sydney CBD, so that everywhere you looked you seemed to be looking at an alien. I have come to call them Star People. But at the time, I saw the book in our local bookshop and was terrified. I told myself not to be silly and purchased the book and read it. I lived through every terrifying moment that Whitley wrote about. I decided I also would seek help from a hypnotherapist. I saw myself laying on an operating table with a huge light above me, as if in an operating theatre. I was surrounded by the small alien beings, with some very tall beings there also. I was shaking badly, but then I realised it was something I had agreed to and that there was no need for fear. They were taking samples of human body cells to examine and find cures for human diseases. So, I pulled away from the memory and I knew there was more to learn.

Whitley Strieber wrote more about his experiences in his book, *Transformation: The Breakthrough*. And in a similar way, that is what

happened to me. If I was asked if I would choose to have these so-called 'alien experiences.' I would say emphatically YES. It was very trying for the first two years, but it was an initiation. I feel very blessed that I have been one of many that have been chosen—and I feel blessed and enlightened that I agreed to the experience long before I came here.

The Star People asked me to write, while holding an Indigenous Australian Sacred Stone wrapped in paperbark and tied with string.

I had the sacred Alcheringa Australian Aborigine Stone, wrapped in paperbark, lent to me for two years. The Indigenous people say it came from the stars. It surrounded me with a bright white light when I sat with it. My consciousness was raised so that the stone seemed to speak to me. It came from the planet Sirius, and **I felt I knew it.** The Stone was metaphysically connected to Uluru.

On 5 September 1994, twenty-two people came to our property, named Alcheringa, to paint new symbols that they had been asked by 'upstairs' to take to Uluru and sing the image vibration into the earth.

On that same day, we had the Star People come in a lightship surrounded by cloud in acknowledgement of our work. We felt they were happy with our work. The property had already been named Alcheringa when I accidentally knocked a copy of the Australian edition of the Oxford Dictionary to the floor. As I lifted it, it fell open and the word Alcheringa caught my eye. The next word was Alchemy, the transmutation of base metals into gold. I thought how similar the two words were.

Alcheringa, one of the few Australian Indigenous words in the dictionary was described as the 'golden age' in some tribes, when the first ancestors were created. Alcheringa is an Ancient Creator Ancestor who introduced himself to me while I was holding the Sacred Stone. He began to teach me about the Australian Indigenous Ancestors, and their customs and culture.

The Start of My Mission

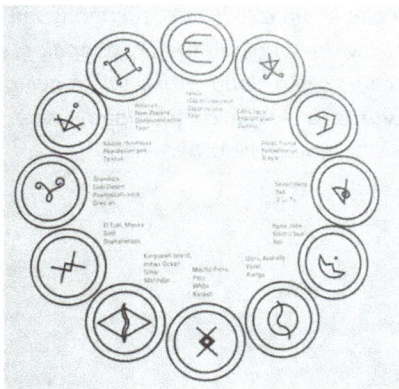

These are the symbols we painted to take to Uluru. They were received in meditation by Rob Sampson, Rosemary Butterworth, and Carol Birch and then asked by the Council of Light, Star People to paint them. Twenty-two people came to Canyonleigh, N.S.W. to help with the work.

Painting symbols at Canyonleigh

As the day wore on, we had a beautiful display of a starship in the sky, surrounded by cloudships and smaller ships sending us a message of approval. There are more images on my website, https://www.valeriebarrow.com/, if you click on the article 'Cloudships and Starships at Canyonleigh.' There is an album with great photos, which were taken by John Butterworth.

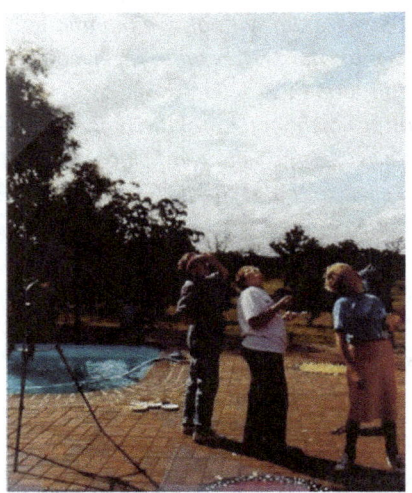

You can begin to see our reaction when we saw the whole of the sky changing. We could see a cloud with a tail, moving towards us—while all the clouds were going the other way!

A clearer picture of the cloudship on the right of the tree. You can easily see the starship hiding inside, and a slight cloud mist trailing behind.

In the photo **below,** on the left of the tree, are smaller scout ships, off the larger mothership, forming the image of a 'Serpent in the Sky.' The starship looks clearer on the right, with a little dot just above it, near the top of the tree.

The Serpent in the Sky was the perfect acknowledgement from the Star People when we were planning to take the symbols to Uluru. After we arrived there on 5 September 1994, we were all initiated into the rainbow serpent energy, well known to the Indigenous people of Australia.

This next photo shows the Serpent image eventually dispersed and we could see the smaller scout ships off the large starship. You can see them looking like black dots in the sky. The mother starship is on the right just out of sight. We agreed, what a marvellous blessing for our work. There is a much more complex list of photos on my website.

Black dots in the sky

A friend was visiting Uluru and she took this picture. You can see what looks like a rainbow serpent energy in the photo on the left. The rainbow serpent energy is very important in the Dreaming stories told by the Indigenous first people of Australia.

    As I have said, the Star People asked me to write while holding the Indigenous Australian Sacred Stone. The magic stone spoke to me the through psychometry—the gift of holding something and reading the ancient record held within it. I was advised it was like I was holding a little piece of Uluru itself.

My diary, based around holding the sacred Alcheringa Stone, was published as The Book of Love, and is now republished in Part Two of the Starlady book.

The manuscript was written like a diary. I took it to the Ashram in Puttaparthi in India and our group was called for a private interview by the Avatar, Sri Sathya Sai Baba, in India in 1995. He took the manuscript and placed it on his knees, turning page after page. He said he would continue to assist me with it, but it was not finished. He blessed the manuscript—but telepathically asked me to use it with discernment for the time being, because at the time, talk of Star People was not readily accepted even when He tried to speak of them. He trained people like me to speak of the Star People after he left his earth body. Now I know it is time to speak openly—no holding back—about my personal 'Close Encounters.' He blessed the manuscript and, remember, he said it wasn't finished.

Three years before, I had visited the Ashram when He manifested a green diamond ring and placed it on my finger. He said when I looked in the ring, He would be there. Even though I was standing in front of Sai Baba we were still communicating mind to mind. He said the diamond had been created by the Star People the same way humans made industrial diamonds. I treasured the ring and kept it in a special jewel box when working, until a friend called me one day and said 'Valérie, Sai Baba came to me in a dream last night and asked me to tell you to wear the ring all the time.' So, I do. I realised the blessed ring had introduced me to an initiation to prepare me for the work I was being asked to do. I receive monthly transmissions from Cosmic Sai Baba, through the ring, which have been going online for ten years at www.cosmicsaibaba.com. The ring comes from the stars, which I know now comes from our next Galaxy Andromeda M31.

After I received the ring, I had become very ill and had returned home in a wheelchair from India. I was never afraid; I knew I was being looked after all the way home. When I recovered, I felt renewed, uplifted, and ready for my continued mission with increased awareness.

These drawings are interesting—Lt Grey went on to be the Governor of South Australia. My husband John Wynford Grey Barrow is related to this man George Grey, on his mother's side.

These cave paintings are from the area of the Glenelg River in Kimberly, Northern Australia. These photographs are taken from the book, "Journals of Two Expeditions of Discovery in North-West and Western Australia 1837, 1838, & 1839", by Lt. Grey. Lt. Grey led an expedition and came across these cave drawings. The local Aborigines know these figures as the Wandjina. Again, just as has been found all over the planet, notice the same halo-looking objects over their heads. Also, notice that other than the halo-type object, the eyes are the dominate features of these beings.

The ancient image in orange has a very similar likeness to Sri Sathya Sai Baba in his recent life. The drawings were made long before that. The true God Beings from the Source of all Creation say they come into a race—looking like the race—so that they can teach and uplift the consciousness of a planet. And so there will not be fear in the people they have come to assist.

This is what Sri Sathya Sai Baba has done, saying, 'I am God, and I come as a man, to take man back to God.'

Sri Sathya Sai Baba

You will note his hands and part of his face are blue; that has happened since he personally blessed the photo. The writing is "Why fear when I am here." – Baba. The V of Light in his hand is for me.

Then came Andromeda Val, and Cosmic Sai Baba asked me to continue messages with her from Andromeda M31.

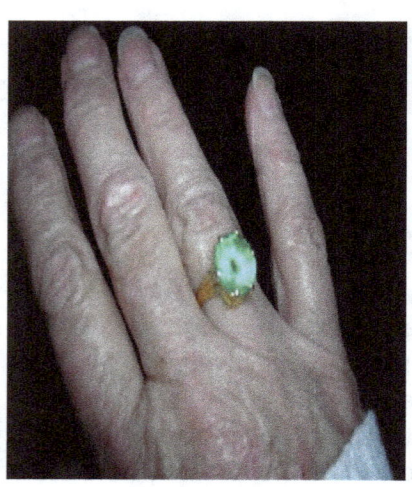

The green ring Sathya Sai Baba gave to me—first placing it on the 4th finger of my left hand and then removing it and placing it on my right hand. I saw that it was made by Star People, similar to how humans can make industrial diamonds on earth. They are calling them Prema Baba rings—ready for the next incarnation of Sri Sathya Sai Baba.

The image below is a LIGHT BODY, which is what we all are—like Sathya Sai Baba is now—only on Earth, we are still cloaked with an Earth body. He has always said, 'His Life is His message.' He achieves a great deal more now from the 4th dimension with His devoted assistants still in the 3rd dimension, than He could when limited wearing an Earth body.

INNER VIEW

Sri Madhusudan Naidu is a medium that Cosmic Sai Baba works through with no limit. You can read about Cosmic Sai Baba and his achievements since he left his body in 2011: SaiSurya@SukshmaBabaReport.Org

Exploring Australian Aboriginal Mythology and connections with the Aliens

Our dear Aborigine friend, Gerry, who first took us to the Hieroglyph site at Gosford/Kariong is, along with me, interviewed on this documentary—

along with others. I have spoken to Graham Archer, the publisher, and he says he can make copies of the DVD **below** should anybody want to purchase a copy. The cover speaks for itself. I personally never use the word 'alien' now—I much prefer the words 'Star People'.

Graham Archer – Attitude Productions/films at Tamworth N.S.W.
MOBILE: 61 2 0419 817 215 PHONE 61 2 6769 5737

Alcheringa tells us he is the CREATOR SPIRIT ANCESTOR of EARTH and is well known to most of the Indigenous people of Australia, who know they are the first humans and the oldest living race, and know their ancestors came from the stars. Alcheringa resides at Uluru in the centre of Australia. I was first introduced to him when holding the sacred Alcheringa Stone back in 1994.

He asked me telepathically if He could borrow my voice box. He used to awaken me, usually when my husband was away on business, and then with my agreement he would practice walking with me and talking through me with a strong, dignified male voice. He taught me many things. It was as though I was going to a university already operating in the universe. I have come to understand that it is a Universe City operating from Andromeda and that many people are being taught from there all over our galaxy, the Milky Way.

This image below is the book cover that continues from holding the Sacred Alcheringa Stone. Sri Sathya Sai Baba has personally blessed this manuscript also. He called it 'Ah...the booku.' This is what he was referring to when he said the first diary manuscript was not finished.

Three

Kariong/Gosford

John and I lived at Canyonleigh, NSW, for eighteen years. The area is in the Southern Highlands, and it is a major Stargate. Alcheringa told us the Alcheringa Crystal was directly in line with Uluru—and here, in the first photo, you can see a faint blue line that appeared in the photo of the Alcheringa Crystal, leading straight out of the front gate and on to Uluru. We believe it is also a Song Line all the way to Giza and the pyramids in Egypt.

The second photo of the Alcheringa Crystal shows the extended light in the same direction 'out the gate of the property—and eventually onto Uluru and the Pyramids at Giza.'

The Alcheringa Crystal

This is not to be confused with the Alcheringa Stone, wrapped in paperbark, and tied with string, that I worked with in 1994. I never opened the package nor took a photo of it, out of respect to the sacredness of it belonging to the Indigenous people. The Sacred Alcheringa Stone has now been returned safely to its correct place in the red centre of Australia, closer to Uluru.

The Sacred Stone was originally found in the early days of European settlement, inside Cave Hill known as the Seven Sisters, GLOWING, 100kms distance from Uluru. As mentioned earlier, it was first found by an Afghani cameleer who tried to give it to the local Indigenous people, but they were frightened of it. It remained with his family for 150 years until it finally found its way to me.

The 80kg crystal was given to us by our dear friend, Gerry, and placed over a 'point of light' coming from crystals within the depths of the earth at the property at Canyonleigh.

Gerry, the Indigenous healer, first took us to see the Egyptian-like glyphs at Kariong in 1995—the same year the avatar Sri Sathya Saia Baba blessed my diary, *The Book of Love*, which was written when I was holding the Sacred Alcheringa Stone and when Alcheringa introduced himself to me.

It was then that many people came to me, wanting to know more about the Glyphs at Kariong and how Gerry, our friend Helen, and myself had experienced the memory together, of being Star People off a huge mothership named Rexegena with 50,000 Star People onboard. It was attacked and only ninety survived. Those ninety were the ones that were back on Earth to tell their story.

Thousands have remembered the story since the book was written. It was written and later blessed by Sri Sathya Sai Baba in 2001 in India. It was the same time as the Twin Towers were attacked at New York City, U.S.A, when thousands of lives were lost.

On visiting the Egyptian Tomb at Kariong/Gosford N.S.W. and touching the Glyphs cut on the stone walls of the tomb, many people entered a spontaneous past-life memory of being Star People. They remembered travelling from the Pleiades in their magnificent mothership named Rexegena to Earth, or Mu, as the Star People called the planet. There

The Seven Sisters from the Pleiades.
There was a Grand Plan from The Hierarchy for Good known as 'The Garden of Eden, the whole Earth.' (Eden means Steppes, which is layers of consciousness taking place for it to return to its Original Plan).

had been an agreement with the reptilian race that they would leave and return the planet to its rightful owner: Andromeda M31.

Andromeda M31 was the benevolent Star People who created the planet Mu in the beginning.

The reptilian/Dinoid/Draco reneged on their agreement and attacked the huge mothership with 50,000 Star People onboard. Only ninety people survived. The Grand Plan had been to establish a settlement of Light and raised consciousness in this dark corner of the Milky Way Galaxy. This happened on Earth about 900,000 years ago.

When Gerry, the origine healer from Bundjalung, first took us to the Kariong Tomb Glyphs, he asked if Alcheringa would come to speak with us. He did. He said the Glyphs would mean many things to many people, that the stories would be shared, and he would release the keys.

The Egyptian Tomb held another story from ancient times when Egyptians/Phoenicians used to visit ancient Australia to learn from the origine people of Australia. The Egyptians/Phoenicians knew of the story that Alcheringa had given them about the creation of the first humans. There is a story recorded in other writings on the tomb walls of when two brother princes from Egypt came with a team to visit the ancient land of Australia about 4,000 to 4,500 thousand years ago. One of the princes was bitten by a snake and sadly died. It is customary for all Pharaohs, or their families, to be buried with great ceremony on their own land, and mummification is carried out for the body to be held in a sarcophagus. Attempts were made to bury the prince, mummified to the best of their ability, in the Australian foreign land.

It was near three thousand or so years later that King Tutankhamen took an armada of ships to reclaim the body of the ancient prince and return to Egypt to bury him properly.

A tomb had been prepared for their return from Australia to Egypt. Unfortunately, King Tutankhamen was accidentally killed soon after his return and was buried in the same tomb that had already been prepared for his ancestor. Interestingly, there is evidence of Australian artifacts buried in the tomb in the Valley of the Kings. There is also a belief that there are hidden rooms in that same tomb, which we believe hold the first prince's body that had been rescued from Australia.

The grandmother tree stands as guardian to the Ancient Egyptian Tomb at Kariong. Photo by Lavinia Smith-Lewis.

'Omni'—The Grandmother Tree

'Omni' (omnipresent) The Grandmother Tree artwork now hangs in Parliament House, Canberra, ACT, AUSTRALIA. The drawing had a positive energetic impact being in the hallowed halls of Parliament house, playing a part to save the land of Kariong from the developers.

Lavinia Smith-Lewis. Pretty Beach, NSW. Australia.
Graphite & Wash Drawing
Artist. Educator & Creative. Ph: 0421-669-614

KARIONG TOMB ENTRANCE

The Kariong Tomb entrance has 250 or so Egyptian/Phoenician glyphs drawn on the cave walls; our Star mentor, Alcheringa, has advised that the glyphs mean many things to many people. You can hear his message given in video at Kariong in 1995 on my Home webpage, www.valeriebarrow.com.

*Top left and right: Back entrance to ancient tomb
Middle: Glyph cleft – View from front – Quite a difficult climb
Bottom middle: Entrance from rear – View as you climb into the corridor holding about 250 glyphs carved into the stone walls. It is believed the corridor was once covered by a roof.*

There are many images of the glyphs if you search the internet under 'Gosford Glyphs, NSW'.

References

Reference is given to Steven and Evan Strong of Forgotten Origins, who have spent many years scientifically researching to prove the glyphs were and are authentic, and that the site is an Ancient Egyptian tomb. Their research was all done with respect and with the first Australians, the Indigenous people. The Strong's work with Uluru is also notable.

https://forgottenorigin.com/

Our Indigenous friend Auntie Minnie has given two objects found on the floor of the Kariong cave to trusted friends. One was a piece of jewellery. The other has been examined professionally and found to be a piece of ancient human bone. I feel it is a piece of bone dropped from the attempted mummification of the Egyptian Prince who died, and from where the so-called Mummies Tomb is held at Kariong (when collected by King Tut's entourage on his visit to Australia to collect the ancient prince's remains). King Tut knew he was an ancestor and so in my understanding, the professional genetic evaluation of the ancient bone would show a relationship between their DNA.

The King Tut journey to Australia was given to us by three separate people in regression. It is recorded in the *Starlady* book, Part One.

Hans-Dieter von SENFF 'Ancient Egyptians in Australia: The Kariong Glyphs, a Proto-Egyptian script deciphered' at: http://www.valeriebarrow.com/?p=164

Colin HAYTER eighteen-minute videos at:

https://www.youtube.com/watch?v=cPPhsNJVgHo

https://www.youtube.com/watch?v=FMK6tDedCbU

Mohamed IBRAHIM &Yousef AWYAN Two-hour, three-part video at: http://www.valeriebarrow.com/?p=538

These are good references, particularly the last one from Egyptian professionals. These are all to do with the Egyptian Royals visit. However, psychics visit the area and are aware of a special energy. They come from Cosmic Consciousness and the hieroglyphs trigger memories of a different (but similar) story of the Star People coming from Pleiades. A door was opened through the Stargate back in 1994.

And it was no coincidence that starships (UFOs), now called UAPs, showed themselves to the people of Gosford around the same time. A compass does not work properly there either. Google 'The Gosford Files' Moira McGhee and Bryan Dickeson UFO sightings 1994 and 1996.

The Out of Australia Theory: Authors, Researchers, Progressive Archaeo-Historians, Speakers, & Our Alien Ancestry Conference Founders.

As stated above, Alcheringa has said the Glyphs would mean many things to many people.

For us, it released the Star People's story of visiting nearly a million years ago on the magnificent mothership, the Rexegena, from the Pleiades, which links with the Dreaming stories told by many of the Indigenous elders. They point to the seven stars in the sky and say, 'That is where our Ancestors came from.'

Four

The Sacred Alcheringa Stone

We were unexpectedly advised by Alcheringa that this cave was where the cameleer had first found the Sacred Alcheringa Stone so long ago—it was glowing with light...

I was invited to join a young family to travel to Cave Hill, known as the Seven Sisters by the indigenous people, which is about 100km from Uluru. The father, Paul, had read the book, *Alcheringa*, about when the first ancestors were created, and felt strongly to research more. He is a gifted medium.

We travelled with a group led by a white ranger; normally it would be led by Indigenous rangers, but there was a funeral. It would have been hard to recognise the cave, and when we climbed on top of it, we found the rock looked the same as Uluru with feldspar peppered through it. After the ranger led everyone through the cave, she explained how important it was to the Indigenous people who held a Dreaming Story of the 'Seven Sisters from the Pleiadean stars and how they were their ancestors.' The cave was covered with ancient drawings and was cool and serene inside. I explained to the ranger that I was a medium and asked if we could meditate in the cave after everyone left. She agreed and said she had to cook lunch but would love to have stayed as she was interested. There is a fourpart article on my website about the following.

Once Paul, after agreeing to speak with Alcheringa, settled, and the girls were still present, I invited Alcheringa to make his entrance. I called him with a song.

Alcheringa: I am here, and I am very pleased to be here ... thank you for inviting me, and I have been with you all day and it gives me great pleasure to be able to speak with you—and also my son, if you want to ask questions, I will be happy to answer any that you may ask.

There is much history here in this cave and the lady (guide) has explained many things; it has many visitations from the Indigenous people, but even before that the Star People were here. So, it is well known to us, this area.

So rather than me go on, because you do know the story of the Alcheringa and when the first humans were created, is there anything that you would like to ask?

Paul: I would like to ask—this looks to me [paintings on the ceiling] like a map of the stars. And that it is a map of the star races and the journey through the galaxies. I am just wondering if that is accurate. To me it looks like the main players are what I call the Children of Lyra, who come through the Lyra/Pleiades series and the Draco reptilian and the whole story seems to me, today, to be the story of that galactic journey and it has also been played out on earth.

Alcheringa: Indeed it is. This Earth, if you like, began as gasses and each process of its evolvement was overseen by the Elohim. It was a plan to be created as a Garden of Eden. There were many races that came to help that transformation to take place. That is a long story, of course, and there have been developments on the planet that were not meant to happen, but they still did...and so, because of the will of Elohim to allow everybody to evolve, they allowed that to take place—the visitation from the reptilian people. There is nothing wrong in that, and the dinosaurs were created, and you know the story of how they were destroyed to help bring the planet back to what it was planned to be—which was the Garden of Eden.

Alcheringa: The Australian Indigenous people were created here. They are the first humans. And they know this. They know they did not come from anywhere else. They began here on this planet, even though the stock of the race, shall we say, which was the upstanding ape-like creature, came from elsewhere.

But the human was imbued with a Being of Light—with a God Man if you like—and that continues, even though there has been further evolution with the human race since. There have been many changes, but they are Beings of God. Creations from God the Source ... and the Star People have helped that ... in the beginning, they came from the Pleiades. There are other visitations from other worlds, other star groups ... the Indigenous people were very clever at watching the stars and knowing and understanding what was taking place in the cycles that happened with seasons and within the solar system. You could say they were the first astronomers because the Star People helped them to understand this. In a telepathic way, they spoke to them—particularly the clever people—and so they were able to pass on their knowledge to other members of the tribe. The Storytellers, initiated by the Star People, were handed down through the ages into different tribes. And this is where the Dreaming Stories came from.

So there has been a long time of development with the Australian Indigenous race.

And so, you are asking if it is true that they understood the existence of other worlds. They spoke of them as Gods, or Star People from other worlds. Perhaps they did not use the word Star People, but that is the way they saw them, as beings more advanced than what they were, and they were willing to learn from them. So, does this answer your question?

Paul: Yes. I think also what I feel when I look at this, although I don't quite understand it—it seems to be not only a map of the stars and its history, but it's just like a clock that works its way around a cycle. Perhaps even a Cosmic Record of how things unfold. I suppose in the same way the Mayans have a clock. And so, when the Zodiac moves from the sky, certain things happen because it has happened in the past. It seems like there is a bit of that here too.

Alcheringa: Indeed, it is; indeed, it is. There are cycles, within cycles, within cycles. Some cycles are small, some are large, some are very large. And it's now time for a cycle that is coming into being, which has been prophesied by many. All who tune into these prophecies remember a time of heartache and pain, with the world being turned upside down— and they still have those memories within their hearts. But that does not necessarily mean that it is going to happen again. People here as humans can be creative—they create what they want, whether they realise it or not. They are creating their own lives. They are being guided, that is true, from the blueprint that they come within their soul. You understand that, and that gently influences their life as they come to live here on Earth.

And so, the smaller cycles are going around within the evolution in the larger cycles of the Earth and her solar system, and it is slowly aligning with a core of suns that go back to the Creative Source of All. And from that place there will be an upliftment of consciousness, and humans all around the Earth will begin to realise just who they really are. And they are not just a physical body, or a human body, but rather Light Beings—Star People. You understand?

Paul: These suns on the ceiling trigger the memory ... I see alignment of these circles which, to me, look like alignments of the stars, and when they line up then the energy can be supported through those stars so that if Earth is to bathe in that it will be an awakening.

The rock art at Mutitjulu Springs, at the rock Uluru also suggests an alignment of the suns and the solar system.

Alcheringa: It is, and it is a slow alignment that is taking place for it would be too much if the energy that is coming onto this Earth was to come on in its fullest power—it would knock people out because some are not ready to receive it. But there are places upon the earth that are opening, and they are Points of Light. The Centre of Australia is one of them; it always has been, and there are many others around the Earth. People come and stay and then they go—they are touched by it—this new Light, this new energy ... this upliftment. This will eventually cover the whole of the earth when the alignment of the suns take place. And this is the turning point for the cycle to move into another cycle.

And this will be, as it was meant to be, when the Garden of Eden was first designed.

Paul: So how can we assist? We have been called here—we have come here—we have tuned into things ... surely there must be more that can be done. I just feel ... I feel frustrated because I have these memories, but

I don't have the ability to go with my memory; but I feel, still, things to be done.

Alcheringa: There is indeed. And you will be prompted ... this is today, there is still tomorrow. And the next day. You will be prompted, and I would like to reassure you that you have the ability—very much so—it is your destiny to help with these changes, to help uplift the consciousness on this Earth, because you come from the stars, and you come with much power—and you can use this power if you acknowledge it and accept it. That will help you with the uplifting of the energy.

Alcheringa: The binding of the times—of the time when the Earth almost went backwards—from the time when the dinosaurs were destroyed, and also at the time of what is generally known as The Fall of Atlantis. It happened all over the Earth and these times are still written very strongly into people's hearts, in their memories, and your role is to help them to accept the changes that took place then. Recognise that it does not have to repeat itself, but rather they can lift their consciousness to their Soul Consciousness and then be able to move forward with the true understanding of who they really are—and that is, they are Star People. Does that make sense?

Paul: The image I have just had is on the beach with the waves coming in and you have a child; if the child is hit by the full force of the wave, it would be brutal indeed, but if you just lift under their arms they can sail up and over the top of the wave and have great joy in the fine experience.

Alcheringa: Exactly ... There are many waves that are coming all the time and in particular Solar Waves so there is some misunderstanding with some people.

When they look at prophecies ... a prophecy is just a warning saying this could happen again unless you uplift your consciousness and realise it, that you are creators ... you are God Beings, and you can make the Earth become what it is truly meant to be. Does that make sense?

Paul: Yes.

Alcheringa: There are many here on this Earth now who can do just this, as you are, my son.

Paul: The girls who have come—Liz and Judy—they are part of this puzzle. They are still trying to find their way. Do you have any words for them? They have abilities still coming to the surface.

Alcheringa: Well, the girls have already been through some girls' business—women's business if you like—but I joke ... so is there anyone else who would like to ask a question before I take my leave?

Judy: My question is the same as Paul's. What are our roles?

Alcheringa: This is an exercise that I am encouraging you to do—to listen to your inner voice, which you do—trust it. You will be guided. You are being downloaded even as I speak. Okay? And you will be able to follow this ... you will know much more by tomorrow.

So this is a little interim of my visiting, but really the main thing is to reassure you and ask you to have faith in your abilities and trust the feelings of what you are being asked to do and then just follow. Is that alright? (*Murmurs of agreement*).

Alcheringa: Then I will take my leave and I will come back if you really want me to come back ... but I am already with you. So, the energy is going out to you—and it is infiltrating you—and you can feel it ... and I want you to know that you can trust it. Thank you, thank you, my children and God bless you.

This whole session at Cave Hill, the place Indigenous people speak of the Seven Sisters from the Pleiades, has never been published in a book. You can read more here: https://www.valeriebarrow.com/?p=57 . This consists of four parts and is named, 'Visit to the Sacred Place at Cave Hill, Central Australia, November 12, 2011 – A five-hour journey from Uluru and back.'

Bob and Jan Wright's story

> **WARNING:**
> Aboriginal and Torres Strait Islander visitors are warned that the next page may contain images of deceased persons.

https://www.valeriebarrow.com/?p=54 'Uluru – Bob and Jan Wright's Story, November 12, 2011.' Bob and Jan Wright were managers of Ansett Lodge, Ayers Rock, 1967, and managers of Glen Helen Lodge, West Alice Springs.

Jan and Bob Wright managed the Ansett Lodge at the base of Uluru over forty years ago. This was before the area was established as Uluru-Kata Tjuta National Park and given World Heritage status. It was before the village Yalara was created.

Mick Whaggo, who was an elder, whom we knew quite well at Glen Helen, another tourist area, and Mick Whaggo used to refer to the fact that the Rock was" ... ... he stopped speaking for a moment and added, "And there was also Uncle Jack who was the tribal 'Shaman' – they both used to talk about the rock plunging from the sky and sinking into the desert. I have heard that only 1/3rd of the rock is showing above ground level – that would be 1,473 ft above the ground and the rest below the ground."

*Indigenous man dressed for spiritual ceremony pointing to white paint, representing spirit and the **Rainbow Serpent***

This is Maggie Springs showing the water cascading into the waterhole after rain. The mythical story tells of Goolagaia *living in the rock. The Aborigines say to look at the rock and see through it as energy. They say you do not have to take photos – you can take a photo with your "inner eyes".*

I took this photo from another Lodge named Red Lion when it was raining and cold. It looks blue white.

Five

The Reunion at Canyonleigh

Group photo of those who remember being Star People and the particular story written as 'Alcheringa when the Ancestors were first Created.'

This was the day of a reunion at Canyonleigh in 2002; many of the people had not met before. They all remember the mission of the mothership Rexegena. There have been hundreds more who have remembered the same story since. Alcheringa advised that all in this galaxy knew of the story—even though not all were part of the mission. Most have returned to finish the mission that began nearly 900,000 years ago. They didn't have to travel to Kariong; just looking at the photographs of the Glyphs was enough to trigger them into a cosmic consciousness and remember being Star People.

When I first visited Uluru in 1994, when taking the painted symbols there, we were all initiated into the Rainbow Serpent Energy. But just before that, as we sat on the sand, I saw a huge black spirit figure take long steps from Uluru towards me. As she came near me, she shouted 'White woman, white woman, close up your legs,' which were separated with a thorny bush. She laughed out loud, and I heard other women laughing too, and she again repeated her message. Then when I shifted to sit with my legs tightly closed, she said, 'Take off your shoes and come with me.' Next thing I was in my light body at the edge of the sacred waters of Mutitjulu Waterhole, at Uluru, and she asked me to walk into the sacred water that flows under the great rock. It was an initiation. Then I saw myself returning to the others sitting on the sand hill and putting my shoes and socks on again. The ranger told me that she was Goolagaia, the Black Giantess who sleeps at Mt. Wollumbin on the North Coast of N.S.W. and when the morning sun hits the mountain top, she travels to Uluru.

Months later, she came again to me at Canyonleigh when a group were meditating. She announced she was the eighth black sister sleeping with the crystal and now she was joining with me—the eighth white sister from the stars. I was the messenger. Another time I visited Cave Hill of the Seven Sisters, and she came to me again saying the Sacred Alcheringa Stone had been originally found in that cave by an Afghan cameleer in early European's settlement. And now when I visited Mutujulu Waterhole at Uluru—I called upon her. And this is how she presented herself: a beautiful, magenta pink orb with seven other rainbow orbs who were her sisters. Egarina is the eighth white sister from the Pleiades; she has returned from the stars and some of her messages are presented in Part Three of the *Starlady* book. Egarina was the wife of Alchquaringa (Alcheringa) when he was a Star Person as commander-in-chief in charge of the mission that came from the Pleiades.

I know now the magenta orb is from Andromeda. The colour magenta is not in our rainbow but is the first colour shown on the electromagnetic spectrum. It is the vibrational colour that will lead into raised consciousness to connect telepathically to Andromeda M31.

This photo, taken at the sacred waters of Mutitujulu Waterhole, Uluru, shows seven rainbow orbs representing the seven sisters, and the magenta orb that we now know is the overseeing eighth sister from Andromeda. The bright white orb at the top of photo is not the sun.

We had moved to Moss Vale, New South Wales, not far from Canyonleigh. One morning was very foggy and when I looked at our rose garden, I found it to be covered in spider webs. I was amazed how thick they were. So, I took photos and as I did, something unseen momentarily took over my camera and snapped a few more photos.

When I uploaded the photos onto my computer, I found that a magenta-coloured image had begun to appear and then saw that it was a bright orb—exactly the same that had appeared on the photo at Mutitjulu Waterhole, Uluru.

I then asked the Star People—Alcheringa—if there was a message coming with the amazing spider web photo and was advised, 'We would like you to publish your work about Star People on the World Wide Web.' Needless to say, it was within a day that I was offered help from a webmaster to create a web page. www.valeriebarrow.com

I awoke one morning to find the rose garden covered in spider webs—I had never seen so many. Can you see a pink light forming in the photo?

THE MAGENTA ORB SHOWED UP IN THE PHOTO

The magenta orb again. I was taking the photo and my camera began clicking by itself.

Before, we had the reunion at Canyonleigh, with all the people who remembered being Star People. When I had just been given the Sacred Alcheringa Stone in 1994, friends came—Rosemary and Brian, both gifted mediums—and asked if they could hold the sacred stone. We decided to meditate, and they began speaking alternately about Alcheringa as an Ancient Creator Ancestor. That was the first time I had heard the name Alcheringa, who was also known as a spirit ancestor.

I lit a large candle on a saucer and we began. First Rosemary channelled one sentence, and then Brian with the next sentence, and then Rosemary again, and then Brian again, one after the other, who both said they were channelling Alcheringa himself. Here is his message and his way of introducing himself to me:

Alcheringa: The dead centre of Australia is the burnt centre, with the marrying of the father (from the stars) and the mother (Earth) energies in the country, the Son (Sun) has been born and the Son (Sun) energies have been released from the heart of the nation, which is Uluru. All work must be done from the heart, all feeling is done from the connection to the heart. Nothing can be done but by through the heart—the heart that is made manifest in this world, that is connected to the heart of all that is.

All the time these messages were coming through the mediums, the candle had caught fire and was burning with leaping flames, although we were not in any danger. We watched the wax run from the candle to the saucer underneath, and flow onto the glass tabletop, eventually forming into a shape that looked at first like Kata Tjuta and then on to look like Uluru.

We were amazed at the time, but I see now it was symbolising the burning of the rock Uluru coming into our atmosphere and landing on the earth as a great fire ball, and after the tempering, it would have been like a phoenix rising from the ashes, the energy of which was transformed into a sun, a Rainbow Serpent of permanent Light—which was, as we know now, 'charged.' The number of rocks were used as bombs, but later transformed into sacred energy, on song lines after the dinosaurs were destroyed.

Uluru is the heart of the nation, like phoenix rising from the ashes as a huge portal of Light. A Rainbow Serpent of permanent Sacred Light.

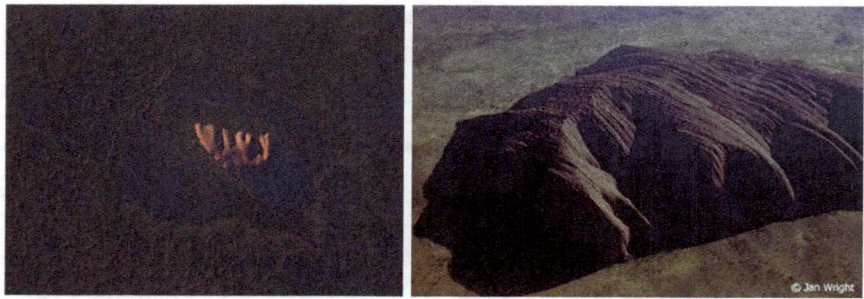

The photo on the left was taken from outer space by NASA Astronaut, Thomas Pesquet. It was something he wanted to take for a very long time. 14 February 2017.

This photo from outer space is looking like Uluru landing into the Eromanga Sea that first existed in the area.

Six

Alcheringa and Andromeda Val

Alcheringa as he presented himself on my computer

I have been asked by Alcheringa to share his talk on the cosmic view of the origin and formation of Uluru. He spoke on 21 December 1994, while I was holding the Sacred Alcheringa Stone. It is interesting that in 1994 there was mention of the energy coming through from another galaxy; we now know he was referring to Andromeda M31. (21 December is an interesting date as it was repeated in 2020, sixteen years later at Uluru, at the Cosmic Consciousness Conference).

Source: *The Book of Love by a Medium* (Now Part Two of the *Starlady* book.)

Alcheringa: I am very pleased to be here, my child. Thank you for inviting me. You have been wondering about the energy from Uluru, which also could be seen as the energy of the lion, which is why you have been given the image of the sphinx. Does this help you, my child, do you understand? You may remember you were prompted to see Uluru also looking a little like a sphinx.

It is true, the energy that has come through from another galaxy, at another time, filters through into the Earth and comes to various points at its surface. What you call Egypt is one of them and it is at those points, pyramids were built in many places. These too were also built at another time.

It allowed the Star People that came to Earth at that time to use the energy to manifest and to create. It was a network that filtered through the Earth. It is no coincidence that the rock known as Uluru came to this planet. We, as the Star People, brought it here to bring that energy and to help make changes upon the Earth so that it developed. This was at a time before humanity. I, myself, as an aspect of a Star Being, have remained in the Astral (dimension) to help with the changes and the understanding to be filtered through to humanity until a time that the Earth reaches back to a dimension that existed when the rock Uluru first hit this planet.

[(Now that all 'the dots' had come together for me, I knew he was speaking of the Star People, The Leonines from Sirius, who were called upon as the cosmic cops from the Angelic Realm/Galaxy Andromeda M31]).

Alcheringa/Sanat Kumara: [The sound of his voice changes here] For your own understanding, Alcheringa is an aspect of Sanat Kumara and it is really Sanat Kumara that speaks with you at this time. I am part of the Council of Light. I want you to understand this, my child.

You are asking about the energy being known as the Lion Energy? It could also be seen as a play on words. It is a particular line of energy and influence that comes upon this Earth from another galaxy altogether.

There is also the *cat* that is involved, and *hair*. This is from the level of the cosmic consciousness, which you understand is where the Star People exist. There are different dimensions, and different shapes and forms. Hair was introduced onto this Earth in the form of mammal. Up until that time it had been a reptilian form with no hair. The time of the dinosaur—and yes, you're feeling that when Uluru hit this Earth it was a time of wiping out of the reptilian form of dinosaur that had manifested to a point where it was out of control—it had to be reconstructed.

It will help you if you think of energy as influence. The energy and the influence are what were created here on Earth into a form. It is very simple really—but of course the form that took place is very complicated and in many forms.

It was experimental from the Star People's point of view. We were creating what is called, or what we call, the Garden of Eden. We were able to reproduce these forms because of the vibration that existed here on this Earth. At a later time, the humanoid or the Form of Man was created and evolved so that senses were experienced—because of that heavier vibration. There was a separation between the positive and the negative and the sense in between could be felt. In the World of Light, the energy seen as negative and that of positive operate together so there is no separation—but there is power. The power was lost to some degree when the form took place on this Earth in the dimension—where the separation existed.

But with the slow vibration it allowed the form to take a heavier existence. This could be experienced in a way that we were not able to experience in the World of Light.

It is unfortunate that there were those that chose to pull away from the Will of God and the Universal Law and so the development and the involvement upon this Earth went astray—against God's Law and understanding.

When it all ended at the time of what you call the fall of Atlantis, which was not altogether an accident, it allowed that form, that energy, that vibration that existed here on this Earth to evolve into what was meant to be on this Earth.

The formation is now coming into being and it will herald the New Age and operate within the Will of God and the Law of the Universe. It has been an edict from the Council of Light that only those that choose to walk with God and that energy will be able to walk forward into the New Age. All that goes against God or chooses to walk in a different direction will be defused, meaning returned to the Source, or replaced elsewhere.

Remember all that exists in this world of yours is of a created energy and form—it is not … the reality.

---oOo---

Below is a message given at the end of an afternoon interview sitting on a sandy hill overlooking Uluru, on 21 December 2020: http://collectivegalactic.com/valerie-barrow.html

Uluru—Solstice with Valérie Barrow & Ivan KNEZ

Alcheringa: I am here, my dear, and I am very pleased to be here. I am delighted (he coughs with the wind blowing). Yes, I will be very, very happy to speak, and I am glad that this is taking place.

Because it is allowing more and more people to come to know and understand the existence of Star People, that people talk about as ancestors, as we are all Star People.

Anything that is not of the earth is extra-terrestrial.

ETs exist, you understand that? So, it is nothing to be afraid of, at all, and when it's the truth it will feel right, it will feel good. Aren't you feeling pleased with my presence being here? In fact, many people who visit this area feel uplifted because there has been a lot of work with the beautiful Indigenous people with ceremony and song and storytelling and holding the energy of connectedness.

It is Source because it is created in itself, do you understand?

It's very simple really. Life could be very complicated if you want it to be complicated, or it could be very simple. And the Indigenous people, bless them, have kept the stories down through the ages.

It does not matter about time. Time and distance do not exist when you enter the time of time with the mind connection. There is no separation.

In an example, when Valérie does work with people on Skype, and they may be on the other side of the world, and they talk and that might be a different time, but they are connected at the same time. And talking at the same time. And when I say time, I mean face to face. That is it. So, if you can understand that, and take it further and further away, time and distance do not exist. However, intention and focus are important, and that needs to be also focused with truth, not playing around, but total focus without any interruptions at all. Total focus like a sword of light through the darkness, does that make sense?

Then people can see, I think, that the fellow that created the internet did say that humanity would move on eventually, and you did not need all this technology, that it would be easy to communicate telepathically or 'mind to mind.'

Already people are talking about the veil thinning and they are getting interactions with people, and certainly, in the past, there were abilities in Ancient Egypt, such as walking through walls, that type of thing. Certainly, they were very, very clever people within the Indigenous race of Australia, or Mu as it was, or Lemuria if you like, or Gondwanaland. It was all very different, but they are the same people. They have not liked to get involved with technology.

They communicated with one side of Australia and would be advising the other side of Australia: the east side, and the west side. But they would all know of a meeting place that was going to happen and they would gather. How did they contact and communicate with each other? Through telepathy. Mind to mind. They could do it.

Unfortunately, it's a little lost now, but it does still happen. And it is important that the Indigenous people be respected and acknowledged, and that people understand why it is not easy for them to be able to adjust to, shall we say, the new ways of the white man or whatever, that have come with technology. They are not interested really, but they do adjust.

There is change, and this is something that will need to be sorted out and agreed to, but certainly they should be acknowledged because they have held in their Dreaming stories, the very source of creation, that have been real. They have not embellished it. They have gone through initiations, and even had near-death experiences, then come back and known they have been communicating with the Star Worlds and Sky People.

They knew all these things, and they know it, and they need to be accepted and treated with great respect. Because not everybody could do these sorts of things that they can do, and know. They're not out to prove anything at all. And so, I have wanted and hoped that the existence of Uluru and its magic, if you like, and the reason it's here and how it was brought and why the Indigenous people know all these things, and they tell stories in different ways from what I would have talked about from a scientific way, but it's still the same and they know it. So, I would ask everybody to think about what they can do and what they have done in the past. The clever ones have said, in various tribes, that Uluru came from the stars, but there are scientists that say that it hasn't. So, they don't say anything out loud anymore, but they know. And they don't want to cause arguments or disagreements; they just quieten down.

Their truth, and their ways, are coming out. They know they have been considered the first astronomers—and they are. It is important they are all honoured for these things. They have a belonging, to the connectedness of everything upon the planet, and the sky, and the Star People, and the universe.

So please consider, please consider, it has been very hard for them to adjust to the new ways. So, I would ask for all to respect them and understand them more, read about them, learn about them. You will find they have a wonderful sense of humour. So, my dear, I won't stay any longer. I've just come to say I'm very happy with what has been taken place. The hierarchy is very happy with what is taking place, and I would like to say yes, we are going to show our faces everywhere so that there will be no doubt that the Sky People exist, that we exist. Everyone is Sky People; it is important that you understand and know this.

Thank you, my dears, thank you. God bless you.

Alcheringa, the ancient creator ancestor wishes everyone to know he is also a Star Person and his other half is Andromeda Val. At the Source of all Creation, they are all androgynous but can separate in different incarnations. Andromeda Val comes from the Adonis race who reside in the Galaxy Andromeda M31. She tells us she is 6,000 years into our future. Looking human, she and her race would like to present themselves on Earth to speak of the planet's history and the history of the human race. She is my future self.

Andromeda Val

Please see the 6 February 2018 message from Cosmic Sai Baba introducing Andromeda Val to readers on the www.cosmicsaibaba.com website, which continues to introduce her every month for messages from the Andromeda Galaxy. Cosmic Sai Baba's messages from the last ten years are published.

Valérie: So, with great love and respect in our hearts we are calling upon Cosmic Sai Baba...

Cosmic Sai Baba: I am here, and I am very pleased to be here. I welcome this opportunity in coming and conducting the introduction, shall we say, to Andromeda Val. You all know of her and her reason for coming and that is to help lift the consciousness and show that there are beings—races—that exist in other worlds that are very human-like, so that there is really no need to be afraid. For they understand and know many things and they can assist you and help you if you want to ask. I suggest that you do just that.

So, with great love and respect I am presenting Andromeda Val. Thank you, my dears, thank you. I God bless you.

Andromeda Val: I am Andromeda Val, and Valérie is asking me to speak up, so I shall try to speak a little louder. I have difficulty, of course, in communicating telepathically; to using a voice box, and we have spent the last year in practicing and adjusting to that. So, I can speak now, more clearly. I am still having a little bit of trouble when I hesitate, but that is the reason. I hope you will make allowances for that. I love you dearly and I welcome the opportunity for coming in your time. I come from a distance far ahead, 6,000 years, in fact. But do not let that phase you because it depends on where you are as to the distance and time.

That is why some say there is no time, and er, in a way it is a measurement, so if you think of it as a measurement then that would perhaps make more sense.

There are many things from where I come from, which is not unlike your planet Earth. The energy is different. The frequency of consciousness is raised and there is certainly no wars or unhappiness because people have come to understand and respect each other. No matter what difference.

The race that Valérie has come from is the Adonis Race. It is a hybrid race from the human race that you are in now. This human race has been going now for about, we could say, nearly a million years, perhaps a little less. This is the problem, measuring time and putting it to something that differs so much. It makes it difficult to communicate exactly how old something is and there is a lot of argument and disagreement.

Understanding will come to scientists as we move on in raising your consciousness and they will realise it depends a lot on different things as to whether something can be measured at one time, or a length of time, and measurement of another thing could be measured at a different time but seem to come from the same time (she laughed), if that makes sense.

So, in other words, it is a broad thing and perhaps would be best if it was not considered so intensely, but rather by saying something is very ancient or something is very new. Or that something is set for the future.

I do not want to sound like I am making fun of anyone. But I do have the memory of being in the race, the human race, through Valérie, for I am she in the future, if that makes some sense.

You can ponder that a little if you like. Valérie, like quite a few other people at this time and before time as it is now, when there was a lot of genetic engineering going on to people who claimed they were abducted.

I could say it would seem they were abducted, but they had, at another level of consciousness, given their permission for some genetic material to be taken from the human body. Valérie will say she has had a little embryo taken also.

So that is who I am in the future...or at least the generations that follow on from that. It can sound a little complicated. But what I wanted to say was that there were malevolent ones who did this abduction thing at the same time, with a lot of experimentation, and caused a lot of fear and physical pain among the human race. Unfortunately, it was allowed at the time, for a while, but it has now stopped. It is no longer happening.

They were just repeating what they thought they could do, when the Benevolent Beings were carrying on the human race as it is and into the future to exist on the Galaxy Andromeda M31.

So, I will invite questions now. Three questions will be allowed as we are on a time (she chuckled) limit. Would you like to ask any questions about that, anybody? (Long pause.) The silence is deafening. Perhaps I could ask then if you have another question that you would like to ask? Anything at all.

Question: Given that we have a planetary Earth hierarchy of ascended masters (The White Brotherhood), is it more beneficial to focus on communicating with them, rather than giving time and attention to off-planet (extra-terrestrial) beings? I'm thinking of beings such as Sanat Kumara, Maitreya, the Boddhisattva, Kuthumi, El Moyra, St Germaine.

Andromeda Val: I understand your question. My first question is why would you see them as different? I know these beings well. They do reside at Andromeda, they do come and go, they go to other places, other galaxies, other worlds in other universes. But when you think about what I am speaking about as the Star People you could see the Earth planet will become part of the Star System. Valérie has just explained that and that is what is happening, and so could I suggest that you don't see them as separate. Or am I not understanding what you are asking?

They are at different levels of frequency, we on Andromeda Galaxy have wise ones—so perhaps if you think of them as the wise ones, I will say very happily that they are. Does that answer your question?

Question: It is a complex question. The White Brotherhood are focused on the evolution on planet Earth, where the ET Beings are more concerned with the galactic scene. Is it better to focus one's attention and efforts to the immediate Earth scene, rather than the larger picture galactic scene?

Andromeda Val: I can understand what you are saying. Can I say these Beings that you speak of are very like Sri Sathya Sai Baba is and was? When he was on Earth, he said, 'My life is my message' and he was without limit. He was able to appear and disappear in many places around the Earth. It is the same with these Wise Ones from the White Brotherhood, for instance, that you speak of. They are here, but they are there all at the same time. There is no separation. So, I am not suggesting that I am the Wise One, but I am not limited in that I am there, and I am here too with Valérie at the same time. Does that make sense? And is there a question you would like to clarify there? Because I could remind you that Earth is terrestrial, right? Then everything outside our planet is extra-terrestrial. In other words, it is from the Star Worlds. So why is there a limit in not understanding that other beings can live in other worlds, very similar to this world, and still be able to have abilities of others that have come here and shown it is telepathically possible to communicate no matter what the distance is. Does that make sense?

The separation does not exist; everything is One. If you think of one wise Being, such as White Eagle, he is part of the White Brotherhood. He did not make his appearance here, he worked through others did he not? Just the same as I am working through others.

Well, Valérie. I am Andromeda Val, but our story, as Valérie has already said, is a little different—but there is no limit. Can you not see that you are creating a division where there is none? Does it not seem like everything is unified, everything interacts, and everything is One?

Perhaps, there is a little need to think more about that or perhaps ask another question if you like.

Question: I think I will digest that for a while.

Andromeda Val: So is there another question anyone would like to ask?

Question: Is the Earth quarantined from an interstellar council, because of the violence on this planet? Are we here meaning to add our spiritual support to grow awareness of higher spiritual values?

Andromeda Val: The consciousness—can I say there are different levels of consciousness, and can I also say some are wiser and some are not. There is no judgement here; the only judgement you have is upon yourself.

If I could say as it is in Andromeda, there is a frequency of consciousness that exists where a thought just does not enter anybody's head to sort out a problem with a weapon. And so, they, meaning weapons, do not exist. Do you understand?

Coming to a planet, such as your own, it does exist. There is a sense of responsibility for those in Andromeda in that they have already said, the Angelic Realms have said, that they created your planet Earth in the first place. It was to take place of another planet that had been destroyed and there was a vacuum and that needed to be replaced so that the Solar System would continue operating the way it always had.

Andromeda Val: So, with the creation of the planet Earth, it was created with a higher frequency of energy to try and help lift this corner of the galaxy (Milky Way). Which is very dark when you look from a Universal

Point of View. And the races that had grown in this corner of your galaxy. Does that make sense?

And so, the frequency of the Earth then became a place of where Andromedans, and many others working with them, wanted to help it to grow. It has been referred to as a Garden of Eden, and it was.

Then it was overtaken by others that had no right to it, but they made it their own. Although some effort was used to try to get them to vacate the planet, it didn't happen, but a war was avoided. So, there was a lot of evolution that took place upon your planet first and since then there have been many ways that the Star People or the Angelic Realms from Andromeda have used to help raise or hold the new vibration that was coming from Andromeda onto this corner of your galaxy.

Am I explaining that well enough? Does that make sense to you?

I would like to make a point about the age of the Earth, so you realise how long evolvement has been taking place and how it is changing and growing and evolving in consciousness. The Earth herself is a consciousness and that is evolving also. It was a beautiful being, but it fell back because of misuse and the way it was treated, and to some degree it still is being mistreated.

It is a little hard to think about seeing one thing happening and then seeing it now because there is such a distance in time. Even though we talked about time not really being 'time'. Shall we say, it is a measurement and from where you are looking. So, if you are looking at Earth and where it is now—you could look back to when all the dinosaurs were all created, and they were here upon this planet—and the very difference now, here on the planet without dinosaurs, although there are bones, and knowledge that they did exist at one time.

That was not meant to happen, but it did. And so, the Great Plan was adjusted to help for that growth to maintain and still happen, but with changes. Does that make sense?

I think for now, my dears, we will have to leave this questioning. I would like you to, if you would, and if you are interested, write your questions and ask them when I come next meeting and it will give me great joy to answer them if I can.

It would be a good way to connect to your intuition, or your soul consciousness to make a suggestion for a question because we are working to communicate knowledge to the masses if that makes sense.

So, if I may, I will leave this now and I have had great joy in being with you and I hope you all welcome me when I return on our next meeting. It is a platform that has been set up so that all the necessary technology is put in place for the communication to take place.

Thank you, my dears, thank you very much for having me, I God bless you.

Seven

Reflections After Channelling

Valérie Barrow—Human/Star Person speaking after channelling had finished.

I have absolutely NO DOUBT about the existence of Star People. I remember being one. In fact, I am one...that has walked into an earth body (with God's permission). **There are a lot of us—144,000, in fact—that have come voluntarily to Earth to assist with the raising of consciousness on the planet.** When you come here you forget quite a bit, but the memory comes back as the frequency and vibration of the earth raises. That is why there is so much more talk about Star People these days. The younger humans coming into earth bodies now can remember more easily.

Way back, before Atlantis fell to the 3rd dimension, the earth was in the 4th dimension (about what we are coming into now). Star People used to come and go easily to this planet, but they had different bodies. Not Earth bodies. Or earth race bodies, if that makes sense. They were highly advanced in their technology and ability.

People have asked why don't they come now? Or are they all coming into Earth bodies this time?

And I can say, yes, they do come and go all the time in a different frequency of Light that earth people cannot see yet. And they are coming into Earth bodies also—that is much harder for them. But they want to help us. They are our brothers and sisters. Our family.

Even though there is a mixture of DNA that makes us look different from their races. We, meaning the earth race, the human race, is a mixture of all sorts of DNA that has come from the stars in the first place. Some, shall we say, are from a heavier frequency, ready to learn, and a lot with advanced frequency are ready to move into the 5th dimension. When we finally leave our Earth bodies, we all return to our home in the stars.

The Star People would come now, with greetings, straight away, if they were welcomed. Now, they are not being welcomed! The advanced Star People can easily disappear out of Earth people's sight.

The 5th dimension is the frequency where all on Earth, and the earth herself, are heading—it has the same frequency of Crystal or Christ or Christos—and it is the level playing field for all Earth Souls to attain in consciousness. It is known as the GOLDEN AGE.

The book, *Starlady*, is a true story about me and my husband remembering many past lives together, and how we came to remember, in Part One.

I also speak of a green crystal tektite known as a Moldavite stone that advised, when I held it, that I would be 'going home.' In ancient times, it has been known as a Grail Stone. This is explained in Part Two of *Starlady*. Understanding goes on so that we are advised that the tektite that fell to the Earth is the remains of the mothership, Rexegena, which was blown up and still holds the energy of bringing Light and wisdom to those who come in contact with it.

Also, sometime after that the Sacred Stone, wrapped in paperbark and then covered with cloth and tied with string, was lent to me and I cried in recognition of it. It belonged to the Australian Aboriginals and the origine people of Australia—but its role was to come to me and introduce me to Alcheringa, who is well known to the Indigenous people as an ancient ancestral creator spirit, and for me to share its knowledge about the evolution of the Earth and its creation.

It was shortly after that I learnt of the mission I was asked to write about, as the return of the eighth sister from the Pleiades, to speak of a time, nearly one million years ago in ancient time, when Star People from the Pleiades came to this planet to establish a civilization with a raised consciousness in this dark corner of the Milky Way. Their huge mothership was attacked and destroyed, and the survivors, using genetic engineering, managed to uplift the ape-like, weapon-wielding form of slave person—to one of Light—our human ancestors, the Australian First Peoples.

If you were to ask how far back our DNA goes, Alcheringa says billions of years to when our planet was first created. Man, or the 'animal man', was genetically engineered by the Star People and known as the snake, and lizard people in the first place, under the guidance of the Draco Hierarchy. The human race was created by the Star People who survived the attacked mothership that had come with love and blessings from the Pleiades and always used genetic engineering with permission from the Source of All Creation. God, if you like. As already explained, our Earth planet, or Mu, was created by them to replace Maldek that had been attacked and destroyed in an ancient Star War.

The solar system had been disrupted and needed to regain a balanced cycle.

The Draco/Lizard People had taken over this planet and believed that the Planet Earth (Mu) belonged to them.

The Hierarchy/Angelic Realm for the Good of All, through the Andromeda Galaxy, created a plan of a Garden of Eden to replace the missing planet that had been destroyed. This means a place of raised consciousness—where a civilization could live holding the raised consciousness energy in this very dark corner of our Milky Way Galaxy. A place of peace, love, compassion, and goodwill. It was foreseen that it could eventually spread the new Creative Divine Light and influence the existing lizard races in this dark arm of our Milky Way Galaxy, corner. The lizard races had been created by the Draco Hierarchy *without* the blessing of the Source of All Creation, and who had an agenda of control, power, enslavement, sacrifice, and only good for the few.

'Eden' meant a place of Steppes. A raising of consciousness, layer by layer, as steps back to where Earth was in consciousness before the catastrophic fall of Atlantis, which led to the Great Flood and lowering of our energy, frequency, and vibration and when humans had to survive in caves.

This was a long time ago, although the scenario is still being played out.

Just of interest:

These photos are of me, back in 1994, when I was introduced to Alcheringa through the sacred Alcheringa Stone. The camera used was an infrared ray, which picks up the 'aura' energy surrounding people.

Orange energy showing Alcheringa behind me *One minute later I asked Alcheringa to step into my body*

Now see what they look like below, raised to *magenta colour*. I did nothing to adjust the photos to that colour—it happened by itself on my computer! Alcheringa had a hand in the change, I am sure.

Valerie calling upon Alcheringa in 1994 standing behind her. His wings can be seen in the right-hand image after overlighting her body 2 minutes later.

The colour magenta, linked with the Electro Magnetic spectrum, is magically prominent in the photo these days, now that Valerie has been given knowledge of her connection to Andromeda M31 –for we are advised Andromeda M31 created the Earth planet in the first place.

And Egarina tells more about the eighth sister, in Valerie's book STARLADY - Part three……….

It is magic.

It is also evidence that the consciousness of the earth and its people has raised again from 21 December 2012 (The Turning Point) to 21 December 2020…and still moving forward.

Eight

The Beginning

I have just been shown by Alcheringa, the spirit ancestor, this beautifully written article by one of our Indigenous people. It is recommended that our readers do a Google search for it. The stories told from their 'Dreaming' are spoken by them in such a beautiful poetic way. The paintings are superb. It is unembellished truth.

https://starlore.com.au/2021/04/21/alcheringa-the-beginning/

Alcheringa—'The beginning'

Alcheringa Island—Moreton Bay—East Coast Australia

The traditional lore of the *Yoocum-Yoocum Moiety* is *Matristic* Rainbow Serpent Culture. Commencing from the Alcheringa it is the marriage of the fresh waters and the salt waters.

I am going to share a *'Boogaram'* [creation lore] with you about the **Alcheringa** and why it is SO important...and how it starts in the land and waters [geology and hydrology] of the ancient **Clarence Moreton Basin** of east coast **Australia**...the lore of_*Warrazum/Warrajam*—Grandmother Rainbow Serpent.

Alcheringa is indelibly linked to the *Rainbow Serpent [water serpent] fertility cult* of the Old-World tribal culture of Australia. It is the most ancient of the continent's cultures. It is a matristic culture—not matriarchal, not patriarchal. It is the Dreamtime matristic waterlore.

The song[line] of creation commences on the continent's most easterly geographical sites and then travels right across Australia, following the stars...but the sea levels change throughout time, and so the ancient lore sites move here on Earth. However, the stars remain the same, and so the higher lore NEVER changes.

As above, so below—the creation lore of *Grandmother Rainbow Serpent and the Seven Sisters* can be read every evening, across the night sky, like a book...and corresponding terrestrial sites can be visited and rituals performed to commemorate the creation of life on Earth.

Copyright – Stellastarlore – permission given to share.

Stellastarlore also talks about the Autumnal Equinox from the ALCHERINGA here: https://starlore.com.au/2022/03/22/autumnal-equinox-from-the-alcheringa/

Nine

Uluru from a Scientific Point of View

Presentation for scientists to consider

Now, I have been asked to work with a scientist to help with understanding how an asteroid could hit the earth, leaving a huge impact crater, and *not* disintegrate.

I have come across many people who 'know' that Uluru is much more than just sitting in the middle of a desert. But none could explain this to me from a scientific point of view.

I was in a quandary and a bit sad, not knowing how I was going to find a scientist—so, I asked Alcheringa to assist me. The next day my mobile rang and there was a friend saying to me, 'Valérie, your image came to me in a meditation this morning. I was feeling you needed help. I am here to help you!' I was a little tearful with joy when I explained how maybe he could help. Well, as a geologist he was doubtful at first, but after sharing all the information and clues Alcheringa has given us, he began to see that it was possible that an asteroid could come to Earth and not break up.

So, we—Alcheringa, the geologist, and I—have been working together for about three months now, with Alcheringa and I sparking thoughts and ideas to the geologist, and him responding as a scientist. It was then that Alcheringa began explaining how the origine people can speak of Creation Stories (that they receive in the Dreaming) from a time before ancestors lived on Earth.

I intend to explain the 'Dreaming' further into this book. I am not Indigenous in this life, but I am a 'White Fella Dreaming' along with many other mediums on Earth. Actually, remember, I am from the stars...

The geologist, Alcheringa, and I have published a PowerPoint presentation on my website, www.valeriebarrow.com. We honour all the work that has been done by scientists, but some are still questions, meaning theories and hypotheses. We hope they will give consideration or advice, even if they need to consider metaphysics, for the existence of Star People has not been officially accepted in existence yet in the Western World.

This presentation hopes to bridge the gap between scientific and metaphysical sources, and encourage more study (geology, metaphysical, cultural) at Uluru.

PowerPoint Presentation for Scientists

Dreamtime of Uluru—The Asteroid

A story told by a non-indigenous spiritual medium, who comes from the stars.

Introduction

- The purpose of this presentation is to recognise the importance of Australian Aboriginal culture and the dreaming stories that tell of Earth's creation and evolution. Uluru is a sacred rock that has come from the stars, which transformed the country from the Cretaceous to now.
- Valérie Barrow's version of the origin of Uluru is told from a different perspective, which is inspired and guided from her communication with the Dreamtime creator spirit ancestor (Alcheringa) who resides in Uluru.
- Uluru is located in the heart of Australia and is important for Aboriginal culture. In fact, Uluru-Kata Tjuta National Park is included on the UNESCO World Heritage List for both its natural and cultural values due to its spectacular geological formations, rare plants, animals, and outstanding natural beauty. Given the significance of Uluru, Valérie examines the cultural, scientific, and metaphysical perspectives regarding its origin and evolution.
- The origin of Uluru given by Valérie is similar to a past-life regression where she has a vivid recall of the giant asteroid hitting Australia's red centre approximately 65 million years ago. The asteroid dramatically changed the landscape, wiped out the dinosaurs/large reptiles, and formed the beginning of mammal species.
- *Key words: Uluru-asteroid, Alcheringa spirit, Cushioning of asteroid by inland sea/sediments, alignment of red rocks (3), basin formation*

The VISION of the Asteroid

The following is a medium's description of a catastrophic event that occurred some 65 million years ago.

- Valérie received a vision while holding the 'Alcheringa Stone' of a huge asteroid, known today as Uluru, which hit the Earth.

As viewed like something like out of a science fiction movie, Valérie's vision was of a large, rocky asteroid in our solar system, which was directed towards Earth. The (Uluru) asteroid was made of rock and ice.

- The asteroid turned into a scorching hot fiery rock when it entered the Earth's atmosphere. The asteroid had the appearance of a fiery spearhead, which was projected at a low angle to the earth. The asteroid was followed by a string of smaller meteorites (like a tail), which broke off from the main asteroid. The meteorites behind the asteroid Uluru were pieces that broke from it as it entered it into the earth's atmosphere. Two of the meteorites landed at Cave Hill (Central Australia) and Mt Burringurrah (Mt. Augustus, Western Australia). The three rocks are red in colour, have similar lithology, and are aligned (E-W).
- The asteroid (Uluru) landed in the centre of Australia and a shallow inland sea, now known as the Eromanga Sea. The asteroid hit the sea and sediments from an east to west direction at an astronomical speed and a low angle (not perpendicular). The asteroid impact was substantially cushioned by the shallow sea and sediments, which protected the rock from breaking apart. A massive impact crater formed in the Euromanga sea.
- The shallow sea in the immediate impact area vaporised while the asteroid sunk deep into the seabed; sediments and earth crust sent an explosive wave of gas and rocks upwards and outwards like a giant mushroom cloud. The impact caused surrounding volcanoes to ignite.
- The massive force of the impact also pushed waves of the seabed (sediment/layers of dislocated earth's crust) forward of the asteroid impact area. The buckled seabed formed a mountain cluster, now known as Kata Tjuta (the Olgas). A remnant of the smaller meteorite tail (fragments of asteroid) is approximately 100km from Uluru and known as Cave Hill (location of the found Alcheringa Stone).

Note: The asteroid 65 million years ago caused major changes to Australia and the planet, such as the destruction of dinosaurs and beginning of mammal life. The Cenozoic (65 million years ago to the present) is also known as the Age of Mammals, and demise of the dinosaurs. Cave Hill tells the story of the Seven Sisters Dreaming. Anangu (local Aboriginal people) know how Uluru and Kata Juta formed. This knowledge comes from the Tjukurpa (the stories and lore that explain and govern Anangu life). But much of it, particularly about Kata Juta, is secret, and cannot be presented. Geologists have their own explanation. (Source: Uluru airport display at the departure lounge.)

Uluru—Mostly Below Surface

Similar to an iceberg, Uluru sticks up above the ground some 348m; however, the monolith extends several kilometres underground and is surrounded by dune sands. Uluru's shape underground is mostly unknown.

Dreamtime Story

The asteroid/Uluru occurred before humankind on Earth. However, Aboriginal people consider Uluru as sacred and part of their culture and initiation ceremonies for thousands of years. Many stories of Aboriginal Dreamtime are secret and passed down verbally.

The geological view of Uluru is a western and scientific view that is also understood by some Aboriginal people. Some Aboriginal people believe that Uluru comes from the stars, and the rock is a reminder about our cosmic origins. Just as the features and imprints on Uluru have meaning for Aboriginals, the rock itself tells a story about the Dreamtime/ancient past and evolution of Australia (e.g., extinction of dinosaurs). The planet, including Australia, is peppered with asteroid impacts and extinction events that have shaped the unique flora and fauna we have today.

Our earth is part of a solar system and galaxy of which Aboriginals may be the first astronomers to recognise (e.g., Dark Emu in the Milky Way). The purpose of the following PowerPoint is to recognise Aboriginal culture and to understand the earth's evolution as part of the Dreamtime that is kept alive with Uluru.

The formation of Uluru and the gap between our metaphysical view and science

- Our asteroid (Uluru) theory is presented from a metaphysical viewpoint with some preliminary scientific evidence. The established scientific view considers the rock features at Uluru to be related to sedimentary processes (alluvial fans) derived from the Peterman Ranges Orogeny, which started some 550 million years ago. Many scientists believe that an asteroid would disintegrate during impact, and the three rock formations—Uluru, Mt Augustus, and Cave Hill—have different rock types and ages dispelling an asteroid origin. However, scientific gaps and difficulties occur in age dating due to weathering and lack of suitable samples.

- The asteroid (Uluru) would have had variable composition (e.g., sandstone-conglomerate) with varying influence from the impact sites (water, sediment thickness, rock type) to connect the three rocks with our estimate age (65 million years). The cushioned landing in the Eromanga Sea and east–west alignment with Cave Hill and Mt Augustus support our asteroid origin.
- Further scientific studies are required to support our asteroid origin. The asteroid concept of Uluru/Mt Augustus/Cave Hill is considered alternative and based on a metaphysical information source (i.e., Alcheringa, the ancient creator spirit who resides at Uluru).

Note: Uluru 25° 20′ Atila (Mt Connor) 25° 29′ 100 km E of Uluru
Kata Tjuta 25° 17′ 40 km W. of Uluru
Burringarrah (Mt Augustus) 24 ° 19′ 1,450 km W of Uluru

The asteroid—and why it remains today

The rock, just like the dreamtime, is still alive, today, past, and future.

- Uluru represents the miraculous intact remains of the original asteroid from 65 million years ago. The reason why the asteroid didn't disintegrate like most other asteroids is due its size and the impact conditions; i.e., cushioning from a shallow inland sea and flexible sediments.
- The inland sea contained thick sediments and mud, which absorbed and cushioned the force of impact. The low oblique angle of impact

- trajectory and muddy seabed protected the asteroid from the disintegration during impact.
- The asteroid's large size (3.6 km long, 1.9km wide, 10 km circumference) and composition (iron and ice) formed a protective shield during the fiery entry into our atmosphere.
- Cooling and hardening of the asteroid occurred after impact due to ingress of seawater and sediments.
- Uluru exhibits obvious resilience relative to the surrounding landscape, showing minimal weathering over geological time. The rock was honed by the extreme heat it experienced when it first fell into the sea of water.

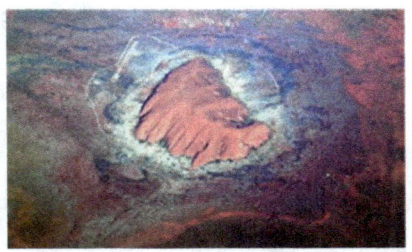

Evidence of the inland sea (Eromanga) during the Cretaceous (65 million years) has been documented by geologists and palaeontologists. Opalised fossils (marine and land-based) verify the ancient inland sea, together with the Shield Shrimp trapped on top of Uluru and the seashells on top of Mount Connor. The Great Artesian basin has up to 3km thickness of sediments.

The Asteroid and Impact Site

Scientists have proven a paleo valley exists between Kata Tjuta, in the west, and Uluru, to the east.

I refer to my vision and now ask you to imagine how Uluru has landed into the ancient sea and pushed the seabed up and forward into mounds. Kata Tjuta is a conglomerate of seabed rock—and it is different to the Uluru Arkose, which is unique.

The impact crater has filled with mud over time. The planet earth also experienced other catastrophic events from different asteroid impacts

(e.g., Henbury Meteorite crater, Shiva impact crater near India, and the Puerto Rico plateau).
Aboriginal elders do not permit testing and drilling of sacred areas.

Uluru's resistance to weathering over time

View of a vertical face of Uluru Rock with some exfoliation occurring like rusting. The red covers the original grey rock.
The rock is hard, smooth to touch, and shows very little weathering and erosion given its age.

Aerial Imagery—Kata Juta

Scientists have various theories on how the Uluru rock and Kata Tjuta rock were formed. Material eroding happened and the materials were later buried, compressed to the coarse sandstone (arkose), and later, large areas of the sandstone was uplifted into mountain ranges by earthquakes and folding the sandstone, tilting it to an angle of 80 to 85 degrees.

Kata Tjuta was formed at the same time, but it is of conglomerate. The strata are tilted at ten to twenty degrees.

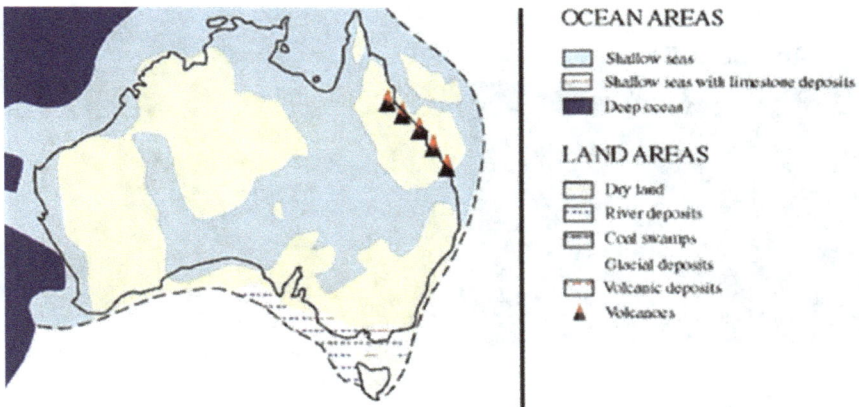

Metaphysical view: result of asteroid impact & buckling of sediments/earth's crust from Uluru.

Palaeo—Map of Eromanga Sea

The Eromanga shallow sea dates back to the Cretaceous (110 million years ago). The image above is a superimposition of the shallow Eromanga Sea over ancient Australia. The Eromanga Sea contained thick sediment to cushion the asteroid's impact.

The Great Artesian Basin

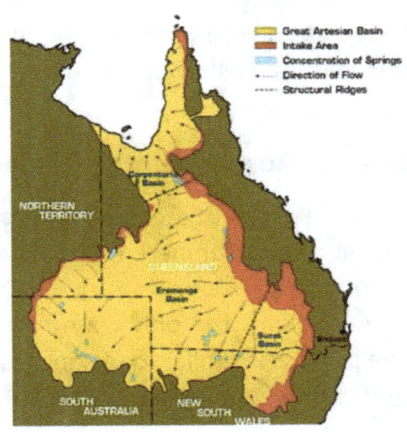

The basin represented a source of thick sediment to cushion the asteroids landing on earth.

Scientists suggest the dinosaurs were destroyed 65 million years ago, during the late Cretaceous period.

It is likely that Uluru (asteroid) destroyed the dinosaurs in Australia. The paleo-channel and valley discovered between Uluru and Kata Tjuta provides groundwater resources for the community. The paleo-valley extends east to west and was formed from 65 million to 10,000 years ago. The paleo-valley is situated along the asteroid impact zone between Uluru and Kata Juta.

The Amadeus Basin

 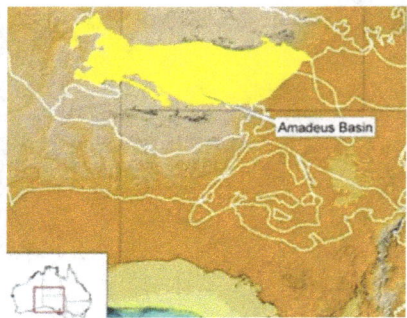

Area of Uluru and Yulara Resort town extract groundwater from The Amadeus Basin (image from space by NASA in 1994).

The Amadeus Basin is a 170,000 km2, intra-cratonic sedimentary basin in central Australia, lying mostly within the southern Northern Territory and extending into Western Australia. Local deposition of up to 14km of marine and non-marine sedimentary rocks took place from the Neoproterozoic to the late Paleozoic, along with other nearby sedimentary basins of similar age (Officer Basin, Georgina Basin, Ngalia Basin). The Amadeus Basin is believed to have once been part of the hypothetical Centralian Super basin. The basin and aquifer systems are informed to reflect the impact of the asteroid (Uluru).

Opals in Australia (asteroid made)

The unique opals in central Australia relate to the asteroid impacts. The extreme heat tempered the minerals and sand within the bones and formed opal.

Australia is the only country with fossilised opals (dinosaur, plants). The process is similar to making glass from sand; extreme heat is required to turn sand into glass.

This map shows the opal digs in Australia; orange dots mark the digs.

Australian fossilised opals

Relics from the age of dinosaurs and the asteroid that changed the face of Australia's landscape and evolution

Australian fossils provide new and fascinating information about Australia's ancient heritage and the evolution of plants, animals, and environments on the Australian continent.

Of all the Australian opal fields, Lightning Ridge and some boulder opal fields are the only places that have opalised fossils of land-living and freshwater plants and animals. The other Australian opal fields have fossils of saltwater or marine organisms, which provide other important information about Australia's past and the ancient Eromanga Sea.

Australia is the only place on Earth that produces opalised bones of land-living animals including dinosaurs—and most of these are from Lightning Ridge.

At the heart of the Australian Opal Centre is a magnificent collection of 100-million-year-old fossils, from the Early Cretaceous period. It was a time when dinosaurs and other ancient creatures lived where Lightning Ridge now stands, and when ancient reptiles swam in a shallow sea (Eromanga) covering much of inland Australia, including where the opal fields of White Cliffs, Winton, Coober Pedy, Andamooka, Mintabie, and Lambina are now.

Lightning Ridge is the only significant dinosaur site in New South Wales. Opalised bones from fields like Coober Pedy, Andamooka, and White Cliffs are from plesiosaurs, ichthyosaurs, and pliosaurs, which are marine reptiles, not dinosaurs.

Legacy of The Ancient Inland Sea

 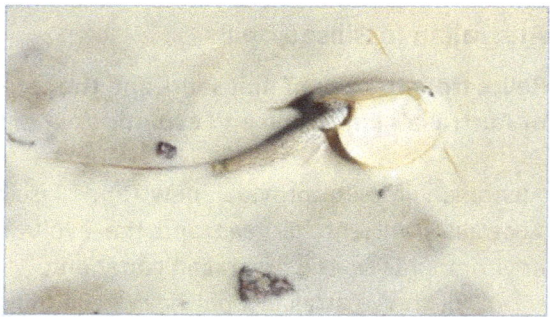

This unusual desert crustacean is Australia's only known species of shield shrimp (found also on top of Uluru in temporary water holes). The shield shrimp is seen in a temporary waterhole in the Australian outback (IMAGE: Robert Pfeife). The Mutitjulu Waterhole is considered a perennial water source at Uluru.

The Eromanga Sea was originally a cool sea, but in the late Cretaceous period, the sea become hot. The heat, derived from asteroid impacts, changed the surface water, but particularly the groundwater temperatures.

This map shows plutonic waters in Australia seeping through sediment into The Great Artesian Basin and how hot the waters rise through Artesian Bores—from 30 to 100 degrees Celsius.

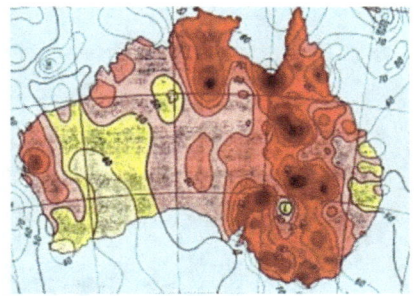

Uluru today

The photo everyone hopes to get at sunset

Uluru is well known for its iconic red glow during sunset. This relates to its asteroid origins and the great heat and powerful entry into this earth.

We hope that scientists are open to understanding our metaphysical view of Uluru as an asteroid and its importance in understanding the evolution of the Australian landscape and a period of the Dreamtime.

Ten

Interview with John Barrow

The Star People had the ability to maintain order within the universe: there were many Star Wars in the past.

Himel the Warrior, Part 3 (past-life recall of John Barrow). John has three other interesting past lives as a warrior that you can read about on the home page of my website, in 'John's Corner.'

22 July 2017
In this section, I am taking my husband, John, through his memories of being a Leonine, from Sirius. This race of Star People (many humans have Star People memories) were directed by the Angelic Realms to maintain order in the galaxies, in the different universes. In this recall, John is describing the powers of the space vessel, and what they could do with asteroids and laser beams to wipe out unwanted races or remove beings from planets (if not an entire planet). I am watching and questioning him, while he is in a theta state of consciousness.

Valérie: How did they destroy the dinosaurs? Because the Earth was a big place.

John: I don't think they were just on this planet. There were other planets where there were dinosaurs also. They all had to be brought to heel, and as it turned out they were demolished. I think that was the enemy.

Valérie: Please stay in that space for a minute. Ask God to help you to see the technology you used to exterminate the dinosaurs.

John: We had the power of being able to direct meteors. That was like our artillery, like our bombers. And we had laser beams, which you could equate to infantry. Those laser beams could petrify the dinosaurs, or any other creature for that matter, into fossil, instantly.

Valérie: How did they catch the meteors? (All this time, John was holding his hand to his brow and rubbing his eyes—just like the image of the thinker!)

John: Didn't catch them. We had the technology to divert them. If you wanted to aim them at something we could do it. I know now what we were, of which I was, if not the total commander, I was a very senior commander. I think I know exactly what these Leonines were. There was a High Being, probably God, above all this. I can't define that, but I know exactly what we were there for. We were Cosmic Cops. No fooling, we were sent on missions throughout the galaxy. We had an arsenal of meteors we could aim wherever we wanted to.

We had laser technology that could just flatten the dinosaurs. We were much smaller than the dinosaurs obviously, but we could knock them out. Zap them out. Or any other beings which were malevolent or that had turned malevolent. Because God's creatures start out, as babies do, pure, and then they become corrupted as they develop. We were totally devoid of any evil. So, if there was a problem in the galaxy we could go and sort them out. Cosmic Cops that's what we were!

(John's theta consciousness popped back into this world, and he said the next sentence with his eyes still closed).

It's funny when I was commissioned in the army in this dimension. In this life I was like a colonial policeman, to help protect the Empire. (John was in Malaya during the emergency—and Sudan before that). There's plenty ships flying around up there, it's going on all the time. It's not just this Earth; it's going on now, right now.

Valérie: Are the Leonine people still around?

John: Yes. (Spoken without any hesitation.)

Valérie: Why don't they show themselves to us here on this Earth now?

John: In an indirect way now, I think they do, with the cat families. So, if you think it through, cats are highly therapeutic, and they can really change people's lives. I now know why I have this very strong affinity with cats.

John Barrow says, 'There's plenty ships flying around up there, it's going on all the time.'

Valérie: It has been said that Uluru is an asteroid and has been brought to Earth to help wipe out the dinosaurs. Does that make sense to you?

John It's very probable. And that's a small meteorite—there are much bigger ones than that. There are some so big that if you impact them on a planet, it will shatter the planet.

Valérie: Have you ever had to do that?

Comet 67P/C-G and Uluru size comparison approximate. Photos: European Space Agency and Parks Australia

John: I know it's possible. We don't just sit and create tidal waves and all that sort of stuff; we could literally fragment a whole planet. What they can do is hurl one planet into another—they have the technology to do it.

This is the Leonines, or their bosses, whoever they may be. (He came out of the meditative state, the alpha state. He still had his eyes shut).

Valérie: Ask God if there is anything else he would like you to understand.

John: I think the Leonine people have been there for ever and they are Cosmic Cops. I don't know what happened with the hieroglyphs and the crash landing here—I mean, they weren't completely winning everything. The dinosaur people had the capability of retaliating...and what I can see in my heart was huge. A very big ship. It was damaged by the enemy. You talk about nuclear bombs and atomic and hydrogen bombs on this earth; they are like peashooters compared with what goes on up there.

(He had jumped time to seeing the mothership Rexegena attacked nearly a million years ago).

I think we had a fleet of ships up there after the mothership was blown up. (John wanted to know if what he was talking about fitted in with the dinosaur time).

Valérie: Yes! That was 65 million years ago, and the time the mothership was blown up was about nine hundred thousand years ago.

John: (sounding quite definite) Well, they were here to sort something out and they got clobbered. I think the Aborigines know something we don't know.

John Barrow says, 'I think the Aborigines know something we don't know.'

81

Perhaps the Wandjinas shared information with the forefathers of the present-day Indigenous Australians?

Earth humans' technology is so behind it's not funny. So behind the rest of the galaxy. The other galactic races kicked the dinosaurs off the Earth and made man the predominant creature here.

It was a highly developed attacking force. It was there not to attack but to police, but if it had to attack. It was deadly. It could blow stuff away. They could pull down a meteor and redirect it. And they still can.

Valérie: My understanding in working with the Lord of the Universe is that he is wanting peace to prevail right throughout the universe, in all different dimensions, across all different races, and he wants this to be so.

John: Nothing has changed, it's just that man has got completely out of control. He's hopeless.

I then explained to John how aspects of the entire universe are in the little body of the earthlings, which holds who they are in that other world with a veiled consciousness so that while they are in the body here, they don't remember, but it gives an opportunity to experience family life with children and learn to love and have compassion. To experience that—because some of those races out there just didn't understand that—I am speaking from a bigger picture here, bigger than the cosmic cops. Because you can't go round now blasting people off the Earth. They don't want that now. The hierarchy, God, is wanting peace to prevail throughout the universe by choice, by people really coming to understand and experience the energies of love and compassion. Not all of them understand or know it—that's why you have people still with an aspect from the cosmic reptile and animal worlds in them, that they can still pick up a gun and point it at someone and in cold blood just shoot them dead, feeling no remorse at all. There are beings like that in the Cosmic Worlds.

John agreed to ask God to release the aggression he had in him from the Leonine being. Today he seems a good deal calmer—I can feel a difference in him. We give thanks to God. John then wanted to have his dinner. So be it.

John said, 'In past lives, I don't think I have ever been anything but a warrior, but now I ask what is the point of war? Both sides see themselves as right—but nobody really wins; all suffer.'

Samasta Loka Sukhino Bhavantu: 'May all beings in all the worlds be happy.'
A song sung at Sri Sathya Sai Baba's Ashram in India.

Eleven

Giants of Earth

John's memory of the Leonine Race immediately came to my mind when a friend, Rebecca, sent me these images (below) that Bruno Teste took in the Fontainebleau Forest just south of Paris.

'We had the power of being able to direct meteors. That was like our artillery, like our bombers. And we had laser beams, which you could equate to infantry. Those laser beams could petrify the dinosaurs, or any other creature for that matter, into fossil, instantly.'

Alcheringa has also advised that the rocks taken from the 'Planetoid Belt' were 'charged'—raised to an advanced energy, frequency, and vibration so they would not break up when they hit the Earth.

Bruno Teste has given me permission to place some of these images in this book. When I first saw them, I asked Alcheringa if they are images of past dinosaurs that had been petrified.

He said, yes; there were also giants that had also been caught up in the war. At the time, the Fontainebleau Forest was the Stampian Sea—the salt water assisted the petrification to hold their shapes. It began 65 million years ago, and the water did not disappear until 23 million years later.

I thank Mr Bruno Teste for allowing some of his extraordinary photos to be shared.

His work is astounding…and is truly impressive. His book is noted at the end of this chapter, along with where to purchase a copy. He is looking for a publisher interested in publishing his work in English.

Alcheringa advises it was the time Earth was inhabited by giants. Some of them were human-like, from Mars.

https://www.facebook.com/profile.php?id=100024081344105
Amicalement, Bruno Teste

Giants of Earth

Giants of Earth

> **Oligocene Epoch | geochronology | Britannica** www.britannica.com › ... › Fossils & Geologic Time
> **Oligocene Epoch**, third and last major worldwide division of the Paleogene Period (65.5 million to 23 million years ago), spanning the interval between 33.9 Million ... & 28.1 Million Years.
> There are hundreds of these fossilised Rocks in the Fontainebleau Forest – South of Paris, France. There was also the Stampian Sea.

- Wikipedia says: The boulders in Fontainebleau are erosive remnants from the Oligocene age, relatively young in geological terms. Their appearance may have been accentuated by localised mineralisation (silicification) of the sandstone rock, forming large nodules that are resistant to erosion.
- What I can gather is that the Stampian Sea (this word comes from the town Etampe nearby) was there during the Oligocene period about 33 million years ago, now called the Rupelian age instead, and that when it retreated it left sand and shelly limestone, which has a supposedly been eroded by wind and water to create the boulders. The Rupelian is, in the geologic timescale, the older of two ages or the lower of two stages of the Oligocene epoch. It spans the time between 33.9 and 28.1 Million Years.
- The Paleogene spans from the extinction of non-avian dinosaurs, 66 million years ago, to the dawn of the Neogene, 23.03 million years ago. It features three epochs, the Paleocene, Eocene and Oligocene.
- The Cenozoic era meaning "new life" is the current and most recent of the three geological eras of the Phanerozoic Eon. It follows the Mesozoic Era and extends from 66 million years ago to the present day. It is generally believed to have started on the first day of the Cretaceous–Paleogene extinction event (also referred to as the K-Pg, or K-T, extinction event) when an asteroid hit the Earth.
- The Grande Coupure, or "great break" in continuity, with a major Europe an turnover in mammalian fauna about 33.5 Million Years, marks the end of the last phase of Eocene assemblages, the Priabonian, and the arrival in Europe of Asian species. The Grande Coupure is characterised by widespread extinctions. Another speculation points to several large meteoritic impacts near this time, including those of the Chesapeake Bay crater 40 km and the Popigai crater 100 km of central Siberia, which scattered debris perhaps as far as Europe. New dating of the Popigai meteor strengthens its association with the extinction.

- I found a couple of late resting websites with bits about Fontainebleau:
- http://int.com.phile-soph4s42.html
- Look at these interesting petroglyphs that were found there, do you recognise them at all?

George Nelh

It is interesting that some of the symbols drawn above are also drawn on the walls of the Kariong Egyptian Tomb near Gosford. The cross within the circle, the 5-pointed star, and the wave-like one is also similar.

John, in his memory of Leonines, remembers the Draco/Hierarchy and lizard people had not left the Earth. After a short time spent underground, they experimented with the Leonine bodies that they had recovered from the war when the dinosaurs were destroyed.

They began experimenting with genetic engineering and created animals with hair they used from the Leonine bodies. They tried to retrieve their DNA soul Light, but that had already returned to Sirius.

The lizard people became quite adventuress with producing furry animals—it is interesting that such a complicated mammal as the Duck-billed platypus was created in Australia or the land now known as Australia.

And then there were all the other hairy animals. With a little imagination, it is not too hard to recognise how some animals' genes were crossed with a new creation of species, again and again, until they looked very different.

Some species were brought to the Earth planet by other races.

So, it was like 'Let's try a little bit of this and then a little bit of that from somewhere else—and over millions of years, there was an amazing collection of animals, birds, insects, and reptiles.

Then came the time when experiments were made to create an upstanding being that could answer to the call of their Draco Hierarchy to do work and mine gold, et cetera, and as it came to be, they were used as a sacrifice to their Gods.

Archaeologists can name many different species of early upstanding ape-like man, who had quite a bit of different DNA over millions of years, all because of evolvement or genetic experiments of the lizard people... until...

Homo Sapiens, or the human race as it is now, have all sorts of DNA that are found in just about all living beings on this planet. Some of the life would have been brought to our planet by visiting Star People. It was the time humans were blessed with a soul consciousness as well as a brain, and a Light body was also connected directly to their Oversoul/God-Self from the Source of all Creation.

Our human race is of great interest to other Star Worlds. It is so different, and the Benevolent hierarchy has taken the opportunity to bless the race so it can be used as physical beings to hold many types of other races from other worlds, be it warm blooded or cold blooded—so that they can experience what it is like to live in our world and feel the emotions and the nervous reactions. Hence, beings from other worlds have been coming into an Earth body under the guidance and agreement with the Karmic Board. This overseeing board exists to always help and remind people of their agreement. That means, of course, that no Earth being is ever alone. The Angelic Realm is there to maintain Universal Law as best they can.

Everyone on Earth has free will, instead of allowing themselves to think or be used as slaves. That means the choices they make are their own.

Twelve

History of Humans on Earth

I have been asked by Alcheringa to review the evolvement upon our Earth that the Star People have given to me. When I was first called to work with them, I was advised that they couldn't give me all the information, as it was too much. They were giving information to various people around the Earth, and it would all come together eventually and weave together like a tapestry of truth. That time is now.

I was also advised not to worry about what the others have written, just the evolvement in how I have been given it.

Differences, when respected and discussed, would probably open to further truth.

My mission is to advise about the main evolvement of the Earth and our human race—as I have learned from the Star People's knowledge, and how the Indigenous Australian people have held the creation stories down through forever—and to encourage that to be accepted and honoured.

Brief overview of important evolution information regarding our planet Earth, given by the Star People from the Andromeda Galaxy M31

The reason Uluru was sent to Earth as an asteroid was to destroy the dinosaurs who were destroying Earth's atmosphere. The dinosaurs had been created by the 'Cold-blooded Star People and the giant race that had come from Mars,' known as the reptilian, Dinoids, Draco, etc., who had taken over our planet from its early inception. It was the time of the Giants on Earth.

There were many Star Wars.

There were five major ice ages upon Earth.

There were many Star People coming and going upon Earth for millions of years—some just visiting; some staying and creating advanced civilizations. Alcheringa has referred to it as the 'Old Empire.'

900,000 years ago, an agreement was made by the United Planetary Nations, with the Reptoid races, to handover our planet, which was originally planned and created by the Angelic Realms in Andromeda M31 to replace the planet Maldek that had been attacked and destroyed. This is evidenced by the asteroid belt in our solar system.

50,000 Star People from the Pleiades, also known as the Seven Sisters within the Taurus constellation, volunteered to come to Earth and establish a point of Light in a very dark corner of our Milky Way and establish a raised consciousness society on our planet Earth.

Our beautiful, technologically advanced mothership, Rexegena, was attacked by the Reptoid/Draco Star People and only ninety Star People survived. They tried to establish the planned new society and accepted help from some of the reptilians who were very upset about the turn of events.

The existing upstanding 'animal man', who had been created by the Draco people as slaves and sacrifices, were used genetically by the surviving Pleiadeans to create the beginning of the human race, which went on to evolve to who we are now, with a *Blessing from the Source of Creation. As for the age-old disagreement with scholars, as to whether humans were created by God or evolved from animals—both are correct*.

700,000/800,000 years ago, the Angelic (angle-ic) Hierarchy from Andromeda wanted to overview the new human race as it was gradually spreading around the world from the 'animal man' interbreeding with the up-lifted HU-man (Light man). Evidence in archaeology shows the many varieties of Homo Sapiens, Neanderthals, Denisovans, and more ancient upstanding ape-like creature skeletons that are given various names.

A Grand Plan was decided upon by the Hierarchy from Andromeda to set up platforms to overview each child being born onto this planet Earth. They were given a *soul*, which is a little like a computer chip that is held within the Hypothalamus and links the Pineal gland to the Pituitary gland in an arc of Light straight to their heart (refer to the Ancient Eye of Egypt and the Eye of Shiva or God).

Each soul consciousness is linked in a divine way to their *Oversoul* or *God-self* from the *Source of all Creation*. It is easily observed by benevolent Star People who monitor the evolution of their creation upon our planet Earth. Understand that these Star People are far more advanced in technology than what currently exists on our planet. They have only ever wanted to assist our human evolution.

The Universal Law gives them the right to assist but not take over. For that reason, we need to remember to *ask* first for assistance at all times and they—the Benevolent Beings—will come straight away.

The new humans, 800,000 years ago, were gradually evolving around our planet Earth. The benevolent Star People were teaching ceremonies, song, and dance to the Indigenous people, to honour their *creator* and to take care of their planet Earth.

The Australian Indigenous People are the oldest living human race on Earth. They were of the Lemurian time, and taught the early ceremonies, song, dance, stories, and how to create fire to cook, as the Star People had taught them in the beginning.

300,000 years ago, the Blue Star People from Venus volunteered to come and establish advanced ways of living and to create centres for honouring the Creator as well as using advanced ways of building and using earth materials in technology. The Earth was still in a layer of consciousness that communication with benevolent Star People was easy and took place with telepathy or 'mind to mind.' This was the Atlantean time.

It has been recorded in the Book of Jubilees that the Gods mated with humans. The Blue Star People from Venus mated with the Cro-Magnon hairy ones. This took place over that period and was the Cosmic Origins of the Hebrew race and other similar races. They went on to evolve into the Race of Atlan. The Atlanteans. They had advanced abilities and knowledge. Some played with their ability of genetic engineering and began to create all the strange shapes of animal and man together. The images have been recorded in Greek mythology.

Some Atlantean scientists experimented with creating another moon surrounding Earth to make it another easy place for Star People to land on their way to visit Earth. They were warned against it, but it took place and sadly broke loose, crashing into the planet Earth.

The Hierarchy from Andromeda had to immediately hold the disruptive atmosphere on Earth within its own atmosphere. The Atmosphere Grid was tightened to contain that disruption to Earth only, and not the solar system. It is slowly being loosened and opened now through star gates.

Atlantis Fell

The time was around 12,000 years ago. After the Earth nearly died, dropping from the 4th dimension to the 3rd dimension, the Ancient Egyptians held a lot of the knowledge of the Star People. The Egyptian Royalty were not actually Star People, but they genetically held the genes of the Star People with elongated heads and bodies shaped like theirs.

They understood the pyramids. The pyramids were built long before the Earth nearly died. The Ancient Egyptians built over them.

The pyramids were points of Light that held the connection of the Earth's energy in direct alignment with the 'core' of suns, linking with the centre of creation of all—the Absolute.

After the fall of Atlantis there was a shift in the alignment. After that, the pyramids were a little off key—for the key was holding the Earth's alignment, heralding the Golden Age. The Golden Age existed on Earth several times before. There have been advanced civilizations upon Earth a few times before the existing civilization. We are now on our way back to a Golden Age where all will be peace, harmony, and goodwill upon our Earth.

The Amarna Period was an era of ancient Egyptian history during the latter half of the Eighteenth Dynasty when the royal residence of the pharaoh, Akhenaten, and his queen was shifted to the city of Akhetaten in what is known as the Amarna Period, 1346 BC to 1336 BC.

Some of the mysteries surrounding the end of Egypt's Amarna Period can be explained by the existence of a tsunami that came through from the Mediterranean Sea and covered very much of what had been created there. You can see the sand covering the sphinx up to its neck—that was further inland. The place that was set up to worship One God was covered in sand and everyone had to leave. Akhenaten also left and was then known as Moses.

The giant tsunami had closed easy entrance by ship travelling from the Mediterranean Sea into the Red Sea. It enlarged the Mediterranean Sea. Many developed lands have been buried in the sea and part of the Nile River was relocated because of that huge surge of sand.

You can see a huge amount of sand filled the area behind the sphinx up to above the base of the pyramids...which are all on the same level.

In recent times, when you first visit this same area, you can see the sphinx ground level is well below the level of the base area of the pyramids. There is also evidence of a pontoon outside the Temple of the sphinx, where the pharaohs use to alight from barges travelling the Nile River. The Nile river is now partly relocated because of the ancient tsunami.

Thirteen

Another Challenge for the Scientists

I feel compelled to repeat this story: when Atlantis Fell, the Earth nearly died, dropping from 4th dimension to 3rd dimension. The Ancient Egyptians held a lot of knowledge of the Star People. We are advised that 300,000 years ago, the Star People from Venus came to Earth to establish a point of light upon this planet. The allegory of Adam and Eve eating the apple in the Garden of Eden explains that some of these Star People mated with the existing human race upon Earth. The only reason it wasn't supposed to happen was the Hierarchy worried it would pull down the consciousness and light within the Venusians. What did happen was that it raised the consciousness of the children who were the jewels of the interbreeding and went on to be clever at music, writing, storytelling, dance, and particularly science. They were the Hebrew children. Over thousands of years the language has changed, as well as the interbreeding, so just about everyone has some of the Venusian/Hebrew genes within them.

When I was holding the sacred Alcheringa Stone, wrapped in paperbark and tied with string, I was given the understanding, as mentioned earlier, that some of the scientists at the time of pre-Atlantis wanted to capture a huge Planetoid from the solar system and create another moon, like the one that had already been created for Earth. It was intended that Star People could continue to visit the Earth planet and use the second moon as a sort of airport. The wiser scientists warned of the danger but were ignored—hence the second moon broke free and slammed into the Earth. Alcheringa advises it hit around the Puerto Rico plateau and caused a major catastrophe to the planet. All visiting Star People left, and the remaining human race went underground or survived in caves. The story is graphically given by Saint Germaine and published in Part Two of our *Starlady* book, and at the end of this chapter.

Artist's reconstruction of Chicxulub crater soon after impact, 65 million years ago.
DETLEV VAN RAVENSWAAY/SCIENCE SOURCE

Updated: Drilling of dinosaur-killing impact crater explains buried circular hills

By Eric Hand Nov. 17, 2016, 2:00 PM https://www.sciencemag.org/news/2016/11/updated-drilling-dinosaur-killing-impact-crater-explains-buried-circular-hills

St Germaine series: Earth's Birth Changes

The book, *Earth's Birth Changes*, provides fascinating reading. I was happy to find a copy as it was *first published* in 1994. It contains an extraordinary description of the fall of Atlantis, channelled by medium, Azena, from the

U.S.A. This was described exactly as shown in the artist's reconstruction of Chicxulub above. St Germaine confirms the information about the second moon, and advises that it created total catastrophe at the end of Atlantean time, causing a major time of Ice Age. It is described as an asteroid that went down over the Atlantic Ocean and embedded itself in the ocean floor near the Puerto Rico plateau.

When I was given this understanding, and permission from the publisher to quote the work, another book was brought to my attention: *When the Earth Nearly Died*, by D.S. Allan & J.B. Delair, published by Gateway Books, U.K. It is an extensive study of compelling evidence of a catastrophic world change around 9500 B.C.

When I visited Uluru in 1994, I too received insight of a second major catastrophe on Earth as well as how one, although millions of years later, had influenced the Earth and its tectonic plates to be so 'turned upside down or moved' in a way that it was difficult for scientists to read the date or timelines of the Earth's structure. This was all before I had been given insight or knowledge of *Earth's Birth Changes* and *When the Earth nearly Died*, which were both published at the same time I was given the same information at Uluru in 1994.

So, I would request that yes, with respect, from a metaphysic understanding of the image above, it is correct—but the timeline needs to be reconsidered to include research into the cause of the Fall of Atlantis around 12,000 years ago as graphically described by St Germaine.

Scientists do say that there have been two major upliftments in the Uluru environs. Is that the same, I wonder with the *Chicxulub crater environs*?

Also, in the link to the article, from which the image is sourced, the last paragraph reads:

'The drilling effort began at the beginning of April and is sponsored by the International Ocean Discovery Program (IODP). To avoid choppy ocean waters, the scientists are using a special vessel called a lift boat that has jacked itself up off the sea floor on three pylons. Morgan, who just arrived on the drilling platform over the weekend, says the mission is the culmination of years of effort that began with her first proposal to IODP in 1998. "I had this dream we would drill this impact crater many years ago," she says. "To see this immense structure and all the people here, it's been really amazing."'

Morgan is one of the team of scientists: I am curious just when she first had the dream? Could it have been 1994? Working with the Star People, I have come to know that there are no coincidences but rather coordinated incidences.

---oOo---

Advice given here, by Alcheringa, is that the catastrophe caused with the giant rock asteroid, Uluru, was not only sent to destroy the dinosaurs but because of the Star War there were many other 'rocks' that were charged and aimed as bombs at selected points around the planet Earth and still exist today—often referred to as 'Places of the Lion'. Various indigenous races around the world have been given insight to those huge rocks and are venerated to this day. Although these rocks were used to cause the catastrophic condition of the Earth 66 million years ago, they were also programmed to heal the Earth itself, and the future human race, as it raised in consciousness.

This catastrophe as shown in the above artist's Chicxulub drawing is in the same place that St Germaine spoke of, to me in 1994. It had affected the area surrounding Uluru and lifted it also; this was millions of years later around **9500 BC** as evidenced by Allan and Delair's work, and published in 1994, 'When the Earth Nearly Died.'

Peter Erbe's book, *Earth's Birth Changes*, of Azena's channelling from St Germaine was first published in 1994, the same time Peter gave me permission to publish it in my book.

Azena's channelling of the event is extraordinary. See the summary of Part Two in the *Starlady* book.

Like Alcheringa has said, the Star People were giving information to other mediums around the world, and it would one day weave together like a tapestry of Truth. As I have said already, that time is now.

Another sign given to us by the Star People was in 1994. NASA was experiencing great joy and excitement watching the Shoemaker/Levy Asteroid/meteor string hit the planet Jupiter and they could see the huge impact crater from Earth. It was called the 'String of Pearls.'

This was a replay of the huge cycle being played out when I was writing the diary in 1994. It was also the year we visited Uluru and were advised by Alcheringa that it was an asteroid that had been brought to Earth to destroy the dinosaurs, and that it was the same time 'hair' was introduced to Earth. Now I understood that as there was a war, some of the Leonines would have lost their lives and the cold-blooded races used the hair from the Leonine race bodies to create mammals. It was much, much later that the lizard races resorted to creating megafauna, which was mammalian, as well as rough skinned creatures that again the Hierarchy had to end— therefore starting more Star Wars on Earth.

The first delivery of Uluru to destroy the illegal giant's world on Earth was the original Lion's Gate, which was again celebrated as a reminder for healing on the eighth of the eighth month, 1988, and continues. Six years later, I began writing the diary while holding the sacred Alcheringa Stone.

On 22 August 1994, Alcheringa had introduced himself to me and the summary of the book ended on 21 December 1994. Another date that coincides with 21 December 2020 is the solstice and the Great Rare Conjunction between Jupiter and Saturn leading to the Gateway of the Lion for the Age of Aquarius.

Fourteen

DNA

Alcheringa is now asking me to look at the various life forms on Earth and see how similar we are in regard to DNA.

A 2018 study found that chimpanzees—our closest living evolutionary relatives—are ninety-six per centgenetically **similar** to **humans**, as can be seen in the following article:

https://www.independent.co.uk/news/science/human-dna-share-cats-cattle-mice-same-genetics-code-a8292111.html

What has the most similar DNA to humans?

Chimpanzees. Although figures vary from study to study, it's currently generally accepted that chimpanzees (Pan troglodytes) and their close relatives the bonobos (Pan paniscus) are **humans**' closest living relatives, with each species sharing around 98.7% of our DNA.

How similar in DNA are we to each other?

All human beings are 99.9 percent identical in their genetic makeup. Differences in the remaining 0.1 percent hold important clues about the causes of diseases.

Which animal is the smartest?

Chimpanzees are reckoned to be the most intelligent animals on the planet. They can manipulate the environment and their surroundings to help themselves and their community. They can work out how to use things as tools to get things done faster, and they have outsmarted people many a time.

Primate family tree

'Due to billions of years of evolution, humans share genes with all living organisms. The percentage of genes or DNA that organisms share records their similarities ... DNA also shows that our species and chimpanzees diverged from a common ancestor species that lived between 8 and 6 million years ago.'
  'Genetic Evidence,' *Smithsonian National Museum of Natural History*, 27 Oct 2020, https://humanorigins.si.edu/evidence/genetics

What percent of DNA do humans share with trees?

We also share a shocking amount of DNA with plants and insects. We share around 60% of our DNA with bananas, 50% of our DNA with trees, 70% of with slugs, 44% with honeybees, and even 25% with daffodils.

In principle, each cell of the tree would contain human DNA. To ensure that it cannot interfere with the normal growth and appearance of the tree, the human DNA is chemically treated to 'silence' it, a standard technique used by plant scientists.

Do trees have genders?

Trees can have either male or female parts. ... In addition, there are also trees that do not contain any flowers at all, making it even harder to figure out the tree's gender. Dioecious trees. If a tree is dioecious, it only has male or female parts, not both.

Do trees have feelings?

According to scientific evidence, trees are way more intelligent than we have ever imagined. ... Trees can feel pain, and they have emotions, such as fear. They like to stand close to each other and cuddle. Trees adore company and like to take things slow.

Why do people have common DNA with most of the plants and animals?

Humans belong to the animal kingdom and there are significant chances that our DNA will match with that of other animals. The advancement in medical technology enabled the scientists to sequence the genomes of all the organisms. This proved all the speculations right as a lot of things were found common between humans and other animals.

Similarly, a recent study showed that humans might have acquired genes from the plants as well. According to the latest research, 1% of the human genome is made up of plants, fungi, and other micro-organisms.

Examples of animals and plants that have similar DNA to humans are as follows:

The genetic similarity of humans with monkeys is heavily in favour of the evolution theory.

Monkey

We are most closely associated with this family of animals. The DNA of different breeds like chimpanzees and bonobos is about 99% identical to the human deoxyribonucleic acid. The emotional expressions of bonobos closely resemble ours. Similarly, the reproductive cycle of the female chimps corresponds to that of humans. Gorillas have 98% similarity while the DNA of orangutans share 97% properties with humans. An interesting thing is that the brain of both the species works in a similar fashion.

Dogs

Dogs are regarded as one of the most loyal animals by the humans. They are also considered the best friends of mankind. The scientific research concludes that there is more than 80% similarity in the DNA of humans and dogs. That's a massive reason why researchers look towards dogs to find cures for many diseases that are common in both the species. Currently, they are being studied for treating diseases like epilepsy, allergies, and cancers.

Cats

If you think that dogs are closer to you than cats in terms of DNA similarity, your information needs an upgrade. Cats share nearly 90% of our genes. This shows why we all love them. Scientists have found enough evidence to suggest that they self-domesticate to make themselves secure and ensure regular supply of food.

Mice

This is another creature that is being used in the laboratories, by the researchers, to find cures for different diseases. The reason for this is the 90% similarity in the genes of the mice and the humans. The most common treatments in which mice are used are gene therapy and gene replacement. The genetic resemblance leads to similar reactions to different medical processes, and this can help us to find some amazing breakthroughs in the field of medicine.

Chickens

The DNA similarity of humans and birds is much less than that of other animals, but a 65% resemblance with chickens has crucial medical benefits. All of us very well know that virus flu is transmitted to humans and birds. Scientists hope that this similarity in gene structure will help them to develop vaccines for better prevention of such diseases.

Cabbages

The source of all life on Earth is the same and that is the reason we have genetic similarity in humans and plants. The percentages are surely not as high as those with animals, but there is a significant resemblance. Cabbage shares approximately 50% of the properties of the human gene. Cytochrome C is the protein that is common in both the species as it is found in Mitochondria.

Bananas

Banana is the most popular fruit in the world. The fact that it gives instant energy is a major reason for this as people, particularly athletes, around the globe consume it for this purpose. According to a study, it is more than 60% identical to our DNA as all the basic cellular functions are common. Cell division and replication of DNA are some of those functions.

Cucumbers

The genes of cucumbers are pretty much like squash, pumpkins, and watermelons. Scientists are hopeful that the sequencing of the cucumber genome will help them to improve the quality of all the related plants. The exact DNA similarity between humans and cucumbers is unknown for now, but there are some common features.

Other plants

There are numerous other plants whose DNA match with ours. Lettuce is one such example as it is 16% identical to us genetically. Similarly, potatoes are like our genes, but the level of similarity is not confirmed yet.

Bottom of Form **Do dolphins have the same DNA as humans?**

Do dolphins have similar DNA to humans?

We have very similar genetics. Throughout studies, geneticists have found that the human genome and the dolphin genome are basically the same. Texas A&M University scientist, Dr. David Busbee, explains, 'It's just that there are a few chromosomal rearrangements that have changed the way the genetic material is put together.'

What percentage of DNA do humans share with other animals?

Humans share more than 50 percent of their genetic information with plants and animals in general. They share about 80 percent with cows; 61 percent with bugs, such as fruit flies; and roughly 90 percent with elephants.

---oOo---

I asked Alcheringa how far back our human race DNA goes and he said billions of years. I said, 'WHAT?!' I was having trouble accepting that, and then that evening I was watching a documentary talking about an 'Ida' fossil found in the Messel Lake, Germany.

The researchers believe it comes from the time when the primate lineage that diversified into monkeys, apes, and ultimately humans, split from a separate group that went on to become lemurs and other less well-known species.

The image below is taken from New Scientist Magazine – 21 May 2009 by Chris Beard

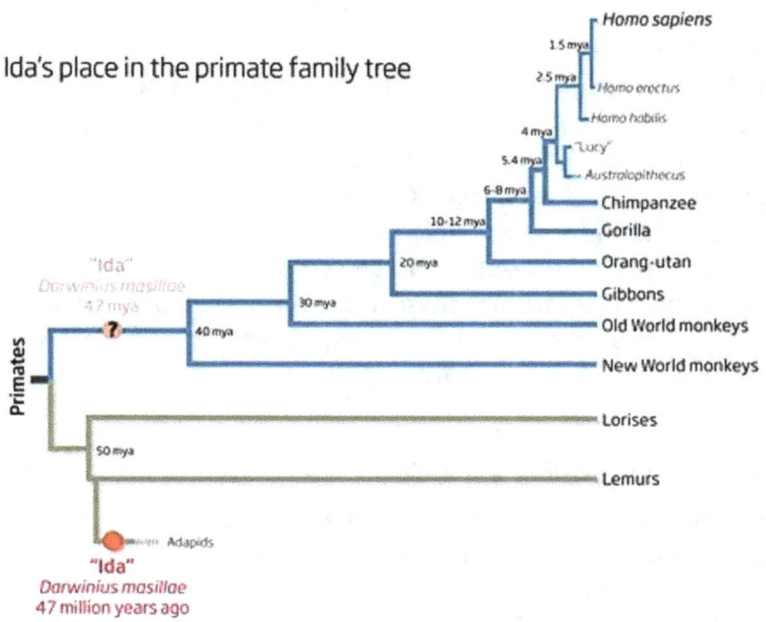

All ancient DNA is within our Earth body, and was finally blessed and raised in consciousness by genetic engineering when man became HUMAN almost one million years ago. Interestingly, the graph of Ida is showing Homo Sapiens at one million years.

Another article, below, from New Scientist, suggests Ida is a species of ancient human, but doubts remain.

By Alison George
Read more: https://www.newscientist.com/article/2282223-dragon-man-claimed-as-new-species-of-ancient-human-but-doubts-remain/#ixzz 6yxuGCyXr

Alcheringa clarifies that all and everything came to this planet when it was created, from other worlds. As he has said, the planet was illegally settled in the early time by the cold-blooded races, Draco and reptilian/Dinoid. They were and still are very clever with genetic engineering (without permission from the Source), so it was easy for them to use a species of creature and genetically transform it—or leave it to its own device, and sometimes changes would evolve because of the environment.

It will be easy for scientists to accept this when the existence of Star People is accepted.

India has held in their legends that a monkey race existed. Alcheringa says they came from another world, against their will. Some were used in experiments to create creatures. Hanuman, the Monkey God, was held in reverence as the one that loved God the most. And yes, they do go back billions of years from another planet.

You could call the result of all these experiments the 'animal man' that was finally rescued and raised in consciousness nearly 1 million years ago, with a blessed soul and Light Body directly from the source of All Creation, which is Universal Love.

Regarding the human race now on Earth

The benevolent Star People have been overseeing us in continued development with genetic influence and natural evolvements as to who we have all become.

The blessed story is given with full event details in the book, *Alcheringa, When the first Ancestors were Created.* Hundreds of people remember they were Star People, and some have contributed their story of the same event. The manuscript was personally blessed by the Avatar of the Age, Sri Sathya Sai Baba in India.

Part Two

THE MYSTERY SCHOOL

Fifteen

The Mystery Schools

12 January 2013

Cosmic Sai Baba: Many people will be a little confused about what has happened and what is happening since 21 December 2012—the solstice or turning point. And there has been talk about Mystery Schools. There are many already set up around this world, but there will be more. There are more that are needed to help people to graduate through the change—the change within themselves.

And so, Valérie Barrow followed the guidance and direction of Cosmic Sai Baba to set up the Mystery Schools.

Cosmic Sai Baba: They will wonder about what you would call 'psychic experiences.' More and more will receive these experiences and not truly understand what is happening. And so, there are many people upon this

Earth who do understand and will be able to help them and given them clarification.

Introducing Mystery Schools by Cosmic Sai Baba

23 November 2012 (Note, this date is Baba's birthday).

Cosmic Sai Baba: I am here, and you do not have to think anymore. The Mystery School it is; the focus is to be on what you started out at Canyonleigh. However, there will be other Mystery Schools and they will evolve—they will begin, and they will evolve around the Earth—for it is time for all peoples to come to know and understand who they really are. And this is how they will know.

We call it Mystery Schools now because it is a mystery to many people as to where they came from, why they are here, and where they are going.

We would like them to know about their Soul Consciousness and how to connect with that resonance so they can communicate and know what their blueprint is.

There is still much more evolvement on the Earth that is needed, my dear. The changes on the 21st of December, 2012 will take place. But there will not be much notice of this, except for all the changes that have already gone and the few that will take place after. I would like this message to go on your website, if you do not mind. Indeed, for I want it known that you are involved with the setting up of Mystery Schools. And more will evolve as time progresses.

21 December 2012 (The solstice)—The turning point

A gathering of seven people was organised spontaneously to activate the Alcheringa Crystal on the property known as Satori Springs (AKA 'Alcheringa'). We poured 'Blessed Water' from the property onto the Crystal. The wind suddenly blew, as if welcoming spirit, and John, the property manager, began to channel a message from the stars.

Then Alcheringa spoke. Up until then it had been a dull day. When he began to speak the sun came out so brightly it was known to also be Divine Light, so bright it almost blinded us. Then three eagles showed themselves in the sky above—always a sign of sacredness.

Most of the people had been present when the 80kg Alcheringa Crystal was blessed from the sky in in 2001. They were visiting the Alcheringa Crystal to find out more. If interested, you can search 'Blessing the Alcheringa Crystal at Canyonleigh' on my website and see many bright lights in the sky.

More evolvement has happened since and will be recorded at the closing of this book, speaking about 21 December 2020.

Sixteen

Before the Fall of Atlantis

Alcheringa has now asked me to study what we have been given by Jalarm 'on the Mystery School.' And to focus on Atlantean times before 'the fall' that is described by those such as Plato.

I would like to explain how this information was received.

The Oracle

Jacqui, Jill, and myself had been invited by Cosmic Sai Baba to work the Oracle, meaning a Ouija Board as most people know it. When we said a prayer, after joining hands and asking for a blessing—we also sang 3 Oms—  the wine glass spelt out the name God. Intuitively, we realized the Ouija Board had been sanctified and was now in the name of God. Then we asked who was there and the name 'Jalarm' was spelt out. He asked Valérie to channel him.

1 February 2013—Jalarm (pronounced Yalum)—Atlantis. (Google: Narayana Oracle website.)

Jalarm: It is Jalarm, and I am pleased to be here. I know that Valérie is wondering if it is the same Jalarm that is on the Internet at the time of Sai Baba of Shirdi, and in some ways it is—but I am coming from a time before Atlantis Fell and I want to speak of that time. I want to give you information about that time, for there has been much written and much speculation, and so, if you do not mind, I would like to try and reduce this speculation and give you a clear picture of how it was on this Earth before Atlantis Fell.

(Alcheringa advised in 2021 that Jalarm was he in a Star Person's body and that he is the same oversoul as Jalarm).

Jalarm: I would suggest to you at times to use the Oracle—but I would also like you to prepare questions, so that when you come to these meetings, I will attempt to answer them and if I am not able to answer them clearly then I can give you a message through the Oracle. For it is the Oracle that will be able to spell out dates clearly, and names and time. So do you have any questions that you would like to ask at this time?" *Andromeda Val (Valérie), Anna (Jacqui), & Daina (Jill)*

(Long silence)

Jalarm: I would like to say to the three of you that you have had lives pre-Atlantis. You have been on this Earth—in many, many lives—and you have a lot of information already in you, but you also can draw upon the records that are kept in the Cosmos and in the surrounding Ether of the Earth.

So, has no one got a question?
(Silence again.)

Valérie: Scientists seem to be unclear of how many years ago Atlantis Fell—in a day and a night, we believe. Is this correct?

Jalarm: This is correct, and it happened, my dear, 10,500 years ago, although there was movement happening around the Earth before that—before it Fell.

The Ice Age started to begin before then. I would like to prompt you with questions.

(We held hands again and he said he would give answers with the Oracle. We then sat in meditation for a while.)

Jalarm: I will put a thought into one of your minds—and then you can ask the question on the Oracle. This is just a little discipline I want to apply. I am asking you to use this to receive the information.

Jacqui: What is the purpose for us coming together?

Jalarm: The purpose of you coming together is to release information about Atlantis before it Fell, and how the civilizations were on this Earth and the abilities they had. And who they were—not just one race but many. They were very advanced when Atlantis Fell. Many of the records were lost. And this is your purpose—this is why we have asked you to come together. Does this help you?

(We said, 'thank you'.)

Jacqui: How can we be of service? What is the goal at the end of it?

Jalarm: The goal, if you are willing to do this, is to itemize the information, as to how it should be presented—and also not too much work for you.

Jill (via the Oracle): How many people were on the Earth at that time?

(The Oracle hesitated and then spun in a circle as if saying, 'it is a difficult question'. Jacqui wrote answers on paper given to and by the Oracle.)

Jalarm: There was a very complicated range of people upon the Earth. Many had been created on this planet and there were many who came as visitors with very advanced information—very advanced knowledge. They did many things that on this Earth have not yet been done. But they will. Certainly, there was flying interstellar interaction. So, there were people coming from other worlds to visit this planet very easily. So, you ask what was the population? And this is why the hesitation of the Oracle. Because they used to come and go. It was hard to say how many. Because some would stay; some would go. So, if you were to ask how many of the Star People have lived on this Earth, how many were born here, then I could give you a number. This is the Star People I am speaking of because they were not made of the earth body.

There were humans that were Earth People who had inherited the hairy ape-like genes. And so, they are a different race also. In fact, it has been said that there was an edict that the Star People were not to intermarry with the Earth women, or men for that matter, because of their inheritance of a lower energy; that was the reason. If they married, they would have reduced their Light and it would have gone against their whole mission of being here, which was to hold a higher consciousness and a higher Light upon this Earth, this planet that was in part of the galaxy that is quite dark. And that was their mission to bring more Light and a higher consciousness of love to this particular area within the galaxy.

So, does this clarify to you how I would like you to ask the question of how many people were on this Earth? There were settlers, you could say, who came to live upon the Earth and have children—so they were born upon this Earth also. They were of the higher consciousness of the Star People.

Humans, that we have told you about before, were an upgraded consciousness and blessed by the Light of God—and they were upon this Earth also.

And then there were still those that had not intermarried with the Star People and so they remained more limited in their abilities and their thinking.

Unfortunately, the Star People who were committed to this Earth did go against the edict from the Hierarchy and found some of the Earth women and the Earth men very attractive, and they did intermarry despite a request not to. It lowered the energy of Light in the children that were born. But in some ways, they were also born with more abilities, certainly psychic abilities, but also intelligence, and they were able to think very cleverly. Those children were special children, really, in that they were able to do and understand things more from the Star People's point of view, rather than the Earth People.

However, the Earth People were taught many things by the Star People and so there was an inter-action of knowledge. And there was also teaching that went out to the Earth People to conduct ceremonies to help balance the energies upon the Earth—to be able to receive energies coming from the cosmos that were assisting this planet to grow and to also to allow the inter-action of visitors from other worlds. It had to be, because in that time, the energy of the whole of the planet was operating at a dimension that was 'higher' than what has been on Earth since it Fell. It Fell to the third dimension, but it is now on its way back up; in fact, it has gone through the turning point into the fourth dimension, which will allow visitors to come now—as they did before—to this Earth planet.

So, am I giving some understanding here? Would you like to ask more questions?

Jacqui: Which planet did these Star People come from?

Jalarm: There are different names with different influences from other worlds. They were from many places. I would suggest you ask the Oracle. But I will clarify the information that you are given from the Oracle if you are not happy with what is given? You could ask about the different Star People living in the different places on Earth. It would be good if you ask about that.

(To be continued.)
N.B. We have come to understand that there was the human race (indigenous people) that continued to live in what is known as Lemurian times alongside the human race that was influenced by the Star People, at that time known as Atlantean times.

Oracle—13 March 2013 (continued)

Question to Oracle: How many civilizations existed at time of Atlantis?
    101,010 civilizations...

Jalarm: Different star groups are still visiting our planet now.
    (Again, we all could not think clearly. We see the need to write our questions down before we come to the meeting.)

Jalarm came again for the second time. *He clarified about the numbers of civilizations on Earth.*

Jalarm: There was more than one Atlantis than what Plato talked about. Had he not given the knowledge of what existed before Atlantis went down, it would have been lost. All that happened would have been lost because it was all covered with water or earth, or just destroyed. Some things have been found that scientists do not understand and that are much more advanced than they would expect from ape-like creatures living in caves. But there was much more.

A figure has been given to you about the number of civilizations that were established upon this planet in the later years of Atlantis. Understand that some of those civilizations were formed originally from Star People and others that have interacted with the Earth creatures—humans. So, there were many different races then that started to form around the planet. This why perhaps the number that has been given to you—of the different civilizations that happened upon the Earth before Atlantis went down—is a little unbelievable, but they existed just as you have many cities on the planet now.

There were fewer Star People, and I say fewer because most of them didn't interact with human DNA or genes. You could ask the Oracle about the number for just the Star People themselves with no influence from the DNA from the ape-like creatures at all.

As I have said there were many different amounts, perhaps this is not quite the right word, but the influence of human DNA was different in everyone on the Earth.

People came from many star worlds. Some didn't stay—they just visited and left—and so this is why there is some hesitancy about the number of Star People and races that existed upon this Earth.

But I can say, that even before the human was created—before the Pleiadean expedition nearly 900,000 years ago came to settle and hold a ray of light and teach the human values—there were other races already upon this Earth that were more of a reptilian nature and Mammalian Beings; there were also beings that came and went from other worlds that were bird-like in their appearance. They helped to create the planet in the first place.

And so, as I have said, it is a little hard just to create numbers because of DNA interaction and many became brothers and sisters to each other. So, the Indigenous people understood this—they have a strong knowing and understanding of the different visitations that have taken place from the reptilian races and Reptoid, Draco, and bird-like people and cetaceans. They have moved on since for there was an opportunity for souls to come into the human, meaning Light Man, so you could say that the Star People came into the Earth bodies and evolved and helped civilizations to grow and interact and come to know the feeling of family and marriage and brother and sister behaviour. The Indigenous people understood this very well.

And it was carried through, and the humans became stronger in the bodies of Earth beings. There are mythologies around the Earth and each mythology you hear about now you will recognise that the influence that has come into them is from afar. For everything that exists upon this planet has existed elsewhere. It was brought here to your planet in the first place.

So, is there another question that you would like to ask?"

(We could not think of one.)

Jalarm: If I could prompt you there are questions that are wanting to be answered from Kariong, which is in your country, that you call Australia now. And yes, those people were created over 900,000 years ago and they have been through many, many changes since—and I am talking about the Australian Origine. They did travel afar on Earth to other places and mixed their genes with other races, around the Earth, but they name and know that this country here, that you call Australia, is their *beginning* as I have said. It is their true *home*, in that it is what they understand as their Earth *home*.

They have been through many, many upheavals that have happened upon the Earth—including the history records of the time of ancient Lemuria. That is not all that long after what was known as the planet Mu, when the Pleiadeans first came here. Although the Star People onboard that mothership came from different star worlds also. So would you like to ask some questions about that?

Jill: *It is a wonderful story—we just cannot think of a question.*

Jalarm: The focus that would be important for the people working with the rock art at Kariong —and it is no accident that they have all come together, for they also have memories within their being of a time before. Long before Atlantis Fell.

In their minds, they would like to give credence to what they know about what is in the rock art in that area. The Lion Island is a very good record because it shows the Star People did visit this part of the world. The ship that sank and is in the memory of the Star People is not that far from the island known as Lion Island near Kariong. The people have it in their soul memory, and it is important to understand that it is in the soul memory of *all beings* upon this Earth. History is recorded and many, many stories are recorded in their soul history.

Jacqui: *My mind is just reeling with how many different Star People have come to this Earth and influenced, and I wonder about Angelic Beings, but I am not sure about the question I want to ask.*

Jalarm: If I can reassure you, the Angelic Realms are very real, and they are the closest to God. The Light is much stronger and brighter, and I have discussed this before and so the vibration is very high. Angelic Beings coming from that place onto your Earth have difficulty. In fact, they cannot put their feet onto your Earth because it is too low and too slow.

However, they can create a hologram and present themselves to people who understand about the Angelic Realms and look like what the people expect to see if they were visited by an angel. Different cultures—different races—that exist on the Earth now have different ways of seeing higher beings that come from other worlds, but they are also transformed into an image that makes sense to them. The consciousness is high—it is God-like—and it gives opportunity to humans to free themselves of heavier energy.

Does that answer your question?

Jacqui: *Yes, it does ... thank you.*

Valérie: *My book, Alcheringa, When the First Ancestors were Created is about a group of humans who remember being Star People after visiting*

Kariong and the glyphs there. And the story of mothership Rexegena coming from the Pleiades.

---oOo---

Watching the video below is like watching something from the star worlds ... an example of new knowledge coming through as predicted.
   https://www.youtube.com/watch?v=IfJemqkby_0
   The Operating Room of the Future – InSightec – Dr. Kobi Vortman, Technion Alumnus

THE FUTURE OF SURGERY: Once again, brilliance from Israel.

Our ex-webmaster Chris Parnell is an interfaith minister with a lifetime of awareness of the higher consciousness. He has worked in ministry as a chaplain and has also given spiritual direction to the new age community in Melbourne. He is a webmaster with several spiritual websites and can be contacted at 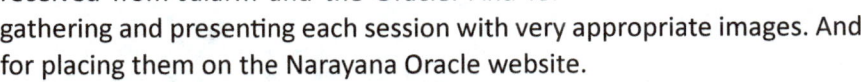interfaith108@gmail.com

   We—Jacqui, Jill, and I—give our heartfelt thanks to Chris for overviewing the messages received from Jalarm and the Oracle. And for gathering and presenting each session with very appropriate images. And for placing them on the Narayana Oracle website.

   Alcheringa is pleased with our work. It was a surprise announcement that he was known as Jalarm, when he lived at the time of Atlan.

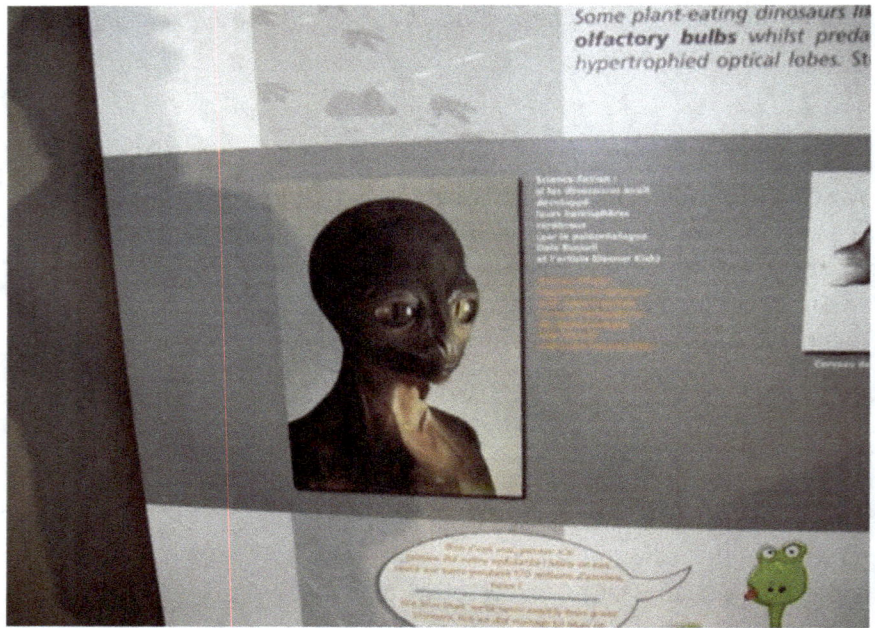

Representation of a Star Being in the Dinosauria (museum) in Esperaza, France.

Seventeen

The Golden Age

Oracle—11 March 2013—Star People coming and going on Earth pre-Atlantis

The locked outside door opened by itself, then the wine glass spelt out BABA. We knew he was here to sanctify the Oracle. Then I was asked to channel.

Jalarm: It is Jalarm, and it gives me pleasure to be here. Sometimes the Oracle is a little confusing because if I spell out something that looks confusing it is because I am asking for channelling to take place. Do you have some questions you would like to ask today?

Valérie in front of Photo of Sri Sathya Sai Baba

Jill: (After thanking him for being with us.) *Is the sphinx in Egypt a lion body or a jackal body?*

Jalarm: It is meant to be a lion—a very strong one, and in some ways a genetic structure of a lion—and a jackal is not that different except that a lion has more hair. So, it's true it could be taken for a lion, and it could also be taken for a jackal. Leonine or Canine—whatever you like. It is symbolic; it is not a true lion in the sense, it is symbolic. It meant a lot to the people who existed upon this planet, long before the Atlantis Fell, and if I use those words, I mean the time that the Earth nearly died.

It was only after the Earth started to work again, if I can say it that way, when the sun came out and more began to happen—people came out of caves, the ice melted, and things were growing—up until then it was an Ice Age. But they then revered the Gods, as they saw them, that came from the heavens looking like Lion People—but there were also Star People that came looking like a jackal or a canine. So, I have clarified that it could be either.

(We said thank you.)

Jalarm: Is there another question?

Jill: *Is there a connection to the sphinx and Lion Island here in Australia near Kariong?*
Lion Island near Kariong; this was linked to the Lion people who came from Sirius.

Jalarm: It is very much connected to the Lion People who came from Sirius. I hesitate to say a date as we, as Star People, have our way of measuring time that is different—it is cyclic—and so it measures differently than from the Earth now. However, there was a time when the Star People did come from Sirius. Not all that long after the time when the people came from the Pleiades. That was, in your terms, something like 900,000 years ago. It was when the first humans were created. The Star People who had survived, the Sirian people, came to assist them because they needed help. The Sirian people were like the 'police' of the galaxy. And so, is there a question you would like to ask about that?

(Sirian is a star in the sky, in the Canis Major constellation, known as the Dog Star.)

Jacq: *Did Thoth come to teach the Aboriginal race?*

Jalarm: There are two major stories that we would like to come out about the site at Kariong. It has been said it is a little like an Alexandria to Egypt. And so it is that Kariong is to the land you call Australia now because it holds history and that history dates back to nearly 900,000 years ago when the first humans were created, and they were the Australian Aborigine.

There was a time for them to 'go out and multiply' and they did go around the world and set up civilizations with other races who were up-standing ape-like creatures, and there has been an evolvement of the human in the very early stages.

Coming back to this land (Australia), it is where the 'beginning' took place of the humans—although they inherited DNA from the ape-like creatures, which is centred more in the land you call South Africa and would, from a scientific DNA point of view, cause some confusion.

For there is a need to accept the existence of DNA that is inherited from the Star People. And the Star People's DNA is now beginning to come into action within the humans. It has gone on for many different developments and evolvements; they are lumped in with what scientists call 'junk DNA', only because the scientists do not really know or understand what it exists for.

It is inherited from the Star People and because you have moved into a new cycle that can now come forth in a vibration that will help humans to develop their psychic abilities and to develop their metaphysical aspects, which has always been with them but held back to some degree ... only because the vibration that they were in—what we call the 3rd dimension—was not light enough to progress into the 'junk DNA' of what they had inherited. Does this make some sense? Do you have a question about that?

Jacqui: A question *written down is from the Emerald Tablets—Messages of Thoth through Doreal, we are asking what is the Mountain of Undal?*

Jalarm: The Mountain of Undal was mentioned in the Emerald Tablets that were recorded by Doreal back in the 1930s—it is written so that people wouldn't readily understand exactly what it was about, for there is quite a lot of lengthy information given by Thoth. He was a God recognised by the Egyptian people as they are now—but pre-Atlantis, they were very real beings.

A bird-like being if you like, because the Star People that come onto this Earth appear from many different races from around the galaxy and the universe, and they look very different from what you see on Earth now. However, they were very talented and very advanced, many of them, in technology but not so much in human values, shall we say.

The Mountain of Undal is 'knowledge.' There is a great deal of knowledge that existed on this planet that needs to come out ... before the great floods came and the time when Atlantis Fell, which encompassed the whole of the Earth. So, there were many little Atlantis's around the Earth. Do you have any questions about that?

(We had trouble thinking of any.)

Jalarm: I know Valérie would like to know whether there is a small spaceship that came from the mothership nearly 900,000 years ago that has gone under the water near Lion Island near Kariong ... and I would say it has.

But over the many thousands of years, it has been covered by silt and perhaps not readily seen by, shall we say, an underwater diver. However, the new technology that is coming from the satellites—it could be picked up from there. And that is what I would like to leave open for all to think about.

Jacq: *Are you one and the same energy of Allan Agnew who came through the Oracle last meeting?*

Jalarm: No. That was just a little play of energy when you were holding your fingers on the glass. You will recognise that the energy was felt differently. We did this just so you would discern about what has been happening with the Oracle.

We allowed *one* from the other side, on my side, to come in to communicate with you—because they also learn as well. It is not just on your side that the knowledge is given but also in the schools that exist in the next world. Or the next dimension. Does that make some sense? It is for the souls who have returned from Earth that continue their learning and they are given information that helps them to develop also, ready for their return to Earth into an Earth body.

But this is more as it is now. What we are asking you to do is to focus on the time before Atlantis Fell and how it was on Earth. Already we have said how very evolved Earth was and how many Star People were coming and going, and that the people that existed on this planet were *up-standing ape-like creatures*. There were also people who had part that, and part Star People genes in them, and they were as you know 'sanctified'—or 'crystallized'—with Christ Light and that made them human.

There are other interactions with Star People further down the track, something like 200,000 years in your time, that were more evolved and more genetically advanced. It becomes a little difficult to isolate each person; for that reason, it is best to look upon this Earth and before Atlantis Fell as being individual. So, they all had a history attached to their DNA. Not all is the same history for each human or Starman upon this Earth. Does that make sense?

(All agreed.)

Jalarm: Would you like to ask some questions about that?

Jacq: *When I think about Atlantis, I always think about the use of crystal. Is that used for electricity or ... do you know how crystals were used at that time?*

Jalarm: Yes, it was used as free power ... not quite the same as the electricity that you know of. It did not need lines of energy points going from one point to another. It was transferred in a different way. That was technology that was used through the pyramids that were built upon this planet long before Atlantis went down. Energy was used at various points around this planet.

Jacq: *Another question: we were talking about the grid lines around the Earth and how the Star People came to this Earth so easily. How did that* *happen? How did they come from such long distances—so many Light Years—and get here quickly?*

Jalarm: Actually, I have just given an image to Valérie for her to see. There were no lines on poles that went around the Earth to align the power or energy of electricity around the Earth. However, the grid lines did just that ... that is slightly under the Earth. There were patterns under the Earth that were used to spread the unlimited power that was used around the planet.

That same way of receiving could be achieved by your scientists on the Earth now, but there is a little more development needed ... and this will come through because the so-called 'junk DNA' will develop so that they will come to remember, or to inherit the knowledge, and be able to go ahead and work from that place. Does that make sense?

(*We reminded Jalarm to tell us how the Star People arrived on Earth from such vast distances?*)

As I have said, there were grid lines under the Earth, not too deep, because there is a magnetic force or crystal (a very large crystal) in the centre of the Earth, which magnetises that energy also. It can go out and interact with the envelope of energy that is around the Earth with another grid line that exists around the outer Earth. This energy field was 'tightened' when Atlantis went down, so that the catastrophic energy would not go out and cause problems with other planetary systems. Solar systems.

But now that has been loosened and opened so that the new energy coming from the Source of All Creation is coming onto this planet through the Star Gate (you could call it) ... where the lines cross (as a net) and that forms a gate—a Star Gate—which allows the new energy to come into your Earth planet.

And with that, the energy coming directly from the Source will ignite with each soul that is upon this earth. Each animal, each insect, and all bird life will raise the consciousness of the life on Earth—but also the planet itself.

And in doing so, it moves into what we have predicted for a long time—the Golden Age, when the consciousness of the Earth will match what is coming from the Source of All Creation. So, does that make sense?

Jill: *It sounds wonderful.*

Jalarm: So in scientific terms, it is a reality—it is not understood just yet by some scientists, but it will be, very well. And once that starts to be understood ... more knowledge and information will grow with that knowledge.

I would like to withdraw for the moment and allow you to operate the Oracle if you would ... because there are more questions that I know you would like to ask?

(To be continued.)

NB. Where the grid line nets cross is the Star Gate. This is always a point of Light stronger than the between area. Not everyone can tolerate the areas of stronger Light coming and going from those places. It can change them gently.

Eighteen

Junk DNA

Those that we call Star People are actually Light Beings existing in other dimensions. They existed in the higher dimensions we had here on Earth. With the fall of Atlantis, the Earth people fell out of the 4th and 5th dimensions. The Light Beings and Star People from different races in the universe had embedded higher vibrations and Light in their children by Earth people. This gave rise to so-called 'junk DNA', which has come back into its own, due to the return of Earth to the 4th and 5th dimensions.

Jalarm confirms that the hierarchy sent the Arcturians to Earth to help the up-standing ape, the pre-humans, to evolve into beings with the Light within them. There was genetic engineering for the Light Beings and the civilizations of Atlantis did not have 'Earth bodies,' they had light bodies. The Nords—those from the northern hemisphere—had very, very white bodies; there was a shade of blue about them.

In addition to the race from Arcturus, there were the Hathors, (a group of interdimensional, intergalactic beings who originally came from another universe through Sirius, which is a portal for our universe). They had strange looking ears, for they were able to communicate telepathically. There was a lot of intermingling between Star People and the Earthlings. Their hair changed colour; their skin changed colour. There are mummies in the Egyptian museums with blondish hair—or even ginger hair.

The Star Peoples' genes came with Light and vibration. When reproduction happened, it was a 'quickening' of the egg in the womb of the mother—and it became embedded with Light. This developed more ability in the children of the Star People by Earthlings, and the children had larger heads. Much DNA, which is called non-coding DNA (or 'junk DNA'), originates from the Star People. We will become more aware now that Earth has raised into a 4th and 5th dimension. It has more reality there—it has more form—and it is stronger than what exists in the 3rd dimension.

Light becomes stronger in the different dimensions, and there are different dimensions of Light as one approaches the Source of Light, the Creative Source of All. It is all power. There is an increase of power on the Earth now due the turning point—the solstice of 21 December 2012; the residual genes from the Star People (non-coding DNA ... so-called 'junk' DNA) is now beginning to flower within humans. The basic vibration on Earth has been raised.

The reason why some people have a higher vibration than others is due to the role of emotions (emotion is putting something into motion), and the quality and vibration of what you 'put out' into the world. These determine the vibratory rate of humans. Everything is energy. The seen reflects the seer, the perceptions, and attitudes within the seer. It is up to the (seer) to choose what they would like.

Measuring time and the so-called 'junk DNA'

We were wondering how the Star People measured time? Jalarm made it clear he wanted to channel through Valérie.

Jalarm: The time is 500,000 years ago, *but* our measurement of time is different from what the scientists say here on Earth. And so, you need to ask the Oracle, *'How long in Earth time'* was it that the Nords (or the Arcturians) came to Earth?

(We were told that flowing between the channelling and the Oracle allowed us to learn and understand in a different way and that was what they wanted us to do.)

Jalarm: For the moment you are asking, and we say 500,000 our time—and how did we get here ... I am saying—and I am now connecting to the early Atlanteans that came here ... They were sent by the hierarchy. They were sent by the hierarchy to set up civilizations upon the Earth to help the little Earthling. The little Earthling was evolving, but they needed help from the Star People. And that is who we are, 'The Star People'.

It is important that you understand that the Star People, or the Atlanteans, did not have Earth bodies; they had Light bodies. In other words, they were not made from the influence of the up-standing ape-like creature. It was genetic engineering that uplifted the ape-like creature in the first place to be en-Christed to become the Hu-man. Man of Light.

So going back to the Nords, and the very, very white-looking people—there was a shade of blue about them, and they were very loving; compassionate. They were not supposed to interact with the Earth people, but some did, and more and more children were created from them, which made it difficult for me to answer your question as to *how many Star People were on the Earth.* Does that make sense?

(*All agreed.*)

Jalarm: We were sent, as I said, to assist the little Earthling and because they became our brothers and sisters—because they went on to be a creation of the Arcturians and the Earth people.

Aside from the Nords, there were also the Hathors, who were very similar to the Nordic people. They had similarities as they had the base of Arcturians, but they were part Earth people as well. And they lived to be able to communicate telepathically, which is why they are drawn on the walls of early Egyptian temples with strange looking ears— that was to show the way they were communicating. So again, those children who interacted with each other still inherited the genes in the first place from the Star People—the Nords—the blonde people. And some of that blonde became (it was white to start with) slightly golden blonde, if you like. You know that mummies are still in Egyptian museums with blondish hair—or even ginger hair. (*But that is another story again.*)

So, there was a lot of intermingling and interaction between pure Star People—and I say 'pure' because I want you to understand the definition of the Earth people as against the Star People. There is no doubt that you are brothers and sisters.

However, it was not totally supposed to be that way, though there was encouragement later for it to happen.

So, I am getting a little lost in how to tell you the story—it is a very large story—so, do you have any questions?

(No questions!)

Jalarm: There are many mythologies held by different cultures or races around the Earth, for once Atlantis went down it was only the people of Earth that remained. The Star People moved on and they are the ones who come to try and support and help the Earth people. Does that make sense?

(Yes.)

Jacq: *A question that I do have is how do people of a Light body and people of more of an Earth body have children?*

Jalarm: The influence of the children comes from what is described as an 'immaculate conception.' There was interaction between the male and the female that was 'heightened' in ecstasy to help procreation to take place. But what took place was the vibration that broke the egg of the mother and began its transformation into the little embryo. But it was also embedded with the Light that they inherited from the Star People, the Light Beings. So, does that make sense? In doing that, it developed more ability from the Star People; the children had larger heads. They had a brain that scientists now examine and say that part of it is what they call 'junk DNA' because they do not readily accept that there was influence from Star People.

The Star People's genes came with Light and vibration. It had form—you will become more aware now that your Earth has raised into a 4th and 5th dimension. It has more reality there—it has more form. It is stronger than what existed in the 3rd dimension. Do you have questions there?

Jacqui: *How do you mean stronger?*

Jalarm: The power of the, shall we say, what happens in different dimensions, you could say the Light becomes stronger the closer you go back to the World of Light and then on to the Creative Source of All. The Light and vibration are so fast; if you were to measure it—or if you could measure it—it is all power. Nothing can exist in that presence of Creation of All if it is not of God.

And so, when I say there is an increase in power to all humans upon Earth now, they have automatically intermixed with the Star People's genes that have gone on to develop into the human and who you are now, and that so-called 'junk DNA' is starting to flower. It is the strength that is within the brain that will release the power that the Star People have and that you have inherited, but it could not be used until now because the vibration was too low. Does that make sense? It was too slow. It could not operate. It could not calibrate—it is now allowing to 'flower.' As I have said ...

So, more knowledge will come more easily and er, your scientists—your clever people—will be able to do many, many things that in previous times were thought not possible to do. So, is there anything else you would like to ask?

(**He left.**)

Jacqui: *I was wondering—how come some people seem to have more higher vibration that others, and others come here and just seem to cause destruction. Is it a karmic thing?*

Valérie: Well, karma means action—the action that you take from the emotion that is actually inside you, that is motivating you. So, if that it is a loving, compassionate emotion then the vibration will be higher. Some people see the word 'karma' as a judgement. It is not a judgement. It is action and you are putting into action your emotions of various levels of feelings.

Jacqui: *I just wonder why everybody cannot get on.*

Valérie: I think everybody will. It is just that the emotions exist whether we are in a physical body or not. That is why ghosts can still get angry. We are actually ghosts walking with an Earth body. Our spirit body is like a photocopy of our Earth body. When it all comes down, they tell us 'everything is energy' so if we work on ourselves and help to release the lower dimension—the lower vibrations that are pulling us into a lower emotional reaction—a not caring, or not thinking of people, putting the self first and not worrying about others—others around the world with their energy of wanting peace and harmony will eventually infiltrate those people.

It will heal. Everything will heal because there are different energies. Say if we see it as light and dark (not that there is anything wrong with dark), a black and white thing. The Lighter it is and the brighter, more compassionate it is ... because we have had it explained how the Light from the Source is the strongest ... it will just diffuse anything that is heavier and lower. And then everything will come together and operate in one vibration or one dimension, which is where we are going—into the Golden Age.

Jill: *So, the new babies will help ...*

We all agreed you can see they know—particularly the new ones ... when they get old enough to speak, they come out with little gems of wisdom. And even before they can talk, they reach out and put their little *hand on someone that they know is upset and it calms them. It is quite beautiful. Wonderful.*

Jacqui said a two-year-old she knew had seen another upset and asked if they needed a 'cuddle.' (How wonderful.) Then we all agreed how lovely it was when you held someone without saying anything, how it seemed to lift our spirit. So that energy has a quality (of caring) and it feels so nice.

So, we decided we would never give up. We are getting there. And we should go around hugging everybody.

Nineteen

The Fifth Dimension

Oracle—22 February 2013—Star People, Pre-Atlantis

Jalarm: So, do you have a question for me?

Jacqui: *Do you have a connection to Sirius? Is that where you are from?*

Jalarm: I do indeed—but then, the beings of Light that come from the Dimension of Light that I come from have been on many, many planets and so you could call it an 'incarnation' if you like. It is the same as taking on a different body when you are on the Earth in a human form—and in a Light Being body you can also take on a form and incarnate into a form that exists on different planets—and yes, I have been on the planet known as Sirius. There are several planets there, of course. So, does this answer your question?

Jacqui: *Yes, thanks.*

Artist unknown. **Sanat Kumara as he was in a Light Body (The Nords) on Earth, pre-Atlantis**

Jalarm: I am Jalarm again. I have jokes (he came in with a 'plomp' and made us laugh), but it gives me pleasure to be here to answer the questions that you have and to also enlarge in your general knowledge. Did you have anyone in your mind when you asked about Sirius?

Jacqui: *How do you mean?*

Jalarm: There are several different races that comes from Sirius—so I am asking is there a race or somebody that you have in mind?

Jacqui: *No, not really. Another thing I wonder is do you come from a certain colour vibration, like a ray of Light?*

Jalarm: All Light is colour and divides into different vibrations, so yes, that is true. We can switch from one to another very easily; in fact, we do ... and so it depends upon who we are working with as to the colour vibration you are influenced by. This is adjusted from a point that you are not quite seeing, but it does help to bring through information that is appropriate for your vibration.

There is also a 'sound' that goes with that as well.

My whole purpose of being here is to clarify a lot of the information, or misinformation, about the times of Atlanteans.

I have said that there are Beings of Light that occupy this Earth, this world; they did so for thousands of years. 100,000 years and 200,00 years have been mentioned. There is varying information coming through. This I will clarify through the Oracle.

It is hard for us to give a time because the time is measured very differently from how your Earth scientists measure it. So, I hope you understand that. But I can give you a time that will collaborate more with the story I want to provide to you. Is that all right?

(*All said yes.*)

Jill: *I am very interested in hearing more stories. The stories sound wonderful, but neither of us can 'think' to ask questions now.*

(*Note: When I, Valérie, was in the presence of the Avatar in India, I found it very difficult to 'think' in his presence. Something similar seems to be happening here today.*)

Jalarm: I know Valérie is wondering about the Nords who are known as the Light Beings that had very white coloured skin and white coloured hair. They did live in the North Hemisphere and that is why they are called 'The Nords.'

They were a race that came, and they did separate and established civilizations, or shall we say various townships in the north. This was all before Atlantis Fell, or when the seas rose, or before the Ice Age.

They came with much knowledge, and they had advanced technology, which has been passed on through drawings in Egypt, places around Europe, South America, and in Australia (yet to be found)—and advanced technology in Africa. In other words, they had influenced many races that had lived on this Earth and they themselves in the north began at the North Pole—but that is not exactly correct; it was an area that was a little warmer than what it is now—but they lived on land in the north of the Earth Planet. In the Northern Hemisphere, in other words.

There was/is quite a lot of inter-communication between various races, for there are other races that came from other star worlds. The Star People from the north came from Arcturus. But then, they were influenced by many other planetary people that came from the galaxy—and so it is a little hard to pin-point where they came from. But as I have said, they had whitish skin, blue eyes, and white coloured hair. As they lived on the northern part of the Earth, they did integrate later with other races and so that still permeates through all races upon this Earth—for occasionally, people are born with white skin, blue eyes, and white hair. So, would you like to ask a question about that?

Jacqui: *The thing that interests me is did the poles shift?*

Jalarm: They have shifted over time, a few times actually, in the progression of the evolution of this Earth—yes. There was a change particularly when Atlantis fell. So, do you ask the question for a reason?

Jacqui: *No. I just recently heard that there was proof of rainforests at the South Pole.*

Jalarm: Indeed, indeed. There was a warmer climate there, yes. I was mentioning the race known as the Nords and they were not purely at the North Pole but rather further south. But there was a change in the North Pole and so the lands where they existed seem to be closer to the North Pole now.

The Fifth Dimension

Jacqui: *It is said that Arcturians do communicate with Earth...and if so, how do they get here?*

Jalarm: They communicate with Earth very much so, yes. There are quite a lot of different beings that are from the generation of the Arcturian that have influenced the Earth and remain in contact with it, so they can overview and assist the peoples who are here. Some of the souls that have come onto Earth have very strong connections to Arcturus and that influences them very easily, but there are others that have been from other worlds—other planets—and all these are influenced in their cultural ways, and their technology, and their understanding of the Creative Source of All. All this infiltrates into the humans that you are now—as Earth People.

Comparison of Jupiter, our sun, and other stars with Arcturus

Jill: *Are we heading for another Ice Age?*

Jalarm: The Earth, my dear, is in a solar system and it is constantly moving. The whole solar system is constantly moving within the galaxy, and that galaxy is constantly moving within the cosmos, and yes, changes come and so yes, there will be Ice Ages more upon this Earth, this Planet, but I would not worry about this if this concerns you. The word 'evolution' means 'evolve in cycles.' There will always be change. You are aware that the Earth has recently gone through a magnificent cycle that has opened into new dimensions for you and is taking you into the Golden Age—the 5th dimension, which is of a golden colour and vibration. It is faster than what you have been used to, but once you get into that dimension it will not appear to be fast at all. Looking from the outside in, the perception is fast ... but when you move into it totally, it will be normal—does that make sense?

(We all agree.)

Jalarm: And we do that work to assist the little Earthlings. They are very happy and pleased about this.

Jill: *When we move into that dimension, will we need as much food?*

Jalarm: When you move into that dimension fully, you will be very aware of the body you carry or that you wear, and you will know what it needs to nourish it and what it doesn't need. And so, elimination will reduce slightly—it depends. It will be a knowing that you do not need to eat as much, or what you do need to eat to nourish the body. Does that make sense?

(All agree.)

Jalarm: You will also know that even now you need to nourish the body from the energy and Divine Light that comes from the centre of the universe, which is the Creative Source of All.

Which is giving life to everything—not just here on Earth but in ALL solar systems, in ALL galaxies, and within the universe, and I say ALL universes. Does that make sense then?

(*We all agree.*)

Jalarm: When the energy is drawn from the Source of All Creation, it is automatically adjusted to the vibration, or the dimension, or the colour that is needed, and recorded in the being that you are from whatever, or wherever, you operate. It has a lot to do with *perception*. Perception is an important word in meaning and understanding about everything in the universe.

Jacqui: *One last question—going back to Abraham in the Bible, can you shed any light on his significance?*

Jalarm: Abraham, of course, represented many people ... and it is a way of telling a story of much how the Earth evolved. And this is written in the Bible, but the actual story itself is much larger and much more involved than it appears from reading it in the Bible. However, the story in overview is correct—and so, if you were to read the Bible you would understand ... if you let your mind be 'open' to seeing and feeling and intuitively understanding what the story is actually telling you.

(Jalarm suggested we work with the Oracle for the moment.)

Notes with the Oracle:

We asked for clarification of 100,000 years or 200,000 years ago when the Nords first came to Earth. We agreed the Nords were white. Were they albinos (no pigmentations)?

The Oracle: Yes! 500,000 their time. (Star People's time.) But with clarification, it would be said to be 200,000 Earth time.

They (human and albino animals) lived on Earth 500,000 years ago, their time. When some later mated with Earth people, the children were born with blonde hair, which is white hair melded with darker pigmentation from the Earth, and so the Nords were white, but some produced children with the Earth people and the children had lighter skin and blonde (golden yellow) hair.

Twenty

Venus

O racle continued ... 1 February 2013

Sanat Kumara and the Lady Venus (artist unknown) from The Hierarchy

Jalarm: I am Jalarm. There is a little confusion, but it is alright because with confusion I can help clarify—and it gives a bigger picture. For you are asking questions that *limit* the answers I wish to give you. And you are quite correct in that sometimes the questions are a little difficult to answer clearly. You understand that now and that is good.

You are asking about the people of Venus and that is good. Yes, there are beings that live on Venus—but, of course, with your physical eyes, from where you look upon it now, it is not visible. But in another frequency, it is. And so, I think this is enough for you to understand; if I start saying about frequencies and the different levels of consciousness and different levels of understanding of how people live in different worlds, it could go into the thousands.

I think for the time being it is enough for you to know that there are Beings of Light—and understand the word *Light*, for Light gives you the different frequencies and there is a lower light that you can still see, and there is a very bright Light that you cannot see for it is too bright. So, are you understanding about different frequencies?

You talk about Divine Light because Divine Light is what gives you life, and so whatever energy exists in Light, it is life. It is the opposite to the darkness. There is no judgment here—it is just that Light is needed for the assistance of life. Although there is some life that can survive in the darkness.

There are many scientific reasons that could be explained as to how life can exist on a planet such as Venus. But it is not coming from a place where you can see it. It is coming from a different place. In fact, it is a beautiful place, very similar to your Earth as you see it, in your $3^{rd}/4^{th}$ dimension. From our point of view when we look at your planet it is in a $3^{rd}/4^{th}$ dimension and that is how we have always seen it. It fell into the 3rd dimension and is now rising into the 4th dimension where more information and more knowledge will be seen by the Earth-man's eyes— but it has always been there. So, it is a little hard to answer a question and clarify it on the Oracle. So, is there something you would like to ask now about the people of Venus?

Jacqui: Are they peaceful people or are they warlike?

Jalarm: No, they are peaceful people. They are actually the people who will help to bring Light, or the Golden Age, that will exist in the whole of your solar system. They have come from other worlds—even outside your galaxy. They are here to lift the consciousness and to assist what has been taking place. They are trying to soften people in their thoughts and their way of behaviour so that they honour each other and respect one another and truly understand about the Source of All Creation. And the love that is so readily flowing from them and there (Venus).

It can infiltrate anyone who likes to reach out and be open to it, but as I have said, this frequency—the Light—is a different frequency for some and too bright for others and so there is a certain level that you can reach in your Earth body and in a Light body. Even Light Beings can be limited as to how bright the Light can shine within them. Does this make sense to you?

(Jacqui said 'yes'.)

Jalarm: So, we have told you about the Beings of Light, the Star People, that were on this Earth. They have lowered their Light to some degree to be able to create a civilization upon this Earth as it was in the 4th and 5th dimensions, and now this Earth is rising back to the 4th/5th and on to the 5th, which is what we will call the Golden Age. It is more like the Star People who came from Venus and the 5th dimension (and still do come from Venus) and the culture and the understanding and the love that they have for all people. They are God People. They understand the Source.

They have influenced the Earth Beings upon this planet and before Atlantis fell there was much given and taught to the peoples upon this Earth, and as I have said they did interact. There is a story about the angels mating with the Earth women. It wasn't that simple. In fact, there was interaction between both males and females, and it is true the children were lowered, and even the ones that mated were lowered in their Light—but they do raise their Light to some degree from what they were as up-standing ape-like creatures. They reached out past that genetic structure and helped one another.

This is really the story, or the analogy, of Adam and Eve in the Garden of Eden and being told not to 'eat the apple' because they were beings that have the reptilian/Reptoid energy in them, and when they mated with them it automatically reduced the Light that was in the Star Beings, and the children to some degree.

But then, on the other hand, the children born from the Earth Mothers, shall we say, increased in their knowledge and their Light and were able to understand much more complicated information. So, for the moment,

I hope you can accept that there were Star People upon this Earth before Atlantis Fell.

I have already said that the Ice Age came upon the planet before Atlantis Fell completely in a day and a night. I would like you to ask a question from the Oracle?

More work with the Oracle revealed there was another planet in our solar system they called 'on'. The Oracle also told us that people did come from Mars when it became unliveable at another time. The people came from the planet Venus by choice and that there are still people on Venus in Light Bodies in a different dimension; they do not eat food as we understand food.

Fourth talk with Jalarm

He came with a loud entrance, which made us laugh but gave us a shock.

Jalarm: I didn't mean to frighten you—I thought I would have a little joke.
(We were still laughing.)

Jalarm: You asked about two moons and yes, they did exist. Two moons were around for a while but not for very long because they were an experiment. There were others on this planet that were coming from scientific knowledge, and they worried all the time whether it was safe … whether it was safely anchored, and this was the problem—it was not and so it eventually broke free from the same journey that the moon (the one that you still see) was making around the Earth. The other broke free and hit the Earth.

I want to reassure everybody that there is not going to be another asteroid allowed to hit this planet.

So, you can put your minds at rest about this. But it was the reason that the whole of the planet was thrown into utter disarray. So, we can talk about this more because I want you to understand that there was an Ice Age before the second moon broke free. But we can talk about this more later.

Thank you so much for being part of this little journey to recall what took place on this Earth before Atlantis Fell. Thank you.

Twenty-One

The Hathors—Gods of Egypt

We asked the Oracle about the mummies in the museum in Cairo and how some have red hair.

Jalarm signalled he would like to speak with us again.

Jalarm: You are asking about the red hair that some of the mummies had in the time of the Royal Pharaohs. And yes, there is an inheritance from the beings that lived on Mars. In fact, they were the giants, as I have said, and the existence of the giants was referred to by the Egyptians as the Hathors. They are depicted in drawings on many of the temples of Ancient Egypt. And this is that connection.

It is said that the Royal Pharaohs were thought of as gods and that they had inherited their genes from the Star People. They knew that. Some of the knowledge had been forgotten, but they had come from the genetic structure of the Hathors. I would like you to remember that the focus of the Hathors was their ears. They were described as Giant Beings and their ears were really representing that they were able to communicate telepathically. And this is the way it was before Atlantis went down. Does that make some sense?

(*Yes, thank you*).

Jalarm: The Hathors had an important influence on the Ancient Egyptians. They drew from their memory of what existed before Atlantis went down. As I have said, there were quite a lot of civilizations and a lot of *beliefs*, what you would call religious beliefs, before Atlantis went down. It has been referred to as Pagan beliefs, but they were very real to the beings and people that lived on this Earth then. I keep saying that because I would like you to remember there were many, many different civilizations on this Earth before Atlantis went down and they had the influences of many Star People from many planets. And so, they were not all the same—it depended upon the dimensions of influence from their teachers, if that makes some sense. For, although they were born on the planet, they still inherited the knowledge and the ceremonies and beliefs that they had from their ancestors. Does that make some sense?

The Red-Haired Giants from Mars evacuated because of a war. Everything was destroyed.

The Beings, the Giant Beings, that came from your planet Mars (and still do), have more of a war-like nature and more of a tendency to fight, rather than to sit down and become aware of each other's point of view and honour that. This was an evolutionary growth even with those people on that planet and I say that because it happened on many other planets.

I say that because a lot of beings that are on this planet, and even before Atlantis went down, were evolving and were still influenced by Star People that came from other worlds. So, if you can imagine that the consciousness was a little like a ladder and that some were just up a few rungs of the ladder and had that level of consciousness—and there were others who were up higher and they had that understanding—and then others reached into the Angelic Realms, which had the true understanding of who they are and where they came from.

So, the people from Mars were evolving. That is the true understanding.

Jacqui: May I ask what you think is going to happen to our planet over the next fifty years?

Jalarm: We have always overseen what has been taking place on this Earth. We have been appointed by a hierarchy that is overseen by the Angelic Realms to assist the Earthling in its advancement. And as I have just described from the Star People that existed upon this planet before Atlantis went down, so too the Earthlings have different levels of consciousness and awareness, and so there is a need for each other to come to understand. And when you understand each other, you can assist each other to see a point of view to the place where there is no need to hurt one another to sort out a problem.

Hemispheric view of Venus centred at the North Pole

While we are talking about Mars, I would also like to mention Venus, which incidentally still has people with it, very much so. And they have contributed to the evolvement of people on Earth down through the ages to come into a Garden of Eden, and by that, it is a suggestion of a beautiful place where beauty grows and that would be not only be in the form of foliage and flowers, but rather the living beings such as animal, birds, and insects, and the humans. It is an opportunity for all to grow upon Earth and the ascension of conscious that is needed will be assisted from the Venusians. They are always here to help. They came again from a different dimension altogether and they wish only to assist the human from whatever level of consciousness they are thinking. They can break through from that, because every human being upon this Earth has been enchristed, with the Light of Love and Divine Energy. So that nobody is missed out as far as an opportunity goes to ascend into a higher consciousness of the being that they truly are, and that is a son or a daughter of The Creator of All. Does that make some sense?

(The others thanked Jalarm; they could not think of anything else.)

Jalarm: I would like to say that the being known as Jesus is known also as Jesus Christ, and the Christ energy is what I am speaking about. He is the Son of God, or the Son of the Creator of All, and that is being assisted by the beings from Venus, which is said to be the Planet of Love.

We asked the Oracle: How long did the last Ice Age last?
The answer was 6,000—yes.
We then asked: How long did the Ice Age last before the catastrophe of 'Atlantis' going down all over the Earth?
The answer was 1,000—yes.

Jalarm spelt out that he wanted to talk through Valérie. (We all laughed and noted that he sends the glass going around, and around, in an anti-clockwise direction when he wants to talk.) He made his entrance.

Jalarm: It is I, Jalarm, and yes, I would like to have a little word with you. I want to thank you for all the work that you do, and the commitment and the focus. And we, in this world, from where I come, are delighted we are able to work with you in this way. You call yourself the 'Harmony Sisters' and I think that is very appropriate. You are all in harmony—your Light melds beautifully and integrates beautifully, and we do not find it difficult to work with you girls at all. And so, we will continue to work with you more as time goes on. We have much information to give you.

We would really appreciate if you would jot down your questions before you come because it is difficult for you to think while this Oracle is taking place—and the Oracle itself is a focal point—if you like. It is connected to the Source of All Creation and so much information can be given to you at ALL levels and so we thank you, we thank you. God bless you.

(*We all liked that message.*)

Twenty-Two

Star People from Mars

Red-haired giants: Star People from Mars

ORACLE on 17 April 2013

Jacqui: So where did the ginger hair come from? We would like to know.

Jalarm: Well as I have said, there have been many that have visited this planet Earth—and they have come from different places around the galaxy. But there was a time when your planet Mars had to be evacuated and the people from there had red hair. They were rather war-like in manner. Does this make some sense to you?

Jacqui: Also, Jill was saying before that people with red hair need more painkillers and anaesthetic and other different things. She was talking about red-haired humans. She herself has red chestnut coloured hair.

Jalarm: It is true, they experienced pain because they were warm blooded, and because of their strength, their warrior strength. They were very large—you could call them giants—and they came to the planet here. So, they were also many of the different Star People on this planet.

    (This again stretched over a long period of time. **Jacqui** *suggested a break, which Jalarm agreed to.*)

We asked the Oracle if there are any 'Martians' on Mars at the moment. The answer was 'yes.' We asked are they in a different dimension? The answer was yes, the 6th dimension.

Jalarm wanted to speak to us. **Jalarm** confirmed it is the 6th dimension and asked us to remember that he said they were very large beings with red hair, compared to the people of Earth. There have been skeletons that have been found around your planet and more will be discovered. Your scientists are not ready to accept their existence yet. They say the photos have been '**Photoshopped**' as you would say—but they did exist.

Jacqui: Well, if they are in the 6th dimension, I wonder what they live on. How do they survive?

Jalarm: Everything is energy—and so it is taken in a 6th dimensional way. It can be presented in form, such as fruit, vegetables. And, in fact, they have a real life, just like you have on Earth; it is just that you cannot see it with the physical eye.

They are well aware of the exploration that is taking place upon their planet at this time, for at another time there were others who lived on the planet in a lesser dimension, and they had to evacuate when war was declared and the planet Mars, or everything that was on it, was destroyed.

Jill: Where did they evacuate to?

Jalarm: Many came to your planet and set up civilizations here; others went to other places. There was a choice—they had starships in which they were able to move around.

Jacqui: The red-headed people came from Mars; the Vikings had red hair—were they (the Vikings) genetically related to the peoples from Mars?

Jalarm: Indeed, they were. Genetically they had interacted with other beings who were on your planet and so they integrated down through time and so, yes, the Vikings are connected with the world of Mars—but they would also have a 'little bit of this and a little bit of that', just the same as your Earthling body has a 'little bit of this and a little bit of that.' I joke a little but, as I have said before, your Earth body is a very complicated structure and has many influences from many different dimensions and many different races—just as the Martians do—but perhaps not so broken down as the

Earthling. However, the Vikings, as you speak of, are Earthlings and they have inherited the influence from the Red Giants from Mars. Does that make some sense? You are talking over a l-o-o-o-o-n-g period of time to cause changes in evolution, but it does show the warring nature of the Vikings.

(*They thanked him.*)

Jacqui: The Annunaki—what did they look like?

Jalarm: Well again, with evolution changes, they did have a reptilian appearance about them, lesser to a degree, but you could say they were like lizard men but not quite so exaggerated as it was in the earlier days upon this Earth.

It was the Lizard people—if I can describe them that way—or the reptilians that took over this planet in the time when dinosaurs existed upon this planet; in fact, they were the creators of the dinosaurs. They experimented many ways, genetically, and created many lizard-like or reptilian form dinosaur beings.

Jacqui: I wonder why they would have created dinosaurs in the first place? And for what purpose?

Jalarm: They were just experimenting, really. However, it got a little out of hand—and many grew so large and were eating all the foliage upon the planet. The planet had been created from a different dimension altogether to be a place of peace. A 'garden of Eden.' It was meant to be a place of peace and Light in this corner of the galaxy. However, when the reptilian people came, they mismanaged it. It was not meant to go the way it did—and that was why the decision was made by the Angelic Realms and, unfortunately, something had to change upon the planet to destroy the dinosaurs. They were eating all the foliage and destroying the planet's atmosphere.

They were so large that they were too slow in dying back into dust and they created a bad odour ... it was interfering with the atmosphere, the oxygen, if that makes some sense, and so there was an asteroid that was brought to this planet that was designed to destroy the dinosaurs that had been created upon this Earth.

It is not something that was done lightly. It was something that a lot of thought was given to, and a decision made; however, there was a lot of resentment from the Reptilian people. Because as I have said, they came from a lower evolvement in consciousness, and they did not readily understand the reason that all this took place.

And so, there was another war that was created—with fighting, arguments, resentment, dissension that was happening upon the planet for quite some time. The Cosmic Police, the Leonines, and Star People from Sirius were sent to help sort it out.

Jacqui: I wonder about dolphins and how long they have been around?

Bottlenose dolphins off the coast of Cornwall, UK

Jalarm: Actually, the dolphins were one of the Star Peoples. They came and lived in the ocean, so they lived in a separate world but on the same planet as the reptilians. They held the consciousness of Light and love and that was their purpose and their mission and still is—to lift the consciousness upon this Earth.

Jacqui: And is that the same for whales, or just dolphins?

Jalarm: Yes, it is very similar for the whales.

Twenty-Three

The Annunaki

ORACLE—17 April 2013—The Light Man that we are as Earthlings. A time we were blessed from the Source with a soul and a Light body overlaying our Earth body.

We joined hands and sang three oms—our voices were harmonising beautifully. The wine glass very quickly spelt out that Jalarm wished to speak through Val.

Jalarm: It is Jalarm. I am very pleased to be here, and I know that you have many questions for me today, and I am happy to answer these for you. So, what is the first question?

(The reply to the questions exposes the different time scales of the 3rd and 4th dimensions.)

Jacqui: What existed in the time between 900,000 years ago and 200,000 years ago, when the Atlanteans came to live on Earth?

Jalarm: We have said that there was a time that the Pleiadean peoples came to the planet on the 'Mission of Love' to establish Light upon this Earth—because this corner of the galaxy was rather hidden with dark energy. We called Earth 'Mu' at that time. And when I say 'we' I am meaning the Star People.

It did not go to plan and the mothership was destroyed, and it was just a few of the 50,000 people onboard who survived. However, they found themselves planted on the area you know of as Australia, and in the area known as Kariong. This was where the little establishment was first set up and when the first humans were created.

Now you are asking about the time. This, as I have said before, is very difficult for us as Star People to say a time that resonates with you as Earth people upon your planet because you measure it in a different way. So, I would say it was a long time before the Atlanteans came to this planet. The time will be clearer as we progress. But it is a long time. So, is there another question?

Jacqui: Actually, Val has written another question asking, 'Is 900,000 years correct for when the story of the first human was created?' But you now have answered that already. There is a belief that the first humans were created by the Annunaki, so that seems to conflict with what we are remembering about the Pleiadean mission? Who are the Annunaki?

Jalarm: The Annunaki, yes, there were civilizations set up upon this planet that came long before the Atlanteans. And so, these people—they were Star People—but I have said before about different levels of consciousness, and the levels of consciousness of the Annunaki was not raised to the point of evolution that is possible for beings to enter a higher form of Light Consciousness. Does that make some sense?

(*They said yes.*)

Jalarm: So, the Annunaki had quite a large civilization established upon this planet. And this was before the Atlanteans came. In fact, I can say this is the reason Atlantean Star People came, because they needed to raise the consciousness upon the Earth. It was getting a little out of hand, and the hierarchy that I mentioned before, which is overseen by the Angelic Realms, needed to be lifted. Mainly because of how the people were being treated by the Annunaki people. Would you like to ask me about that?

Jacqui: The next question written here is saying that genetic engineering and experimenting was said to be carried out by the Annunaki to produce the first cave man.

Jalarm: The Annunaki did do genetic engineering. Genetic engineering was done quite commonly with the Star People at various levels of consciousness. It is important to understand that with genetic engineering—the cells of a body, and not necessarily an Earthling—can be changed and recreated, *but* there is a need for it to always be done in the name of the Source of the Creator of All and in that way, it is *blessed*. But, unfortunately because of ignorance, the Annunaki were experimenting with genetic engineering and there was a kind of 'hit and miss' as to what they created. Sometimes they were creating or trying to create something, and it didn't work out that way, so they would change their thinking and do it a different way. They had a lot of knowledge—a lot of technical knowledge, but they were not using it through the Source of All Creation to help and assist them in their endeavours. Does that make some sense?

Jacqui: It does. Does that mean they created an animal with a human head or say a human-like figure with an animal head, or a bird-like head?

Jalarm: Indeed, that happened yes. They went on to create what looked like a cave man. They went onto produce an up-standing ape-like creature, which was used with DNA from the animal, and this would be what your scientists would say was simply an up-standing ape-like creature. Its brain was limited to quite some degree. The Annunaki had ancestors who were reptilian in form; this, I would like you to understand because they also had the influence of the reptilian beings as well as mammalian beings and so they had hair—but they also had a spine and even with the Earthling now, it still has the spine that once held a tail (though this has been dropped, genetically dropped).

Getting back to the up-standing ape-like creature, that was produced by the Annunaki, so it would assist them in mining gold. You could call them man if you like, because they did have a limited brain function that was able to take orders. They were called in when it was necessary and when they were needed to mine gold; other than that, they were left to their own devices. They developed very haphazardly—again, part of the reason was they were not exactly connected to the Source of All Creation.

However, they were weapon wielding. They did produce weapons that were carelessly used, and you could say that they were mind controlled. Does that make some sense?

Adams Calendar in South Africa. Jalarm gives information about what happened here

Jacqui: Yes, thank you. Do you know of the site that is called 'Adams Calendar' in South Africa?

Jalarm: This is all part of a very large development that took place because that site is just near a very deep source of gold—it still is. And so that was a centre of much activity at that time. This is quite a long time before, as I said, the Atlanteans came to this planet.

The Annunaki wanted the gold because they knew it had an essence to it that beings of a highly developed nature could use to assist them with their connection to the Source of All, and this they were trying to recreate. It is called White Powder Gold. And it lifted the consciousness so that they were able to have unlimited abilities. But unfortunately, they were not quite achieving it as they wanted.

However, they did use the gold for adornment, and so would you like to ask more about that?

Jill: The gold sounds very interesting! What did they do with it? Did they make beautiful articles or what?

Jalarm: Yes, they did. They fashioned it into figurines, into jewellery, into various bowls in which to carry things, to adorn many things ... but also, as I have said, they were trying to capture the essence of the gold to use as a raising of consciousness. They did not achieve this. They did not understand about the quality of being that is needed to be able to create such an essence. Does that make some sense?

(*They said, 'thank you, yes.'*)

Jacqui: Just going back to the Adam's Calendar, were any humans or Star People ever sacrificed there?

Jalarm: They were. And this is linking to a belief of connecting to a Higher Being—but again the teachings were a little misdirected and so they began to overrule the beings they had created, that they called upon, and they thought if they offered them to a higher being that they could be consumed by the gods and sent back to them as an essence. Does that make some sense?

(**NB:** *In my earlier work with the Pleiadeans, we were advised that the Higher Beings that the reptilians offered their creations in sacrifice to were known as the Draco, or Draconians, who had created the reptilians in the first place.*)

Jacqui: When did the humans begin to look like they do now—with hardly any body hair, smaller faces, and larger skulls as compared to cavemen? How long ago was it?

Jalarm: Again, I hesitate to name numbers. You can try this on the Oracle, but again you need to be careful about asking it in your time, rather than the Star People time. There was evolvement of what you would call the beings that were created—you could call them 'man.' It was later that the Pleiadeans came and did genetic engineering that was given by permission from The Source and the Angelic Realms, and the children that were created were imbued with Divine Light and love, and so they were Children of Light in a man's body, now in a human body. That was the difference. Does this make sense? ... This came later.

Twenty-Four

Lemuria

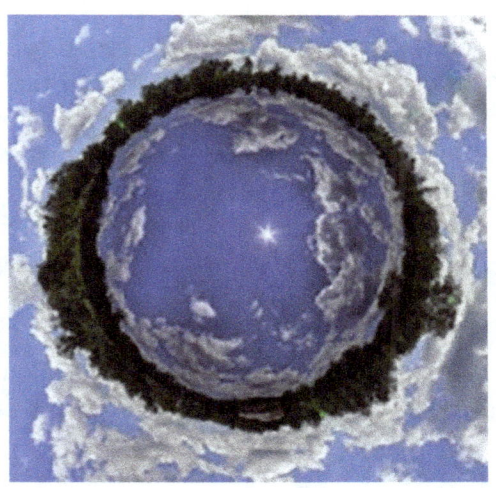

Jalarm: Understand that there are different dimensions on this planet and people can live side by side even though they do not recognise each other. In other words, it is possible to live upon the planet and be superimposed upon another life that is taking place at the same time and same place.

Valérie: In the early days, *before* the first humans were created [*I am speaking from knowledge given when Alcheringa came to us*], we believe the up-standing ape-like creature was eating the carcasses, when they died, believing they were no different from dead fish, or animals... [Jalarm interrupted.]

Jalarm: This is correct, my dear, they had no understanding. And so, we as Star People came; we returned to teach them ceremony. The ceremonies did not begin straight away, but gradually they began to understand. They also came to understand about the fire and the cooking, so as I have said, when the humans were first created and enchristed, they did not have all the knowledge straight away. They needed teaching so, as I have said, the Star People came to teach them ceremony, how to cook food, how to light fire, and how to create a ceremony for their dead so that their spirit could pass back to the World of Light. So does this answer your question?

Jacqui: Wouldn't their spirit have gone back to the World of Light as a natural thing in the Universal Law?

Jalarm: Indeed, it does, my dear, but they needed to understand that so they would stop eating their dead. Understand that right from the beginning as a human, there was a very large selection of DNA from animals, birds, insects, and many any other aspects that are on the Earth—and all of this created the up-standing ape-like creature. This is no judgment of any of it. But the human has inherited that very heavy energy, that very heavy weapon-wielding, animal-like approach to life. And they needed to understand about human values.

Jacqui: This is a bit of a leap away, but there is a question here—it is said that the Aborigine travelled the Earth in the figure eight—when was that?

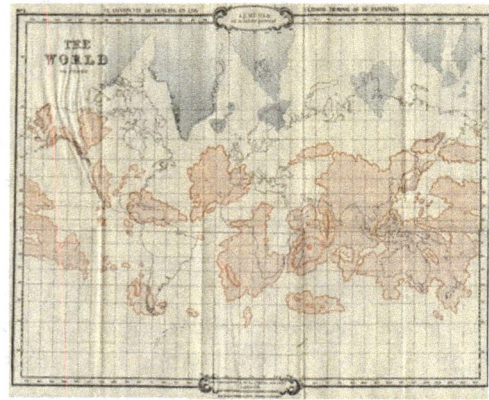

Map of Lemuria according to William Scott-Elliott

Jalarm: This was more of a time in what you call a Lemurian Age, when the Australian Aborigine had evolved and were very much in tune with the Star People and communicated with them telepathically. They definitely had evolved to a place where they were very much in tune with ceremony and the understanding of who they really were (inheriting some of the Star People's DNA). So, they were brothers and sisters—they understood this. And so, they had been encouraged to spread and intermingle with other indigenous people who were upon the Earth and this they did.

They were encouraged and taught by the Star People how to build boats they would sail. They had already been given a lot of instruction about astronomy and how it worked as a star map to help them travel around the Earth. They were given instructions about the currents that existed in the seas, and they travelled these currents more than anything. They travelled one way in what was vaguely a *figure of eight* around the world, which they have in their Dreaming stories. The elders know this, and when they travelled, they interacted with other beings that they came across, and mated with them. Sometimes they stayed and others came. There was a lot of movement around. Some of the movement was assisted by the Star People who already lived upon the Earth.

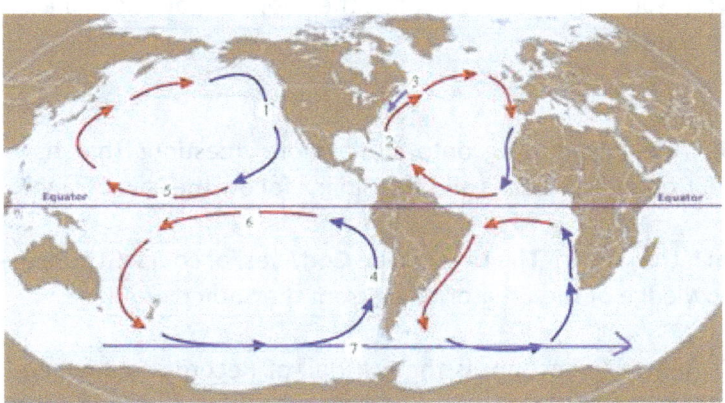

The Earth's ocean currents are like a figure of eight enabling circumnavigation

And I would like you to understand that, for it made it a little easier for them; however, they had to be left to their own devices to some degree so they could evolve and become the true humans, with human values of which they have come to possess.

Jacqui: Do you think the human bodies will change a lot going back to a Light Body?

Jalarm: You are already a Light Body, my dear. This is something that all humans need to remember. You have inherited the Light Being—Star People. You have different weights and measures in everyone upon this Earth. But you are—and have—Star People genes in you. And the weight and measure differ in different people; however, there is a coming together because the Earth herself is changing and lifting and ascending into an energy that will help to integrate with all the beings upon the Earth as it is now. And this is since Atlantis went down, and when all the people on the Earth at that time lived and survived only in caves because a great Ice Age had finally come to the earth, and so they had a difficult time in surviving. The sun was hidden because all the ash came out of the volcanoes and blotted it for a long time. This was before the air started to clear and the sun started to reappear, and more began to grow back to where it was. It was a major catastrophe that happened upon the Earth, and it was only about ten-and-a-half thousand years ago. The time could be questionable; it depends on how you measure time. But it was not such a long time as far as the evolution of this planet. Do you understand?

(*Yes.*)

Jacqui: I am just moving onto some more questions that have been written. Do the Pleiadeans and the Sirians follow the Law of One?

Jalarm: If they mean '**The Law of One God,**' yes, of course. There is always the knowledge of the Creator being from the Source of All.

Jacqui: Another question: Is there a Hall of Records somewhere on an Astral Plane or Earth that we can access? I have heard of a library of Porthologos that is in Agartha that contains the cosmic records of the universe. Is it true that exists? And how can we access it?

Jalarm: I would like you to ask the Oracle about this because it is a complicated question. I would like you to see how it flows.

(*Yes.*)

Jalarm: Thank you, my dear. Thank you.

Asking the Oracle

The Oracle advised that **'yes**, *there is a Hall of Records.'*
Is it in the Astral? **'Yes.'**
Is it within the Earth's atmosphere? **'No.'**
Is there such a thing as civilizations in the inner Earth? 'Yes.'
Does that mean they exist in their astral body? **'Yes.'**
Are there Star People *in* the Earth? **'No.'**
With more questions, it seems the Hall of Records is *inside* the Earth's crust.
Can it ever be damaged? **'No.'**

Fourth talk with 'Jalarm'

I said I worked with a gentleman who saw into the future, 300 years ahead, to 2,300 AD. He said, *'Something did happen on Earth.'* But he didn't know what.

Jalarm: The future is ahead. What has passed is behind. What is important is the now, and to live in the now you need to have faith and complete trust. And to know that whatever happens in your life is what is meant to happen to help you—to assist you to progress to evolve into the true Light Being that you are. You are God and so you can help create a future for yourselves. It is important to understand that because the Law of One is just that. It is a recognition of the ability of every being upon this Earth to create a future for everybody's good—not for the self but for everybody on this Earth. And *'everybody'* encompasses the animals, the birds, the insects, and the reptiles. It is what belongs; the energy belongs to you on this Earth. It has had the evolvement of all those beings on this Earth ever since it began.

And so, my dear, I would like you to forget about the future, for it can change. One person's memory into the future can be another's that is different and not necessarily the same. Understand that there are different dimensions on this planet and people can live side by side even though they do not recognise each other. In other words, it is possible to live upon the planet and be superimposed upon another life that is taking place upon this planet. It is all part of evolvement—it is all part of the edict of change—evolvement and who is ready to leave into a higher consciousness and who is not. Does this make sense?

(*All agreed.*)

I will leave you now, God bless you, my children. God bless you.

Read about 'Denisovans' who were likely a group of primitive humans, related to our vanished Neanderthal cousins. There are also comments about ancient brain genes in this article.

Twenty-Five

Pre-Atlantis Wars

Pre-Atlantis—reptilians, Leonines, and early humans

It was Wednesday, 27th of March, that we met. It was on this day we sat joining hands to unite our energies and called upon God to be present. The wine glass quickly spelt out **'Nara'** and we knew that meant Narayana—Sai Baba's birth name. The Oracle was now sacred.

Jalarm came, but not before Sai Baba had spelt out his name on the Oracle and when asked again, he made us laugh as he said, 'Go,' and then spelt out 'Baba' and swung the wine glass around and around—the signal we have come to recognise that Jalarm wants to borrow my voice box. The wine glass pushed out of the circle of letters and began to move quickly outside of the circle towards me. This made us laugh even more.

The word *'go'* reminded me of the time when I first met Sai Baba at his ashram in India. He had stopped in front of me and then pointed somewhere and said, 'Go.' The ladies around me said it meant to go for an interview.

I have just remembered a dream I had not long after we had been asked by Cosmic Sai Baba to sit with an Oracle. Jacqui and Jill agreed to join together. Jacqui had learnt from childhood how to place individual letters from the 26-character English alphabet on small squares of white paper—numbers one to nine, plus zero, also on separate squares of white paper, and a 'yes' and a 'no' on two more small squares of white paper. They were then laid in a circle onto a smooth table along with a longish stemmed wine glass, which was placed in the centre. We knew it was imperative to ask God to sanctify the circle before we began.

In the dream, I was talking to an interesting man about pre-Atlantis. He said he loved The Groks (?) and spoke about the North Sea and Antarctica. I asked him if I could interview him. I had no idea what that dream was about until we were set up to use the Oracle and were introduced to Jalarm. In a way we are interviewing him.

We have words that have been spelt out by Jalarm on the Oracle—but we don't understand them. We are told it is a language.

Jalarm: It is Jalarm, and I am very pleased to be speaking with you and sharing this little joke with our beloved Baba—for he is my love as well as yours. I know there have been a lot of questions written down and I am keen to answer as many as we can so why don't we just get started and ask the first question?

Jacqui: Edgar Cayce described the Arcturians as being three to four feet in height with bluish/green skin and three fingers on each hand. Is that accurate?

Jalarm: It is, but as a lot of planets are similar in this way, there is more than one race that inhabits the planet. And so, the planet that we mentioned as Arcturus and the very tall, white Light Beings that also live there, lived there long before the smaller beings came. Does that help you?

Jacqui: Yes, I think so. Another question is were there any wars on Earth during the Atlantean time?

Jalarm: There were unfortunately wars, yes. But not in the early days. As more civilizations established themselves on the Earth, there were disagreements that could not be resolved easily and so there were a few wars, yes...

Jacqui: Were there any wars when the humans were first created at Kariong?

Jalarm: This is going back a long time, of course, and yes—where the humans were first created, there were still many of what we call the reptilian races that existed and the up-standing ape-like creatures who had been anointed with the Christ Light were evolving into humans. They were in danger, and yes, the beings from Sirius came to help them and there was a war between the reptilians and the Leonines. Also, the up-standing beings that were tall, white, and without hair that came from the Sirian Constellation. They were of a more advanced being and were able to teach and lead the Leonine race.

The war took place between the Leonines and the reptilians—however, that was resolved.

Jacqui: Thank you. Another question about Kariong in Australia—we are wondering what are the *cup holes* that are drawn on rocks found at Kariong?

Jalarm: The Star People that survived—who had come from the Pleiades at that time and helped with the genetic engineering to take place with the up-standing ape-like creature that then went on to become the beginning of the human race—they taught them many things. They taught them how to make fire, how to cook

The up-standing ape-like creature evolved to the human we know today

food. How to understand where we had come from and that there is a *power* that connects them to the Source of All Creation. They began to understand because we told them little stories that would assist with their understanding; these, they have kept in their Dreamtime stories.

However, we did also teach them about the stars and their movement in the sky and how that was reflected on Earth, and the energy on the planet.

Earth was influenced by that movement, and so they were encouraged to draw circles representing different star constellations from the sky. So, these *cup holes* are part of that map of astronomy, and they were given some sense of the cosmos. They were drawn on the rocks like a star map, so, in just the shape and the number it held what constellation it represented. And so, the evolving human began to understand that. And they were, as I have said, the beginning of the Australian Aborigine. So, does this make some sense to you?

Image: Steven and Evan Strong—Forgotten Origins—Star Markers

Jacqui: Yes, it does. Thank you. Where is the city of Atlantis as told by Plato?

Jalarm: This is an interesting story, and it is very good that Plato wrote it down so that it was recorded ... of what had happened before Atlantis went down and was lost. Plato wrote at the time (about a place located) around the mid-Mediterranean Sea (as you know it now) and that actually—along with an outer edge of evolvement that doesn't show readily above the sea now, but is hidden under ocean—(that place) does come from around Greece, Malta, and other areas close by and reaching out further to the beginning of the existence of Atlantis, as written by Plato.

But I would like to add also that other civilizations had developed around the Earth. And [there] were similar evolvement of cities created by Star People that existed around your Earth. Does that help you at all?

Jacqui: Yes, it does. It's making the hairs on my arms stand up! Another question: How many pure Star People (without other DNA) existed that weren't lowered?

Jalarm: Yes, now this is a question I would like you to ask the Oracle so that you can see its significance, because we are trying to show you there are many ways to connect to the Star People and with God's will we like you to use the Oracle as a way of connecting to other worlds. So, I will withdraw for a while, if that is alright?

The Oracle didn't like the way we had phrased the question; the way it was spelt out was too hard. We had to rethink the question. The Oracle told us when Earth Fell, the (pure) Star People left Earth on starships to fly to other star systems.

We asked how they came and went in Atlantean time. Jalarm called to me to begin a transmission. The word **'GUBAA'** was spelt out, which we think means 'Goodbye.'

Second Transmission from Jalarm

The tall white Star People from Arcturus

(He literally jumped into my body—and made us jump and laugh. We could not see him, but we knew he was with us.)

Jalarm: I joke with you. (*He made us laugh again.*) Sometimes they

They travelled in wormholes.

travelled by what we call starships or motherships—you can imagine you're travelling from, say, the southern hemisphere to the northern hemisphere in your planes. We had ships that travelled from a place on Earth to another star system.

We didn't travel, as you would think, in a linear fashion but rather through what you would call 'wormholes.' It didn't take all that long to go or to come back.

Sometimes people were relieved because it was a little like being assigned to the planet and they were on duty while they were living on Earth because they were holding the energy of Divine Light and love and that was what their mission was. They were also teaching all the different races that were gathered on this Earth, much like what is happening now. Although I can assure you, it was more advanced at that time. You have seen evidence of starships coming and leaving from this planet now, and there has been evidence caught on your digital cameras. So, they do come and go. It is not difficult once you have the advanced technology at your fingertips.

Star Trek animation

There are other ways too—to come and go—because there are some Star People that came and manifested in a hologram upon the Earth so that they could be seen and heard and communicated with, and then they would leave. A little like your so-called Star Trek animations.

There is much that is received in your way of telling stories in science fiction that is true—because the writers in science fiction are drawing from the memory deep within them in their Soul Consciousness of being Star People and how it worked at that time. This all happened before Atlantis went down. And as I have said, there was much happening upon this Earth for the past 200,000 years—but even before that ...

We are talking about Arcturians who came to uplift the human race, and it is why they are tall, white beings and the look that they have with their white hair, white skin, blue eyes, and very similar bodies; it is why they are so close to looking like the human race as the humans look now. But that took a while before Atlantis went down for the evolvement of humans to take place upon this Earth.

From the Star People that existed upon this Earth, they were here to teach and help to balance energy upon this Earth and to create knowledge and opportunities for all the other races upon this Earth to learn and to come understand how to work with Mother Earth—and to live with her, and upon her, to look after her, to care for her—because she was caring for them.

So, it is no different from what the indigenous people already remember. It is those from the so-called *western world* with advanced technology who have forgotten. This, we hope will change. But returning to the Star People and the ones that were living upon this Earth and how they returned to other Star Worlds and then came back—there are many ways. But it was possible to travel by ship—it was always possible to transform the self into one place and then into another, depending upon the level of consciousness and the ability that they had. Does that make some sense?

(*Yes.*)

Jacqui: With all the coming and going, was there some sort of border control?

Jalarm: In a way there was. It was all done through a hierarchy, or a group of beings, to act as a border control if you like to use those words. So, they would come and go without breaking any of the Universal Laws. Unfortunately, some did come, and some did break the Universal Laws. This unfortunately led to the demise of what existed on this planet before it went down. I can add here that some of the scientists decided to experiment, even though they were coming from a place where they really knew better. They scientifically experimented without the permission from the Source and produced beings—*if you could call them beings*. They were alive; they had body parts that were mixed up so that sometimes they had a human head on an animal body or vice versa—a human body with an animal head was not allowed by the Universal Laws. This was deeply going against the edict of what the Angelic Realms and the Hierarchy had as a Law upon this Earth. Because it went ahead, and the scientists were experimenting by misusing the beings that had been created, the creations were victims and still exist in the in-between worlds (a world before the Souls that leave this Earth now). When they (the souls that leave) return to the World of Light, there is a passage that they must pass through and some of these beings are still there, lost. They are referred to as **'demons'** because they are overlorded by a race that is misusing them still. This must go—this is being changed.

Jalarm: This is an edict on this Earth now and it will not be allowed to differ from what the Universal Law has put into place. So, would you like to ask about that?

(Jacqui and Jill both said they couldn't think. The energy was very high. Another written question was about the wars that were said to take place towards the end of the Atlantean Age).

Jalarm: Yes, this was in the later time of Atlantis when the Universal Laws were starting to break down. Some of those in positions of power upon this planet decided to go their own way for power and took control. This eventually happened and is written in the mythology of many Indian and other civilizations around the world. But in the Hindu religion, for that is one of the strongest that has survived since Atlantis Fell.

Jacqui: Can I please ask a question? Lord Ganesh has the head of an elephant and the body of a child in mythology, so can you tell us anything about that?

Jalarm: There are Gods that are portrayed in symbolism—symbolism only. Not necessarily as I have just described as taking place before Atlantis Fell. Many of the deities within the Hindu religion are purely symbolic. So does that help you?

Jacqui: Another question; it is a bit of a difficult one. Could you describe what the cities on Earth were like before Atlantis?

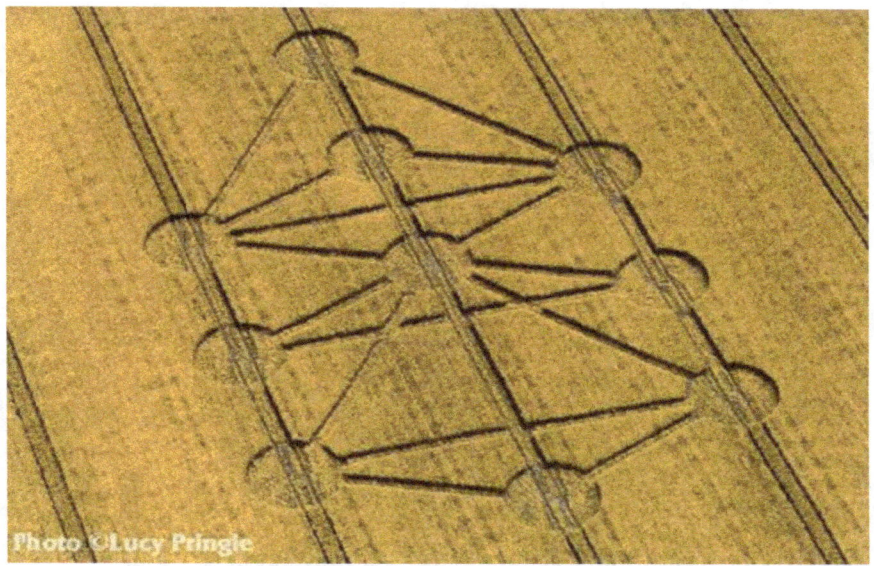

Sacred geometry was used by the Star People

Jalarm: Many of the cities that were created by the Star People themselves had sacred geometry. So, there were a lot of circles and within that the patterns of geometry, but that also interacted with the functioning of the city or the town, depending on how big it was. There were also  areas for a natural ceremony that the Star People gave to the Source of All Creation. And they see it as a sun. They see a group of suns in alignment to the Source of All Creation. And so, the sun, or the Solar Logos, is what they were giving thanks to and drawing energy from to help nourish them as Light Beings. In a way you could see it as a food, but they did eat other things as well.

Jacqui: That was my next question. What did the people eat? And then how was it after Atlantis?

Jalarm: Again, and this is a little difficult to answer because it depended upon the evolvement of different races, some needed heavier food that came from a heavier Light and needed sustenance for their physical body, and the lighter they became the lighter the food that was necessary. And in the long term, they could arrive to a place where they needed no heavy food at all but would survive and live very easily on the Divine Light and love directly from The Source.

Jacqui: Did they eat any animals?

Jalarm: This depended upon the energy of what they have in their physical body. As I have said, if they were heavy then the animal was the kind of food they needed—and the lighter they became literally, the lighter the food they needed. Does that make sense?

Jacqui: There is another question here. Did they eat each other?

Jalarm: Unfortunately, that did happen with the lower energies—by that I mean depending upon the circumstances. But that is another story. I would like you to ask the Oracle about that one.

Asking the Oracle

The Oracle said it (eating of bodies) did exist pre-Atlantis. They did recognise disease and would not eat the body. Jill asked did they kill them to eat. The Oracle said 'no.' They only ate dead bodies so they wouldn't be wasted.

Early up-standing ape-like creatures first created by reptilians misunderstood and were confused. The Oracle said Star People (Light Beings from the Pleiades) came to teach burial ceremonies after the genetic engineering had taken place and the new humans were created.

Twenty-Six

Asteroid Belt

Light Bodies and the Chinese Race

We were prompted by Jalarm to all hold hands to harmonise and allow ourselves to be prompted with insight.

Jalarm: (Confirming we were being prompted.) We are having a little fun here because we want you to be able to receive the messages together. And so, I would like you to rehearse if you do not mind. You have asked how the Light Man—the Chinese Man—came to manifest into an Earth body, and I would like to say, one, two, three.

Valérie (one): I would say that the Earth body was actually created in a hologram. It was a Light body, and the Earth body was much later …

Jacqui (two): All I can see is a huge Angelic Being coming here onto the Earth. (She is going to paint it.)

Jill (three): I am seeing good. I don't feel I am getting any answer, but it feels very pleasant. Thank you.

Jalarm: So how do you feel about the information that has been given? Does it feel not quite right or not all there yet?

Jill: I think it feels wonderful and I am feeling overwhelmed by it.

Jalarm: That is alright, my dear. Now I have said it is created like a hologram—so this was very advanced technology, and it is part of the reason that the Chinese race seem to be so clever; in actual fact they are. Because they have come from a very advanced dimensional energy, which still influences them in their bodies today.

I can confirm now that their Light Bodies became influenced by their Creators into a denser energy field. This may sound rather odd—and like science fiction—but they were created by the knowledge and the ability of the God Beings in full form to start with. And then, after a large core number were created, they began interacting with each other. Is there something you might like to add there?

Jacqui: It just feels like an amazing Angelic Form coming to Earth, that wasn't connected with something already here. It felt it was totally coming from another place.

Jill: It does make perfect sense to me.

Val: I am seeing a physical body being formed in a cylinder, almost like a cloning. I see an image and then the science that came together that formed the being from the energies from Earth so that it became denser. It's like the DNA of the Earth being was copied—and then they were able to keep cloning them. But how they produced male and female, I am not sure. There would have been a separation that took place ...

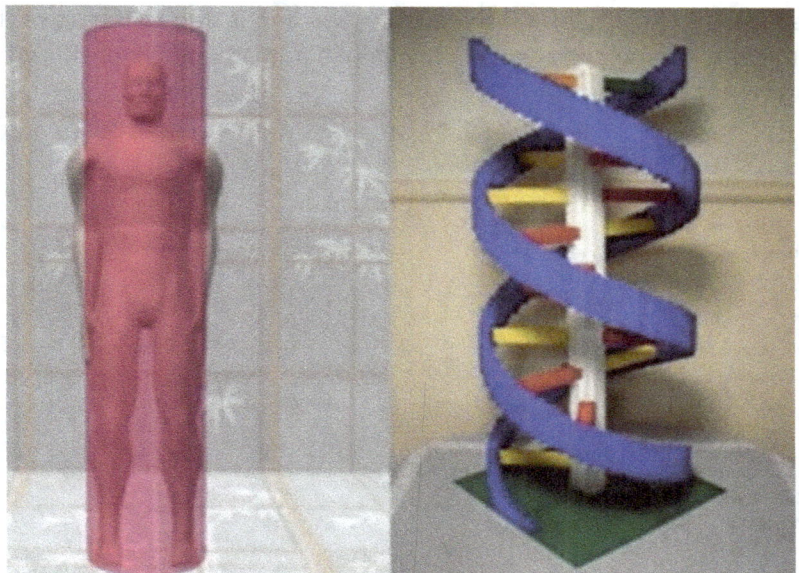

DNA was formed from the Earth in a light body

Jalarm: (interrupting) There was indeed a separation that took place. Again, this was a long time ago. The separation took place in a different dimension from what the Earth was operating. Remember, in the time we are talking about, it was the 4th dimension that the whole of the planet was operating in. It only fell into the 3rd dimension after the terrible catastrophe that happened on Earth. And so all the beings on the planet fell into the denser energy too.

So, I just have to give you an image of how the Asian, or particularly the Chinese race, was first created. When Atlantis went down it was a time of great confusion, and as I have just said the planet fell into the 3rd dimension and all the people who were left on the planet fell in consciousness as well. And so too did the Chinese people, and so they became a little confused about their warrior spirit and they became angry and reacted. They fought wars—but this is not truly their nature. They were basically pacifists, as were the Australian Aborigine and the Jewish people.

---oOo---

We decided to ask Jalarm if the dugong was connected to the beginning of the ape-like man because the image of a human embryo at thirty-two days looks like a dugong.

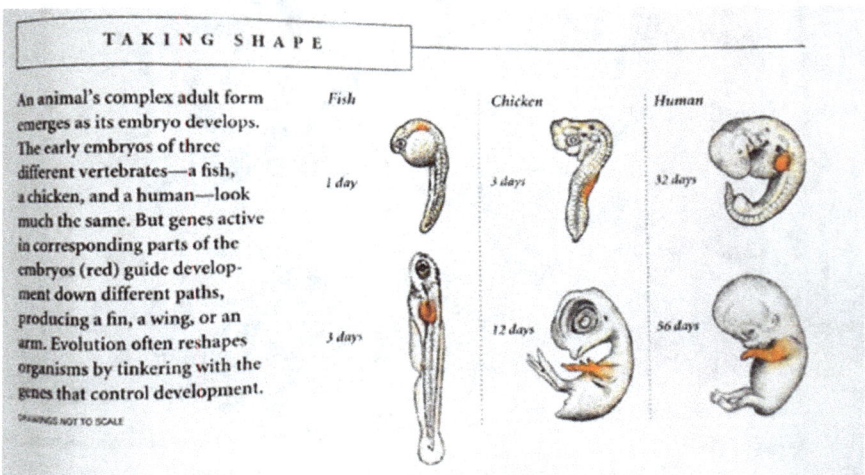

The human body at thirty-two days resembles a dugong. Taken from National Geographic, November 2006, artwork by John Burgoyne. See of interest: 'A Fin is a Limb is a Wing' article by Carl Zimmer.

Jalarm: The question that you ask is a little complicated. It is a fact that the Reptoid peoples did a lot of experimenting with genetic engineering and they were, for a long time, creating many different shapes and forms to try and get a being that would be suitable for them to use virtually as a slave to mine gold. We have said this before. And so they needed somebody. They had a vision in their mind that looked like the barbarian ape-like creature. To achieve this, they used DNA from themselves and from other beings that had come to the Earth and the interaction of the material needed to have a birth mother and so they chose the dugong.

The Reptoids used Dugong DNA to create an up-standing ape-like slave

Mainly because it was mammalian and they themselves were reptilian–lizard-like beings with cold blood and they wanted a warmer blood—really, they felt they might be getting closer to an evolved person because they were using some material from a captured Leonine Being from the star worlds during the war that existed, and this upset the Leonine people. They used some of the genetic material from the dead Leonine and put that  together with other genetic material and implanted it in the egg of a dugong—because that was also mammalian, and they knew that would be a good mother, able to breast feed the baby. And so, the child was born into water. It is the reason why the human is attracted now to having water birth.

However, the being, when born, was very hairy because it had come from Leonine DNA and (remember this all happened when the Earth was in the 4th dimension, so yes, the dugong was ape-like-man's mother. This was the beginning, but the material is also related to the dolphins, which they also wanted to try and capture, knowing they were able to hold light and a raised consciousness upon this planet.

It all sounds rather far-fetched, I know, but as I have said, the Reptoids were very clever in what they could do—and although they were experimenting, they didn't quite understand about connecting to the Source of All Creation.

They understood it to a degree, but there was, of course, an element of the energy of themselves that was not created with permission from the Source of All Creation, so they did not have that blessing. So, this is what they were working at and aiming at when the first man was created, and it goes back a l-o-n-g time.

However, these creatures were what they wanted. They were able to stand up, had some increase in mental capacity, were able to take orders, and had hands that were physically able to mine gold ... and this is what they wanted. And so, they were used as slaves. They were weapon wielding because they had the fighting spirit in them. So, does this give some insight?

(They all agreed it did.)

Jacqui: The only other question we would like to ask is where did the Asteroid Belt come from in our solar system?

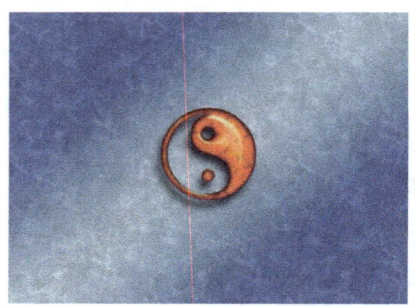
Yin Yang, symbols of the Chinese light body?

Jalarm: Yes, your solar system planet circumnavigates the sun, and there are a few other circles that are not related to the immediate solar system—however, they come and they go; these have been recorded by your astronomers. At another time there was another planet that existed—and because of wars between the reptilians and the Leonines, which were ongoing for many, many hundreds of thousands of years—they attacked this planet, or one of them, which no longer exists. They blew it up and it was caught up in the magnetic force of what exists in the pull of all the planets to your sun and it is still there. So, it was once a planet, but now it looks like asteroids. Does that make some sense? It also had life forms upon it, which eventually moved to your planet Earth.

This was where the Chinese Light Beings lived before they came to your planet Earth! Before it was *deleted*.

Twenty-Seven

Star People Experiencing Family Life

Evolution or Creation

We joined hands to harmonise. Jalarm made his entrance.

Jalarm: I am here, and I am very happy to answer questions.

Jacqui: Yes, thank you. Does the Zoroastrian religion have a connection to the Sumerians and the Annunaki people?

Jalarm: Not exactly, no. In fact, this was brought up at a much later time to the Sumerians and evolved alongside them—it was to help raise the consciousness because the Sumerians were coming from a place a little less evolved. And so, sacrifice was being made and there was a need for the race to

understand that this was not the way to go, that this was not what the Creative Source wanted.

And so, the Zoroastrian's knowledge and their energy played alongside each other to help and bring changes just by their very presence. It did not happen overnight, but changes did happen.

Jacqui: Thank you, and just another question: evolution or creation—can you explain please?

Jalarm: There is much talk about how humans evolved upon the Earth. And there is much cellular examination of many different animals or species of bird, or reptile, that are similar, but even the DNA or genome exists in plant life and shells and so there is a similarity in all forms upon this Earth. And so, there is a certain amount of evolution that took place—adjusting to changes in climate and more than that, really; It was because of climate change that adjustments took place, but then there is talk of Creation and how things were created, not evolved, and there is truth in that also. In fact, it was from other beings from the cosmos that used genetic engineering, which I have said before is very common to the evolved races, or even the races that are not so evolved. They still had advanced technology, much more than what exists even on your planet at this time.

So, there is a necessity for careful study and experiments with genetic engineering. And if it is always done in the name of the Source of All Creation and blessings are asked for—because it will automatically be blessed then—then the changes that will happen will bring great changes to the human race, but it must be sourced by and processed by those that come with evolved thinking. Not those who are just playing with it. Does that make some sense?

And so, the Gods—as races upon this Earth saw them when they came from other worlds—are correct, in that the creation is seen as God bringing the changes ... and this is true. Is there anything else you would like to ask?

Jacqui: There is a question here asking, in the evolutionary tree—which came first, the birds or the reptiles?

Jalarm: If you are just selecting those two, the birds or the reptiles, the birds came first. Because it was the bird race from the Star Worlds that came to help progress the Earth's evolution. Now I am saying evolution in the sense that there were changes that evolved from different scientific elements that came together and changed into something else that was needed in the creation of your atmosphere. But then, the *bird-like-beings*—they were upstanding, they had technology, they were sent by the Angelic Realms, and they came to assist the progress of the planet into a garden. A beautiful garden of Eden. Eden is also connected to sound, which is part of the evolution or growth. Does that make sense? Is there anything else you would like to ask about that?

Jacqui and Jill (after discussing for a while): *Where do the fish fit into the evolutionary picture?*

Jalarm: The fish were a form that were created to be in the sea to feed other forms that were already created on Earth. They have a place to provide energy to other forms—even humans still eat them. The fish came from a race that were fish-like in appearance and although it was not the race itself that was eaten, they did create forms that provided food in their likeness. By that I mean they looked like fish. Do you understand that? Do you see what I am saying? In other words, the fish-like beings—

Star People—produced and created a form that was food, and it had their own image. Just as it is said that the human has been created by God in his image. I would like you to think about that if you would. So, is there another question?

Star People that looked like fish beings

Jacqui: In the study of DNA, it seems that all vertebrate beings have a common denomination in the spine. Would that be correct?

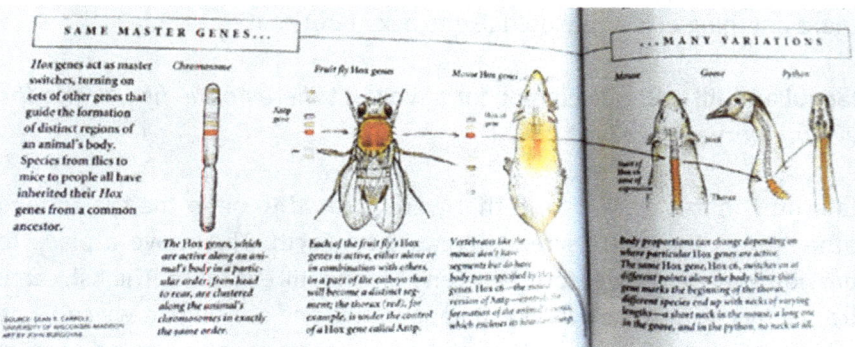

Taken from National Geographic, November 2006; artwork by John Burgoyne

Jalarm: That would be correct, yes. Is there something you would like to enlarge on that?

Jacqui: Would that mean there is not creation, but rather creation from the Star People?

Jalarm: Well, I think I have already answered that—would that be right?
(They agreed.)

Jacqui: I am having a little trouble thinking. Deep within the human mind there is a belief that all creation is from God. Is that because within the psyche of the human they know that higher power has created everything?

Jalarm: All humans have been blessed by the Creative Source of All. And every human upon this Earth has a soul. And with that soul is the blueprint that comes with it and the Source of a Star Being perhaps, or the history of Star Beings that are not as evolved as others—they have the opportunity to come and live in a human body and experience a family life. You will note that all indigenous people have marriages and families, and they love their children. This is what they come to experience. The ones I am talking about are not as evolved as Star People. They have never experienced the warmth of a family and children, and they come to experience that here, and in doing so it raises their consciousness for everybody upon this Earth; the ones who readily understand the love of family and children help to share that love, which comes from the Source, so that everybody on Earth comes from, shall we say, a level playing field. They all become warm, loving, compassionate beings. This is then taken back to the race they have come from or shared with other races. Does that make some sense?
(They agreed.)

Jacqui: Is the first man created by the Annunaki to mine gold, a red-haired ape-looking being? Val says she sees that, and the word *barbarian* comes to mind.

Jalarm: The first ape-like creature, created by the Annunaki, was the man or *'ape-man'*—he did look very hairy, with red-like hair, and yes, at another time, much later, he was referred to as a barbarian. This was much, much later.

The first ape-like creature created by the Annunaki was the man or 'ape-like' man

A rest time was suggested.

Twenty-Eight

Moldavite

I asked about the Moldavite. Jalarm wanted to go back to the Oracle.

The Oracle spelt out, 'faith.'

We asked the Oracle, '*Is the Moldavite stone the remains of the mothership Rexegena?*' **The answer was 'Yes!'**

'*How long ago did the mothership Rexegena come to Earth?*' The Oracle spelt out 700,000 years in 4th dimensional time, and then 900,000 years in 3rd dimensional time.

We asked, '*Was the Egyptian Tomb at Kariong created around 4,500 years ago?*' **The answer was 'Yes.'**

Then Jalarm signalled he wished to speak through me again.

Jalarm: 'It is I, Jalarm. We are talking about the Moldavite stone. It is said to come from outer space, and it does. It is the mothership—and the mothership Rexegena was a very evolved piece of machinery. It was a highly developed technology that does not exist on your Earth even now, even though it was so long ago. *It was raised on the 8th planet of the Pleiadean constellation*. It is organic and the method of building it was through growing it—growing it with the mind. This may seem a bit hard to understand, but it was done that way. And it can be done that way.

Just talking aside, I would like to say that the crystals that are on the Master Crystal at Satori Springs, Canyonleigh, NSW, within the solar/Stargate activities, they are growing—and the ship grew in a similar way—from the result of interaction with Beings of Light and their consciousness.

I reach down to the Master Crystal at Sartori Springs. Crystal offshoots—which are growing—can be clearly seen. This crystal is known as the Alcheringa Crystal, not to be confused with the sacred Alcheringa Stone from the stars, belonging to the Indigenous people of Australia.

Jalarm: So the mothership, yes, when it was attacked it was like a nuclear explosion. It was attacked and melted piece by piece, portion by portion. The 'melted' aspect of organic material that was used from the mothership fell to Earth—not quite all at the same time—but almost. It was very hot of course, and as it entered the atmosphere it found its HOME around the area of Czechoslovakia—Moravia and Bohemia. The Moldavite stone and its transformational qualities have been known for a long time.

However, it was witnessed by beings who were upon this Earth, of course. The rest of the galaxy heard about it and they were very upset, including the Hierarchy, and so the Angelic Realms issued an order that help should go out to assist the survivors off the mothership.

Some were able to get away, and some were shot out of the sky. Others moved further south, crashed, and landed around the area you now call Kariong. But they were still in danger. They needed protection. They laid low for quite some time and tried to survive as best as they could. But then came some reptilians who were very upset also about what had happened to them and they tried to assist them. Further down the track in what would be five years in your time  (which isn't very long really), the Leonines came. Quite a few of them came to retaliate against what had happened. And so, there was a war. I would say the reptilians retreated into what I would call an inner-earth area. A slightly different dimension. They were able to do this, which is why they mined gold—they knew how to transmute themselves.

So, there was a war, but that calmed down very easily and quickly and then the survivors went on to establish a point of Light, which was what their mission was, upon this Earth. They ended up creating man with Light. Man, that came later with souls, were the beginning of the human race. And this is what the Angelic Realms had decided should happen, to help establish a much bigger plan to offer opportunities for various beings that came from other planets—and other levels of different dimensions of frequency (somewhere not as advanced as others). But there was a Karmic Board in the Star World. There were situations where there were many, many homes that were like homes but were motherships that allowed the souls to be downloaded and enter into the new babies that were born on Earth as humans.

And this has been happening ever since.

They have been coming and going, and always in a soul that is connected in its history to many different races. Each soul is very different. Each soul is individual. There are no two souls alike. But some souls have been split and have created what is called a 'Twin Soul.'

There are other souls that like to come and go as a family. And they come from the ship down to the new little foetus that has just been born to a mother, and they enter and then grow to be born human. And then they interact with others who they have known from the World of Light and they assist in holding the new consciousness in this corner of the galaxy—which was very dark but is becoming much lighter with all the activity. So, we shall rest now for a while.

The Oracle spelt out '**OEOK 8 B**' and then the glass kept moving around in a tight circle, anticlockwise. We don't yet know what these letters mean.

Jalarm: (making his entrance again) I am here again and yes, there was a very advanced civilization in the area where the refugees (from the mothership) lived. I would like to add also that the area was not as active as it had been in previous times. It was quite an old, old city. It started with the old empire and that was when the reptilian and Draco held sovereignty over this planet. At least they thought they held sovereignty over this planet, but they didn't really—they just took it.

And that was allowed to develop because they, the Hierarchy, the Angelic Realms, could see that they needed assistance to raise light and this was an opportunity, perhaps, to help them evolve. They had this grand plan all along. For a long, long time.

There were Star Beings that came also, in the time of Atlantis, and lived in that same area (known as Gosford). So, there are quite a number of layers that exist in that place. And it was spread out—up and down the coast, north and south—and there is evidence of this, and it will come eventually. It will be found. It is the plan.

View of Gosford, NSW, Australia. An advanced civilization lived on the east coast of Australia. There are layers and layers of beings beneath this region around Gosford and Kariong and other areas along the east coast.

So, there is really nothing to worry about; it is just a matter of a little time. We are prompting people. There are many working at this, to navigate the study or the research in a way so that the information will come forth.

And yes, it will be known that there was a very evolved civilization all along the east coast of Australia.

Jacqui: Was there another name for Cosmic Sai Baba?

Jalarm chuckled and then left.

So, we decided to ask the Oracle, but the glass moved around, playing jokes with us, and then drew by movement the figure eight and kept going around one circle, and then reversed to go around the other circle. The glass kept doing it—the symbol means infinity. We kept laughing. When we asked if we needed to understand, the glass shot up to the letters 'NO.'

Note: Alcheringa has now advised (in 2021) that Jalarm, the Atlantean, is him.

Twenty-Nine

Your Thoughts and Your World

Written by Chris Parnell, our webmaster.

We know since 21 December 2012, that the world did not end. There is more light upon the Earth, and that light is going to the Earth, our mother herself, and to the different dimensions, and to all the beings that live here in the mineral kingdom, the plant kingdom, the animal kingdom, the kingdom of mankind, and to the beings in the higher dimensions.

There has been a change, an uplifting, a surge of light energy, and a change in the relationships of humanity, between persons, members of a family, in a town, in a society, and between nations.

There are many light workers on our planet now, who are correcting the misunderstanding about 21 December 2012; instead of the end of time, a new energy has come, brighter and lighter from the New World. This new energy—light energy—transmits influence on people. Some are conscious of this new energy in diverse ways; they are taking notice of all the synchronicities happening in their lives. They are aware of how they are creating their lives with their thoughts, words, and actions.

Others are unconscious; they are not aware of the new light energy; for them it will be a gradual change, a subtle elevation of consciousness and awareness. Others will experience sudden sensitivities to the higher energies and some people will be confused by the new energy.

The new energy coming onto this Earth is a divine energy. It is universal love. Everyone and every living thing receives this. It will cause people to think differently, to look at events and situations with tolerance and sort out problems, allowing differences to be.

It will be a time of letting go of the past, a release from the negativity of the past, and memories. These can be given over to the light, to the Angels, and the past can be left in the past. It is now a time of live and let live.

We have reached a turning point in the cosmos; cosmic divine energy is aligning now with the Earth. The Earth herself will feel the difference, as the energies are being anchored deep within her. The Earth is our mother and is available for all beings; for people to live, for animals to forage, for plants to thrive, for minerals to form and offer their gifts. Where would we be without our earth to live upon?

A New Door Opening

With the causation of the new energies onto Earth, there has been a new point of thinking that people will have; it is a time of adjustments. Many will experience confusion and have a need to adjust to the new energies, the new times, the possibilities of harmony on Earth. They will find ways to live together economically; they will find ways to live energetically; they will find ways to live with the Earth without damaging her.

We have all come from the one source: the Creative Source of All. There is really no difference between anyone or anything, for we are all part of the Universe. We are all part of the light that flows from the sun and through the sun, and this is the creative energy from the Source of All. To raise anger within hurts both our own self (a diminution of our life force energy) and anyone—or anything—outside ourselves, for we are all part of the One, the Creative Source of all. So, think about this before you reign anger in you, or allow it to rise within you. Calm it and drink some water and have another think; and find a way to express what it is that is really upsetting you.

Help is Always Given

We are being helped in unseen ways. There is prompting—for thought-forms arise within us and these are given to us by the elementals. They are the unseen lightworkers and the angels. So, when we have a thought, a prompting, we also have freedom and a choice whether to follow this or not. All prompting is for our good; it comes to us from the light and love of the Creative Source of All, who has many workers and helpers assisting us.

They assist us to evolve, to gain understanding, to be aware of our moods and motivations, and to think before we act, and to consider what we are thinking. In this way we can make choices for the good of all, not just for the good of a few:

This energy is around you,
This energy is prompting you,
This energy is helping you to live on this Earth, this planet

Whenever we take up the opportunity for human birth, there is a soul blueprint for our life. This soul blueprint has imprints for the roles we will play, the people we will meet and interact with, and the soul's work for this life. Sometimes, with a soul blueprint, there is a change. This change makes better interactions with others. So, our lives follow the path laid out with a blueprint for a life, like a play with a script and lines of drama and sorrow, humour and wisdom, actors and scenery, curtain rises and curtain falls, and make for interactions with other people that will heal.

We are all Lightworkers

Through conscious management of our thoughts and feelings, we can take up whatever work is needed to release everything that has gone on in the past and move forward. The past is past; leave it there. We can move forward with our thoughts, thoughts that will bring change. Thought is very, very powerful on this Earth. Thought forms have energy, so, have thoughts that will bring change and growth to everyone and everything on this planet. Our thought forms can and will bring forth change for the better and growth:

to everyone
to everything
on this planet...
for all life forms on this Earth will move into the 4th dimension.

We can consciously be of our thoughts, for thought will affect plants, trees, the birds, our family and friends, a society, and a nation. The energy of thought has great impact on:

people, situations, conflict,
trees, plants, birds, animals,
the climate,
and climate change itself.

So, our thoughts, ceremonies, songs, and chants can change the energy so that the Earth's climate and energy is not so severe. Our thoughts can make the climate so that it is gentle. When we give thanks for the rain, the wind, the sunlight, the weather patterns, these things—which are caused by our thoughts and actions—will change themselves.

Self-knowledge of our new identity as lightworkers is significant; we can take responsibility for consciousness of the thoughts that exist here, our own thoughts and attitudes; we can change the thoughts in a group, in general awareness, in what is broadcast 'in the air' as it were. We can move forwards, not sideways, not back. Progress, prosperity, and positivity are in our own hands, our own minds, our own personal mental broadcast.

What you think, feel, and say,
What you text, email, and write,
What you send, chat, and phone,
What you wear, how you style your hair,
What you say to someone face-to-face:
This is your personal broadcast

Everything that happens to a person upon this Earth is an important transition in their growth. Nothing happens by accident—everything has a purpose behind it.

Divine light and the Earth body

Divine communications and promptings come from a dimension where the energy of the divine light vibrates at a faster vibration from what we Earthlings experience in any moment and this may be overpowering. There are different energies that exist in other worlds, and this is why it is not so easy to communicate with other beings. From that place you would not be able to think *at all* for communication is in symbols, phases, energy wavelengths, and vibration.

This vibration takes place in light, an infinitely inexhaustible effulgence billions of times brighter than our own sun. This light is divine light; it is the light force that is both in our sun and flows to our sun and through that to our planet Earth and all the life-forms upon her. It is the same divine light that is within you, the reader. You have the heat from the sun that gives light to plant life and to other beings, such as yourselves ... to human beings, to the animals and the world of minerals. So, there is light and light flows on in the divine sense of light. You are a light being as well as an Earth Being.

When you, a light being suffused with spirit, take birth as an Earthling, you have an Earth body, a spirit in the Earth body, and a light body. The

light body is in fact a carbon copy of the Earth body. The light being that you are over-lights your Earth body and so the two of you meld together and become one—and so you are spirit—a light being—and an Earth body.

The spirit that you are would not last all that long if you were to leave your Earth body; the Earth body would not survive at all. The spirit body then falls away and moves on to your light body. This is worthwhile to think about. Make your life worthwhile, meditate, and think about the Light Being that you are.

Your thoughts, your times, your reality

It is a time when many events are occurring all around the Earth. We have been witnessing them through the media and we have a situation where a whole lot of information is coming out about change. Things don't appear to be any good, but they are changing for the better.

It is difficult as an Earth body to perceive and understand how things are changing for the better. Our thoughts and feelings go out to those nations undergoing trauma and conflict; nobody wishes to see people meet their end in unexpected ways.

Because as things are aired in our worldwide media, people will influence it—here we mean the changes for the better—by their thoughts and by their reactions. We may feel helpless as we watch civil war, read of car bombings, floods and famine, drought, and the pestilences of child polio and other communicable diseases. As we take in these events through different forms of media, we may influence the outcomes with our thoughts and reactions. Thought is the most powerful energy on this planet. Everybody, regardless of what they see, hear, or read, can be positive and send thoughts of love and kindness to everything that happens upon this Earth! Currently, it is important in particular to help change, or ring the changes that are happening here. And it is with your thoughts, apart from your actions, that you can actually help the change for the better, for the good of all, rather than the good of the few.

There is much happening in the cosmos that is influencing our solar system and our planet Earth. And in this happening, it is forcing the Earth to adjust to the new energy that it is coming into alignment with. And when we say 'force,' we mean that the movement of this planet and the energy upon it is changing—there is no choice.

It will move into an energy that is uplifting.

It is raising consciousness of everything upon the planet.

So, if you focus on an energy that is coming from a lower thought-form, meaning something that is not good for people (and this is a choice), then that will hold back what is happening on this Earth now.

The changes will happen despite what people think. What you think will help the changes to move smoothly into a lake—a still lake of calm and peace, and free of the talk of war. And there will be a desire for everyone on Earth to help their brothers and sisters.

All are of the same race regardless of what colour skin you have, or what culture or religion you have—you are the same race and that is what we call the 'Earthling.'

You should be proud, for there has been a long road in developing the human that you are, but make sure that you hold onto the human values. And you will know that the human values are right because there will be love in your heart—it is that simple.

So please, please be careful of the choices that you make, and the thoughts that you have and listen—listen to your heart, for it is connected to the Creative Source of All and holds love and divine love within you.

Many people are feeling pressure for the changes are taking place even though they cannot see it. They are taking place within themselves, and society, and the Earth herself. The changes are difficult at times, and they will be easier at other times.

Be assured that the time is coming when you will be free of all the interactive changes that pull against the Creative Source, leaving only the God and love and compassion and a feeling of unity that will exist upon this Earth.

Be of good cheer. This will lead to change.

If you view what is taking place upon this Earth, it may seem a little hopeless, but in reality, it is giving opportunity to 'open up' whatever different issues there are with different societies or cultures, or belief systems within yourself. And as they open up, it gives movement and freedom to discard:

'Old thinking'
'Old ways' and
'Old beliefs.'

So those changes can take place. Be aware of this, rather than downhearted about what seems like hopelessness. Rather, be cheerful in knowing that the larger outcome from what is happening upon Earth. It is leading to a change where there will be unity and people will respect each other. Societies that may have differences will agree to disagree but will still respect one another.

This will lead to harmony, harmony upon this Earth:

in all its forms
in its colours
in its sounds
in its nature.

Music is a wonderful way to find harmony. It connects to the heart and when you feel joyful in listening to music it raises your heart—it raises your emotions—depending on the music that you choose. And you can feel a lot better very quickly, so we would encourage you to listen to music that is harmonious and lifts that vibration of who you are into a joyful feeling—from the love and the Source of All Creation.

Prayer, Thought, and the Times

Troubled times are still with us on this planet, but the great masters, the Angelic Realms, are also here, along with those that assist the Creative Source of All from the World of Light. They are mingling amongst you or sending messages, or encouragement. You are never alone; be aware of that. The Angelic Realms are with you always. All you need to do is to call upon them and they will assist. Spirit, as you would describe it, is very real. It is the essence of your Soul. It is who you really are.

So, you are readily part of the World of Light. You know what to do at a time of crisis.

But 'times' are difficult at the moment and there is a need for assistance in many places around the world. If you were asked you would assist in some way. The Creative Source of All is asking you if you can assist then please do. Remember that prayers and thoughts are the strongest power of energy that you have within you.

It is your thoughts and your prayers that can do the best for all those around this Earth at this time.

Those that are struggling or are confused, those that are hungry ... all can be assisted. All you have to do is ask and it will be organised. The energy and the thoughts can be put into the thoughts of those that can make something happen. But you must ask us first, before we can do these things.

Thoughts are very powerful, more than you realise. Please be careful about your thoughts. They can interfere with good—good for all—good things that are done to assist people.

It is important that you look at your thoughts.

Think positively for this is what will overcome, anything that pulls away from the good or from God.

Thirty

666

M essage received from Jalarm on Tuesday, 9th September 2013 at Werai, NSW, Australia.

Jalarm: It is I, Jalarm, and I am pleased to be here with you and to know that you are so competent and so professional in the way you work with us, and I/we appreciate that. For there are many that are observing what is taking place with you. You ladies are on an important mission, and I do not want you to get carried away with that, but it is important.

And so ... the message I have is connected to 'six'. The 666 is said to be evil ... but it is not. It is related to the movement of stars—the movement of planets within the cosmos. And it is connected to the planet Venus.

There is what is called a six-pointed star, which is connected to the Ancient Indians and what is called the 'Shaktona.'

It is symbolic of movement, and it is an important beginning for humans upon this Earth. And so, the number 666 is referring to the human. The elevated Man—the Man that holds the Christ Consciousness, and when I say Christ, I mean crystal.

The energy is the same structure that the crystal holds and is also in you and every individual being upon this Earth. Because when they are born they are enchristed with this energy, which makes them human—part of the human race. And this has happened at a time before Atlantis Fell.

This was a creation from the influence from the beings from Venus who hold the majesty and the law of what is to take place upon this Earth.

We have known it as Mu—but whatever you call it, it is the planet that is part of the solar system to your sun. Your sun is, you could say, like a soul to this planetary system. Just as that has been played out in everyone because they have a soul, which is a sun that is a planetary system with all the energies and influences that come from those planets. This knowledge was known in what you call astrology and people upon the Earth are influenced by the different planets upon this solar system, and it infiltrates into each being and their journey upon this Earth. For as I have said before, their journey on this Earth is limited. You come, you live, and you leave, and you move on.

And so, I would like you to think about that. The message is that 666 is the aspect of the different layers of the God Force that is within you. There are three layers, and they influence you all the time. The Ancient Indian traditions taught of the three aspects of God, the Creative Source, and this is what I am meaning when I am say it is influencing you all the time. So, in a way, you are a creation of a planetary system, and I would like you to remember that and think about it.

It is possible for people to live a life and receive a reading from those who are gifted and able to read the system and influences upon different people. However, they need to be very careful and very educated about the influences. And so, I would advise those people who are listening to the 'readers' or clairvoyants—and keep their mind open—but always refer the information to your own Inner Sun, which is in your heart. For it is what keeps your heart beating; as soon as it stops, the Life Force leaves you. And the Life Force is what is given to you in your heart, the same way that the Life Force from your sun in your planetary system—your Solar System that gives Life to the interaction of the planets that evolves or revolves around your Sun.

I have said before that this sun is connected to the galaxy, and the Galactic Sun is very large. That is aligned to many suns and many planetary systems. Your scientists are beginning to be aware of the many planetary systems that exist. Many are very similar to the one that you live in at this time.

My message is for you to be aware of influences—sometimes the influences of evolving planets have a favourable influence upon everything that happens upon this Earth. And sometimes it is not so favourable. It is nothing to do with evil. It is nothing to do with death in the sense that everyone should be afraid—far from that. It is still the movement and influence only.

And my message is that there is an influence coming onto this planet at this time that is not favourable, and I would ask everybody to connect to your Inner Sun, realising that it connects to the Galactic Sun and the core of suns that links back to the Creative Source of All.

This influence, if they connect to it, will help them through the heavier energy that is influencing them in a negative way. I would say negative in that it is up to everybody upon this Earth to decide which way they want to be influenced. This is something they need to understand within them. They have a choice. Everybody on Earth has a choice and they can make decisions that are good for themselves and those around them—always for the good of All. This is important currently.

For now, the planet, your planet, is very vulnerable, and I do not have to explain it or spell out the dangers that can happen upon your planet at this time—but if everybody is positive and sends the positive energy from The Source of Creation of All that is Love, they can change outcomes.

And so, this is my message—this is the message that I want to speak of this day—it is important; and it is a special transmission that is coming from the Angelic Realms and the Hierarchy that works in a positive way to help and oversee what is taking place upon your planet. Not just now but always.

So, I hope you will listen and consider where your thoughts go and how you focus them. The focus is needed upon *love* and *consensus*; talking to people to help understand how they think and what motivates them into taking actions that are not good for All.

And so, I ask people to think carefully, very carefully, about the decisions that they make at this time.

I send this message, I give this message, with great love—for the 666 is not evil, I can assure you. It is coming from the influence of Venus, your planet known as the Venus of Love. And so, it is.

NOTE: This message is given on the 9th day of the 9th month of the year 2013, which adds to 6. And if you add the day, month, and year together it comes to 24, which adds to 6. THIS IS A SIGNIFICANT SIGN FOR US. The hidden influence from Venus, and the energy of universal love is another 6. A delightful co-ordinated incidence.

Thirty-One

Creation and the Journey

Jalarm: It is I, Jalarm. I understand your difficulty in understanding us as extra-terrestrial. We come in many shapes and forms and appearances, but there are really no differences in the thinking of the Earth being— the human—and the extra-terrestrials, as in, some humans are evolved, some are not; it is the same with the extra-terrestrials—some are evolved, some are not. And there is a Hierarchy as we have already explained. And from the extra-terrestrial point, there is a Source of All Creation. And it is true, it is an energy, it is a force. It has a hidden aspect, one of Light that is also an aspect of Creation. From there, there are beings that come forth. There are many, many, many—and as I have said, some went forth in exploration, while others remained on track and sought advice from the Source always. And so, you can see, perhaps quite easily, where there was separation. You could say that some were fallen, but not really. They chose to go a different way. They chose to make their journey in a way that was from their own choice whereas from the God Source it was always overseen with advice and knowledge of the actual being of the force. If that makes sense?

(We said '*Yes*'.)

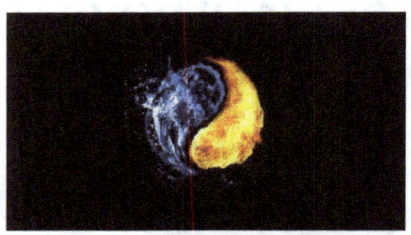

Jalarm: So, that was a long, long, long time ago. Long before your planet, long before your solar system. It was creation of creation. Those few words were begun in the so-called bible that you have. But you have come to think about that, separating from that, not being influenced anymore, and allowing yourselves to be influenced from the true source of Creation of All. So yes, it is an energy, it is a force, and it is of love. When I say love, I mean it is caring. It is not destructive in the sense that it is destructive to hurt, but rather it is destructive just to get rid of the unwanted, otherwise it would be a total mess. It is like someone cleaning up your house; if you did not clear away the dust, it would just build up and take over. You understand?

So there have been aspects of, shall we say, the God Force that have been presented as three aspects. And that is:

1. The Creative Source
2. The one that holds that energy to allow the creation and destruction to take place because it is always there, and...
3. The force that destroys. It is not to hurt people but to just break down and to eliminate the unwanted or to change the heaviness of the unwanted.

Nothing is ever lost. This is from the Source of All Creation and they have beings that have been evolved from that point and gone on to be a what you could say is a God Being—one that controls everything, but not for power but rather to assist, to assist those who have taken a different journey or exploration and another to just hold on to the Force so that all peoples can be developed as they are meant to be.

There is no wrong or right; I would like you to realise and remember that always, no matter what dimension you are consciously connected to. There is no judgement from the Source. You are your own judge.

So, when the human was enchristed, it was to try and bring balance to all beings that had been created, to find a balance and to hold a source of love and compassion upon this planet. This is a long time later. So, when you look at another, as Sai Baba has always taught, try to find the good or God in everybody. Because there are aspects of their mind that are still influenced from other worlds or other lives that they have lived that tend to get them to pull away from the God Source within them. It could be the force of fear, it could be the force of not knowing or remembering what it is that they were fearful of and so they do not make that choice, because it was unknown. The thing is, they are all God Beings. Some of the mistakes (from their own point of view) involve making a decision that is not good for them or for others around them. And so, sometimes they do bad or negative things. But they are still God Beings; they have simply made a decision that is not good for all. This is the opposite to making a decision that is good for all. It is that simple.

There are beings that have come to understand this, who make a decision to the point where they are all knowing and so you could call them God Beings, for they would not dream of making decisions that are not good for others. They hold the energy of love and compassion in them, which is the force that comes from the Source of All Creation.

It is a choice; it came from the Source, which is *one*, and then it separated. And then there has been continual separation down through time and energy throughout.

And so was there a point you would like to ask about God or a God Being. You are asking about a presence that could be looked up to, or be of a presence that is all knowing, all loving, and all compassion. And that would be from the God Source. I can tell you there are beings like that, but they mirror the very thing that you are within yourself, which are God Beings. You are that. Everybody is that. You have been enchristed.

There is room to grow, that is true. But the connection and the energy are there within you. It is there. And it is in your soul, and it is in other beings that you are connected to in other worlds. There is no limit. It is difficult to describe everything, but I can assure you that you are a God Being; in other words, you have the Source of Creation within you. If you did not, you would not be alive. You would not have the Life Force in you. You would not have the Light within you, which helps you to understand and to lift the consciousness of who you are.

You could see yourself just as a consciousness only without any form at all and you would be closer to the Source. If that makes sense? But you have a choice to become a form of some sort. I will leave you to think about that. And now I think it is time to close and God Bless you, my children. And I am so glad you have offered your time to be with me this morning. Thank you.

Thirty-Two

World Peace and Planetary Healing

Jalarm gives a salutary reminder to Valérie and the two ladies who are participating in the Mystery School on this day with the Oracle that extraordinary information requires a certain discipline, clarity, and understanding that languages in other dimensions—along with time in the other dimensions—do not exactly translate to our 3-Dimensional reality here on Earth. It is true that Ascension is happening now, and more energy and more light are coming. But with this, more effort and a certain thoughtful discipline is needed to use the Oracle effectively in order that insightful answers be received. Much of this process with Jalarm and the Oracle are a form of intuition; that is, inner tuition. It is as if these sessions are the Universe-city of the Universe, a place of universal learning!

Jalarm: It is Jalarm here ...
(Valérie waited but nothing came.)

Valérie: (explaining *to both girls*) When he comes it is ... I don't know why he is not speaking, but everything has gone blank. I don't know whether *it has something to do with my age or because he downloads and then speaks and I shouldn't have to prompt him—and I cannot remember what the question was, so I shouldn't have to prompt him. I don't know what is going on. Why doesn't he just take over and start talking?* He wants me to understand something about this...

Jalarm: (suddenly speaking very strongly) It is I, Jalarm, and yes, I have delayed this on purpose because I do want Valérie to understand that it is I talking and she does not have to, shall we say, prompt me. The questions that you ask are important and I would like to respond. Some of the questions could be answered very easily, so if you were careful to ask very briefly something that I can spell out then I will do this. But if it is something you have phrased so that a very complicated answer is needed, then I need to speak through somebody. And so, what is happening now is that I just want you to understand that. So we can use the Oracle more if you ask questions that can be answered with a 'yes' or 'no.' Or in a simple spelling out. Otherwise, it would take far too long on the Oracle.

But **the Oracle** is a very important part of what you are doing here and so I want you to just think about what I am saying—is that alright?

(*We all agreed.*)

Jalarm: So, we shall begin again. I am going to leave, and you are going to ask me a question that I can respond to on **the Oracle**. Will that be alright?

Will there be peace on Earth?
The Oracle: Yes.
How long will it be coming?
The Oracle: 8 AB
Eight years after Baba?
The Oracle: Yes.
Does that mean six more years until peace on Earth?
The Oracle: No.
It's all about religions?
The Oracle: Yes.
Are changes happening because of the Age of Aquarius?

The Oracle: No.
Are world prayer and meditation helping in the process?
The Oracle: Yes (very strong).
Should we form a group and focus on world healing?
The Oracle: Yes—intention is important.
Will there be world peace?
The Oracle: Yes; all religions, all races.
Will there be planetary harmony?
The Oracle: Yes.

Jalarm: (coming through to add on to the above) It doesn't matter how many are in a group, really. It is intention that is important. A gathering of like-minded people with a raised consciousness would do a great deal of good to preserve peace, because this would of course be the focus. And I would suggest that you do this around the crystal that is established at your place as known as Satori Springs in Canyonleigh. This would be up to you and how you arrange it.

Valérie at the circle with the Alcheringa Crystal at Satori Springs aka Alcheringa.

Jalarm: There is a full moon every month, sometimes two, but mostly one full moon—and if it was possible, it would be good at that time—whether it be during the day or the coming night. It is up to you, for what is felt here in the southern hemisphere is also felt in the northern hemisphere. Energy does not just switch on and off; it is influencing over a period around a full moon.

Prayers and good intentions at the time of full moon are always helpful to Earth and its peoples

It is up to you, but if you did follow the moon cycles they would differ in days and dates within the month. I will leave this to you. But prayer going out at that time, or any time, is always helpful for the energy that exists upon the Earth. *For it is an energy* and it does flow out and because of the rays of consciousness that go with it, it will help transmute the energy that is on this Earth. And so, it is *very* important and a very welcomed placement of your emotions and feelings and your thinking at that time ... to help your planet to reach perfection in world peace.

(**Jacqui** *said she kept wanting to call Jalarm 'Swami'. With that, Jalarm jumped in and we all laughed.*)

Jalarm: It is Jalarm, and I am your teacher, and swami is a word for teacher, so you can use the word swami if you like, my dear. So do not worry if it comes to your mind. For I have come to you not just to teach you girls. I have come to teach all those who care to listen and so your suggestion, at my prompting, for a group to meet for a planetary healing is very good.

Anything that suggests harmony and peace is something that needs to be prayed about, for as I have said, *the energy goes out and influences people*, whether they realise it or not.

And so, what is the question that you are asking?

Jacqui: *Will another group of people make this thing work?*

Jalarm: Once you have decided upon the venue, and once you have decided to have your first meeting, you can advertise it and we shall move behind it and bring the people to you. You feel you have an alignment with others, and of course, you do. There are many people on this Earth who are holding meditations and gatherings for world peace. You are not alone here. There are many, and so I can assure you.

Once you establish the venue, as I have said, we will get in behind you. It will then follow. You will be then prompted, if you will allow us, to suggest that you have an extra special meeting from time to time. And we shall get in behind that also. And because there will be a lot involved, there will be a need for donations—or a specific sum, called a donation. It is up to you how you present it, but we understand how it will have to be paid for in this world. But do not worry; we will be behind that. We will behind everything that you do in the name of planetary healing and peace and harmony.

Jalarm: So, does this help you, my dear?
(*We all said 'Yes'.*)

Thirty-Three

History and Karma

Jacqui: *We are asking about when Australia and India separated with water.*

A documentary was on TV the other night (Andrew Marr's History of the World) and answered all that—explaining how the Earth, in the beginning, was one piece of land that was only and then separated at various times into what it is now. There are a number of resources, a book, and a DVD. It was also screened on BBC One.

The Oracle: This is correct.

Jalarm advised that the name Valli had an energy that was very suitable for me (Valérie) to use. Sai Baba called me Val and that is connected to the Angelic Realms, but because of my work upon this Earth and the dimension that needs to go out to meet the mainstream—yes, Valli is a very important name for me.

Chris *asked about what happens to souls after suicide.*

Jalarm: Through the Oracle.

Chris: *It is the same as a natural death?*

The Oracle: Yes.

Chris: *Is there a karmic debt of some sort?*

The Oracle indicated that Jalarm wanted to speak.

Jalarm: Those who have committed suicide have broken their commitment to their soul blueprint and that means those that come have an agreement with the Karmic Board. And so, it is a Karmic debit, if you like. However, it is one that they need to sort out with their own judgement, nobody else's.

They are encouraged to either return into another body or to rethink and learn a little more, or to be able to serve, even from the spirit point of view, to help others. And from their experience they are encouraged to talk to and put suggestions towards those contemplating suicide on Earth. And sometimes they can save people from committing suicide on your Earth plane.

(We had all been discussing about our 'junk' DNA and whether this was being lifted now. Jalarm jumped in and made us laugh!)

Jalarm: It is I, and I have been listening. You asked about the DNA and junk DNA and whether it is being lifted and *yes*, it is, because of the new energy that is coming upon your Earth. It is coming through what I would describe as Star Gates and by that, I mean the ethereal net that is around this Earth that was closed tighter to enclose the atmosphere—but even tighter when it almost exploded as it needed to be contained so that it would not go out and affect the solar system, and the galaxy for that matter.

It was a very, very sad time for your Earth. And so, the Star People, all the visitors, had gone. The only ones left were the up-standing ape-like creatures and the ones in the form of flora and fauna on your Earth.

The atmosphere had to be adjusted and it was. It was quite some time before the sun began to shine again. Because of the haze of the clouds that was formed from your volcanoes raging, exploding, and going into your atmosphere, it became very dark.

But I do not want to go into this. What I want to say is that all these energies are having an influence, and it is a time now for this to be cleared. And so, the energy is lifting and in doing so, the energy in the souls of all the humans upon this Earth, who are the only physical forms of life that we call the Earthlings, that is being lifted also. With that of course the consciousness lifts within their minds and so they are changing.

If you could see the soul as black and white, a Tau, a contradictory thing that you have on Earth, you have been gifted the choice—of your own choice, your own thoughts, your own decisions—and in that way if you look at things having an opposite, it allows you to make a choice, if you understand that.

In some ways, that is what is happening in the DNA in the cells; they are making a choice within the physical body as to what you put in it—

what energy you put into it. And so, it is possible to eat or drink things that will change the consciousness of the cell, of the DNA.

It allows the junk DNA (as you call it), which is a **'limited DNA'** that was inherited from the Star People but not opened yet, and so that is opening. And so, the information and consciousness coming from that is also melding with the consciousness of your Earth body.

So, it depends upon every individual, every person upon this Earth, as to what they want to do to work with themselves. This is their choice. If they eat and drink well and take supplements that will improve their physical being and their immune systems, it will help to change and link with the new energy that is coming upon this Earth.

As I have said, it is coming through the Star Gates, so it is only part of centres around the Earth where that influence is strong. For some people would not be able to cope with it and they have no choice to stay around. That energy is too powerful for them, although their consciousness may not realise it.

So, it is slowly being spread around the Earth. More and more the Light becomes stronger. And this is what the mission of the Earth and all the peoples upon it is: **to raise their consciousness, their light, their energy, and spread it and hold it in this corner of the galaxy.** For that is also going out and lifting and spreading, depending on where the different personalities of souls come from within your galaxy. If they are coming with a heavier energy of consciousness, then that will be influenced by that stronger light, which is now on this Earth. And it will be taken back, when they leave the Earth, and help to lift the consciousness of their races in other worlds. Does that make some sense to you?

(All agreed. There was silence for a while. We all find it very hard to think while Jalarm is around.)

The reality suggests a fixed consciousness with the body—and in our sleep, in fact, we have parallel lives.

Jacqui: *I do have a question. Do we travel back to other dimensions in our sleep, where we might have a real life?*

Jalarm: Yes, you do. You have parallel lives, everybody has parallel lives—some from a different time. Again, everything is a quantum source of

knowledge, of being. So, it depends where your focus is and your mission. Does that make sense? Would you like to ask me anything more about this?
(Silence again!)

Jalarm: The life that you have on this Earth is not the only life that you have been in—or will be in—and it depends on the focus as to where you are thinking. If I can put it that way. Or where your focus is. It is all relative. You understand that. So, when you are encouraged to live in the now, that is important because it helps to hold the focus of where you are specifically in this moment of your travels through the cosmos. Does that make some sense?

Jacqui: *It does, but I am getting a bit confused. I think we are all getting tired!*

Jalarm: That is alright, my dear, it will unfold as you think about it more. For the moment I think we are all a bit confused, and I think we should think about ending our session.
(*He is always so kind in the way he speaks to us.*)
We all said that was a good idea and Jalarm left but not before he blessed us, calling us his children.

Thirty-Four

End of the Dinosaurs and Coming of the Moon

Jalarm: It is I, Jalarm, and I am very pleased to be with you girls and to know that I am welcomed.

I have looked forward to this meeting. And you are feeling I would like to speak with you, and I would. I will accept questions of course, but today there are many things that I  would like you to think about. So, you might like to make notes about this and then we can continue with our work.

Our work, by the way, is significant and it is coming from the *truth*. It is coming from how history really is upon the Earth. And it is necessary at this time because there are a lot of misunderstandings, miscalculations, and misrepresenting of what really took place upon this Earth.

It is time for your mankind to understand and know that there was a lot of activity on this planet (that we as Star People called Mu) and there was a lot of coming and going of Star People. And a lot of civilizations established on this Earth, even though they were not, shall we say, the humans, the Earthlings as we now call you.

For now, the planet is in the hands of the humans and that is an energy that is a little different from a lot of the people who visited the planet before.

In the Old Empire (and I have said all this before, but I am just rounding up my introduction) it was a time of beings upon this Earth, again from the world of the stars, but they were not quite connected to the Source of All Creation—although they did experiment in genetic engineering, and they created the world of the dinosaurs that existed upon this planet.

Now I am going to ask you, if you would please ask more about this situation of the creation of the dinosaurs upon this Earth, knowing it was influenced by the reptilian race that existed here.

Indigenous cultures, or civilizations that are human, know this because they have been given the information in an esoteric way in, shall we say, a *telepathic* way because they have ready communication with the Star People. The Star Worlds.

So please ask your question.

Jill: *Well, the dinosaur time does really fascinate me, and I think we did touch on it earlier that they ate themselves out of existence because of the need for more food, more trees. I am really interested in finding out more about the dinosaur times.*

Valli: *Did this planet move into another place before, in that time of the dinosaur existence on Earth?*

Jalarm: It is Jalarm again and we are talking about the creation of the dinosaurs that existed upon your planet, and Valérie was thinking and wondering if perhaps the planet, before the time of Mu, was perhaps in a different position at another time. And I would have to say that it was. This is a long, long, long time ago before your solar system was in a position of planetary circular around the sun. If that makes sense. However, it was your solar system and in the moving of your planets into the position that it is now—around your sun—the energy has changed and so the dinosaurs were not able to survive into the new magnetic force that was being held by the sun itself.

And so, if you can understand that when the dinosaurs were destroyed it was necessary to take place, for the Earth moved slightly into a different circle around the sun to allow the force of the atmosphere to change and be lifted slightly so that a different form of life in a physical body could survive on this Earth (understand, I am not meaning the Earthling).

It would grow then, into what was planned by the hierarchy as a **Garden of E-den.**

E-den is a sound ... it is a vibration and from the lifting of sound, the formation of life on this Earth became evolved to the point that it was not just cold-blooded life on this planet, but it developed and was able to handle the energy of mammals or mammalian life (which had warmer blood) and that also continued with other life forms.

This is all at a long, long time ago in the Earth's evolution. If you can understand that. Is there a question that you would like to ask about that?

Jill: Well, fossilised skeletons were found here, and they must be so old. Scientists are finding them and saying they are dinosaur remnants, to survive on this Earth. So that would all fit in with what you are saying. That's not a question, but I am sure you would want to tell us more.

Jalarm: No, it is just that I would clarify, of course. What I am saying is the planet still existed regardless of its point of balance (shall we say) in the solar system. It is just that it did move, if I can put it that way.

So, is there anything else you would like to ask me?

(*We all agreed not at this time.*)

Jalarm left for a while. *We were chatting for a while and remarked Jalarm must be very patient.*

Jalarm: (*coming forth again and announcing*) I am the patient one!
(*We all laughed together—and we apologised.*)

Jalarm: I joke with you, but I would like to reassure all of you that the existence of the dinosaurs upon the planet—yes, they did exist—when they existed the atmosphere was a little different. And so, this is what I was trying to explain to you when the planet Earth was moved to a different place within the cyclic life of the planets in your solar system; it did not come from a different galaxy, it was still part of your solar system.

And I know you are wondering about the moon—and I would like to say yes, the moon was brought to also help stabilise the Earth in the new place within the distance from the sun. That played a role to help bring balance. This is why it was very dangerous, at that other time a long, long time later when scientists that had come onto this planet, to here, and decided to bring another asteroid to create another moon to use as a jumping point into the star systems outside your solar system.

By the way, your NASA has been talking about doing this again and I would strongly advise against it. For at that time when Atlantis went down *for that very reason,* we are recommending that it does not take place, because the second moon did stay, for a while, in balance from the sun and your planet. But then it became loose. It lost its gravitational pull and slammed into your Earth. It caused a great, great destruction upon here. It almost destroyed your planet.

So, I just wanted this noted. Thank you, my children.

(He left again.)

Note: *There are dreaming stories of the Australian Indigenous peoples that tell of the presence, in ancient time, of two moons.*

Thirty-Five

The Journey of Souls

The three of us joined hands and chanted the OM. Very quickly, the crystal glass moved in circles, anti-clockwise, indicating the Oracle wished to speak through me.

Jalarm: It is I, Jalarm, and I am very pleased to be here and, of course, you have been aware of my waiting, waiting, and waiting. (We all laughed.) But do not worry, because I am joking with you, and it is very nice that you have all gathered here to speak with me because I want to speak with you also. I am ready for questions, but if you have no questions, I can continue talking. It is up to you what you want me to do. You have that choice and I am at your service and so, *do you have any questions today?*

Jacqui: The only question I have is the one about the incoming spirits—where are they all coming from? There are billions of people on Earth. My husband is wondering where all these souls are coming from?

Jalarm: Well, the souls come in and are given birth, through an Earth body upon this planet, you understand. You understand the process of that. And there are many people, many beings from other worlds, different places, different stars, different galaxies that are willing to come to experience a life here on Earth. As there are many, many souls that are waiting for entrance into this universe of yours. Does that make sense?

(*They all agreed there were no more questions.*)

Jalarm: Minds are very much affected by culture and belief. This is inescapable, particularly the effect of culture, which shapes beliefs. So, when information comes in from the Angelic Realms or from the Angels, who have no abode and may be present instantly, it has to be shaped and presented in a way that allows it to be processed and understood by those receiving and passing on the message. It cannot be too concentrated, it cannot be too cram-packed with ethereal teachings or it would never be understood, and the receiver would be … well … deified—that is, turned into a deity—very quickly.

This is not what we, as a Hierarchy overseeing this galaxy, wish for here, nor anywhere else in any other of the worlds we oversee. Nor is this what anybody that is coming in from another world wants. Because they cannot learn if they don't realise that they are interacting with different ways, different thoughts, different cultures, different customs, different races, different beliefs. And so there needs to be a way of presenting it so that perhaps it can reach to some—not to everybody—but in some way the interlocking of knowledge and sharing can help for the *whole* to come to realise. Because every individual upon this Earth is on their own singular path to find their way back to the path that is who they are—and that is a God Being.

It is true, you are all children of God.

But you are like children, you are still learning, and this is what the role of the child of God is about. The Source of your Life Force comes from the Creative Source of All. And that sometimes needs some consideration or even talk amongst like-minded people—to understand exactly what that means for each individual person on this Earth. And so, is there a question you would like to ask? Perhaps about the souls are waiting to come upon this Earth and do they have to wait until others have moved on from reincarnating on this Earth, or is that how it operates?

I am not saying that is how it is. I am only suggesting a question.

Jacqui: I was also thinking the Buddhists believe that you progress through each lifetime and better yourself, and the soul rises to the next level. I just wondered what you have to say about that. For instance, can you start out say, as being a flea and then reincarnate to a lion or a whale in the next incarnation? What do you say about that?

Jalarm: Now, we rehearsed in the last meeting that we had that opportunity to use the Oracle itself. The Oracle would be able to answer, very clearly, if you were to ask the question very simply. So, I would like to withdraw and you can discuss about the question and then we will carry on from there. Is that alright? (All agreed.)

Question to the Oracle: *What level do all original religious teachings operate?*
Jalarm signalled that he wanted to speak.

The Givers of Light and their teachings

Jalarm: It is I again, Jalarm speaking. And you are asking if, shall we say, the teachings of the Buddha, the Muslim teachings from the Koran (Muhammad), Christianity from Christ, and other teachings that are well known and accepted as the beginning of teachings on the Earth—are they coming from the 6th level, or the 6th dimension? In a way that is correct, in that it is the teachings that are at that level, so they are capable, then, of being easily understood and received by discernment to whoever chooses to draw from that teaching. Does that make sense?

If we had the teachings coming from a place that was so advanced in enlightenment, then the teachings would not be understood, nor would they be able to be received because they would be far too powerful in the Light that they exist.

The Beings that have come through and brought these teachings are not at that fixed sixth level; however, they still influence and carry the *energy* through to whoever wants to reach out and accept the teachings and embrace them as a religion, and they all come from a place of love or caring or concern for others. All these teachings have come from the Star Worlds in the first place. And I would like people to remember that! It is only mankind that has perhaps changed the teachings, the first teachings to something else—for that seems to be a power over those that listen and take it into themselves—then realising that it is not quite right for them.

For the original teachings are from the God Source of All Creation and the original teachings, if embraced wholly, by those that reach out and readily accept them—they would be connected to the Source, to God, in every sense and be guided from that point. And so that would be as one follows God in every way, in every sense. In other words, when you are concerned about something, you let go and let God show the way, if that makes sense. Is there anything else you would like to ask, or shall we go back to the Oracle? I would like to encourage you to use the Oracle more, but it is up to you. (*They agreed.*)

Jacqui: *Okay (we are asking the Oracle with our fingers on the glass); is that the only time you can reincarnate if you have reached the twenty-seventh level?*
The Oracle: YES.

Jacqui: *So, when you pass over after you die, you have to do the work to reach that twenty-seventh level—is that how it works?*
The Oracle: YES.

Jacqui: *So, you have had to have done the work to reincarnate?*
The Oracle: YES.

Jacqui: I do healings on people. I see many levels in their aura going out in rings from the body like a layered cake. *Does everyone who has reincarnated have twenty-seven levels in their aura?*
The Oracle: YES.

We asked: *Is a level the same as a dimension?*
The Oracle: YES.

Valli: *So, are you talking about the 27th dimension?*
The Oracle: YES.

We asked: *Once you reach the 27th level, you can reincarnate and if you want to, you can keep coming back to help humanity?*
While we were still discussing this, the glass flew up to '**YES**.'

Journey of Souls

Jalarm: It is I, Jalarm. You are discussing the souls and when they come into a body upon this Earth, and you are wondering if/when they experience past lives, is it the soul that has these past lives? Or have they inherited the life from another, to help them cope with a life here on Earth? Because for some, that come from other races around the universe, they would find it very difficult to cope with life here. And so yes, some do inherit a life, or the emotions from a life, so they can cope on Earth. This is not a negative thing. It is rather something that is agreed to by the Karmic Board, which exists and allows them to come here to be able to play out a blueprint of a life that they have agreed to with others upon this planet.

And when they leave, they can go on and have parallel lives, or live other lives in other worlds and not be connected to this Earth at all. But they still grow. It is possible for them to grow. And there was talk about levels up to the twenty-seventh. If they want to reincarnate, after they reach a twenty-seventh level of consciousness, then they may do so. Or they may not want to. It is up to them. That is their choice. They have free will as to whether they want to come back to a life on Earth or whether they do not. That is their choice. And this is what is meant by free will upon this Earth.

In fact, the world of the souls and the World of Light have free will. And so, they may want to make an easier life, and when I say that, emotionally it is not as difficult as it is upon this Earth. So, does that makes some sense? (They agreed.)

So, Valérie is wondering also about past lives. And I would have to say that each soul is individual. I have already said this. So that does not mean necessarily that they keep coming and going on Earth, but rather they are reviewed and assisted but from a universal sense not just an Earth sense. So, does this help to clarify some of the questions that you may have in your mind? Is there something you would like to ask about that? (*They said they were happy with that. Thank you.*)

We asked: Do we choose to be a murderer or to starve to death?
The Oracle: YES.

We asked: Do people choose to be murdered?
The Oracle: NO.

Jill: Do victims choose to be victims?
The Oracle: NO.

Jill: Are babies born deformed preordained on the other side?
The Oracle: YES.

Jill: Then everything is a lesson?
The Oracle: YES.

Valli: I prefer to think of life's lessons as an 'experience' and an opportunity to understand emotions. Our feelings. *So that's it? Nothing happens without a reason or a purpose?*
The Oracle: YES.

Jacqui: *So, should we call it an experience?*
The Oracle: YES.

Jacqui: I asked Jalarm about a Sai Baba dream I had when everyone was of a network gathered to do high work to help people. Was it my subconscious or was it real? Was I in another dimension?
The Oracle: YES.

Lucid dreams

Jalarm: It is I, Jalarm, and I listen to you very carefully and I try to influence you with, or suggest to you, thoughts, so if you were to also sit quietly you would also receive some suggestions for your enquiry as this is what is happening here.

Your dream is what you call here a lucid dream. In other words, you are conscious and subconscious all at the same time, which is of course what all beings upon this Earth are leading to—to be able to always communicate at the level of the soul conscious. Does that make sense? (They agreed.) And that, of course, is leading to 'telepathic communication', which is the way we Star People operate. And so, it was with the early indigenous people upon this Earth who inherited the Star People's genes and you know that story.

So, is there a specific question that you would like to ask about your dream?

Jacqui: The main thing was that I had Sai Baba in my dream, and I was just wondering if that was actually Sai Baba or was it my subconscious?

Jalarm: As I have said many times, when (he) Sai Baba was in a physical body on Earth, if he came to anyone in a dream, showing himself in a physical form, then it was really him. If I came to you in a dream and presented myself in a physical form that you know well as Sai Baba—that I come to you—so it is really me, yes.

Jacqui: Thank you.

Prayer, sacred intentions, planetary healing

Jalarm: And I would go on to say, it is to do with what we have requested in the hope that you may gather people that are like-minded to pray, for want of a better word, because in praying it is a very positive energy going out—to help heal the planet, which is what we requested of you. You do not have to do this, of course, but we would like you to—and we will be with you, and I know you are open to this, so it is about Planetary Healing.

And so, my dear, there are things that are ahead of you, but you cannot see just yet, and if you would follow 'step by step' you will find things will unfold. The reason we hold back, shall we say, the main picture, is because sometimes the Earth mind can get off on a little track of its own and can perhaps go running down a lane that perhaps is not quite the right direction. Mind you, it will be stopped and brought back into the focus that you and I, shall we say, as we are wall to wall working together, that we need to take to achieve or to help with the work that you have agreed to do. At another level you have agreed to do it. At another level you understand certainly the outcomes and I would suggest that you leave yourself a little bit in the dark at the moment. It will evolve. Just trust. Is that okay?

Jacqui: That is great, thanks.

Jalarm: Thank you, you dear. Thank you.
So, is there another question that you would like to ask? I know Valérie is wondering about the World of Light and where it is, and to where the souls return when they leave a physical body. I would like to reassure her that the World of Light is a dimension of energy and Light that exists. The Star People work with you and know. The interaction of souls of much higher beings is a little complicated, but we shall give this information as time goes on. So, is this alright for you girls? (*They agreed.*)

I think for today this is enough, but if you have another question, please ask the Oracle and we will take it from there. Otherwise, I am finished for today. I am with you, but I will not speak with you anymore this day, is that alright? (*They agreed.*)

Thank you, my dears, thank you.

Thirty-Six

Consciousness

Jacqui: *What was the understanding of 144,000—do they all have to experience the same lessons before they can move on as a group soul?*

Jalarm: It is I, Jalarm. It is true that there has been reference to 144,000, and the number is important. I have already spoken about the importance of the sacred numbering that exists in the cosmos. However, a group soul— yes, they do exist. There are many numbers in different group souls. A group can be 144,000; that is a larger group. There can be others. The number is important because it is twelve times twelve. And the number twelve is important, as you have already been shown in the visit from Jesus with his twelve disciples. This is a raised consciousness, and it does exist.

Nine has been put forward as a number for Sai Baba and that is the end of the old. To move into the new is another three aspects of God, which is added to nine and that makes twelve. So, the twelve has been around for a while, and it is also known as the consciousness of crystal, and many other crystals for it holds the energy and it does not lower and fall back into a different dimension. For we are working in the plan to keep the consciousness raised. This is important for us as a mission:

for many of you to help raise the consciousness of the beings upon this Earth. And like I have said, it is not just the human but everything else that is on this Earth. Because the mother herself, **your planet**, is raising in consciousness.

The consciousness of the crystal already exists here. There are many other consciousness levels to be raised too. And from that place people will not have to return from the journey they have taken in a soul consciousness. Now, I say this so you understand that you are not just a soul consciousness; you are linked to a being that is more evolved and more advanced, beings that are known as the 'Fallen Angels' though they do come from the Angelic Realms. They have chosen to live a journey or a life (or lives, if you like to look at it that way) from a different place—from not following the inner aspect of the self, which is always there in every physical being, that you have been and what you are.

Some nurture from God—the Source of Creation always; others have explored a different route. And so there should never be any judgement upon who or what one has been because sometimes they have chosen to make that exploration from just one specific life but not necessarily the overview of lives that they come from, from that being that they relate to.

You could say that life in the World of Light is a play. There are many aspects that have gone out to play that journey of Life and Light—there are many, many stories out there from each soul connected to the being from its Source.

For the soul is like a landing point once you have come into a physical body. Does that make some sense? You speak of the 144,000 and that would be closer to the number that exists in the raised consciousness of the 12th dimension. I am hoping that you will come to understand and realise that there is so much separation and yet so much unity that it is hard to explain it, for it becomes convoluted. It becomes difficult to get your head around it as a human being, but it exists.

The good of say, 144,000 is not necessarily coming to learn all the same lessons but rather sharing all the different lessons and coming together as one to unite and become that one being that you are connected to. Does that make some sense?

And so, I could say that everyone is linked to an angelic being. Some have ... I do not like to use the word fallen for it is **not**—for they have chosen to explore a different way. They have chosen to explore a different way, and it is a little harder to get back to the source where it is nurtured readily from the Creation of the Source. But each being, each soul connected to the 144,000 group that they belong to, can do this. It is much more complicated than this. But if I try to explain it, I think I will use this submission: *that it is helping to raise the consciousness upon this planet* and all the beings that come. All are filtered through a Karmic Board. All are overviewed by others in other worlds to assist them in their life's play upon this planet.

It is not for very long, compared to what and who they really are in the World of Light in the Angelic Realms.

We asked the Oracle: What *frequency/dimension does the crystal operate on?*

The Oracle: The 7th dimension. Pure consciousness of that level.

Jalarm: I am here, we are talking about the crystal. The crystal is actually a consciousness of the 7th dimension—it is a frequency, and it was used in computers and radio in the first place. It is used many ways to lift the consciousness that was so heavy and dark in this corner of the galaxy. This was the whole plan. And so, the crystal is not too advanced. If it was too advanced it would not work very well. In fact, it would explode things, if this makes sense? So, we had to find a balance. One energy that would be accepted by all the living beings and by that I do not limit it to humans. I mean all living beings and everything, in fact, upon the planet. And so, it is all a crystal being, Mother Earth included. It all needs to match her. This was created, as I have said, when the planet was first formed.

It was created into mass and then became solid and then became water and earth and then became an atmosphere in which many different forms of life could live. You could understand, I think, if I say, if we brought in a frequency that was too different from what existed on this planet then it would not operate. It would not interact. In fact, in some areas, it would explode and so I think you are understanding what I am saying. Do You? (*Yes.*)

Chris: *The one we call Lord Rama was said to be thirty feet tall. Was he a member of another race of beings? How long ago did he live on Earth?*

Jalarm: He was coming from a different dimension. Like I have said there were different dimensions and different beings. Some came from a much more evolved place. Had they come in their fullest power, again, everything would explode because the Light and the density of Light would have been too powerful, and the atoms would not have been able to tolerate that. Do you understand? And so, Rama, yes, a very tall being when you compare him to the beings that were already on this Earth, but from where he came he was not too tall. He was normal. But then there are many worlds, and there are many dimensions and so for me to say he came from a different planet would not be correct, for it is another universe. Very different from the one that you can see with your eyes, but even with your own eyes you cannot see it completely. You need some sort of scientific object to assist you into seeing into your universe. So, I will just have to leave it at that.

Jacqui: Okay, that is great. Thank you.

Chris: *Many young people now have gender–sexual identity issues. They are in bodies in which they do not relate to their gender. What is the cause of this?*

Jalarm: You could say this is a difficult question or you could say it is an easy one. It depends on how you view things. If I speak from your soul consciousness it has a history of many lives that are male or female, or even other consciousness beings that are physical from an extraterrestrial point of view. And so, if we are referring to that which happens upon this Earth, whether someone identifies as male or female, a soul coming in could be influenced very readily from past lives. Or a life that they have just experienced as female and then find they have been born into a male body (which only differs by one chromosome). You would find there could be confusion when the body is growing as a male, but the soul is still feeling that they came from a female body. It is in their memory, and it is the consciousness that is in them. And so, it is easy to understand from that point of view. And then, on the other hand, if you look from a medical/science point of view the male is very different from a female, but if you think about it there is not much difference; it is just to do with copulating.

There is a reception and a direction into the two coming together—so that is what was created in the separation of the male and female from the physical, which took place at another time in your soul history. And that goes back a long, long time and so understanding is needed for those who find it difficult to relate to the way they have evolved in gender, as a male being feeling like a female; they need to have acceptance and understanding ... because it is possible for two souls to come together and deeply love each other and why should that be held against them if that is what they choose? For love is the thing that is most important.

For people to feel love, to feel love for one another, to care for one another—and I am not suggesting that these differences should be taken as a guideline for what was meant upon the Earth—I am merely saying that perhaps allowances should be made and understanding as to why two males show much love and affection for one another, or two females show much love and affection for one another. Once you come to understand about soul history, you can readily accept and see how it is possible to have that confusion. Everybody needs to act and respond to the God within and how they feel, and if they come from the truth within and they feel happy and good about themselves and those that they share their affection with, then what harm is that, I ask you?

Jill and Jacqui: (gently) *Agreed.*

Thirty-Seven

Roles of the Sea and Land Creatures

Jacqui: *Thank you. Jill is curious about mermaids. Is there anything on Earth that are mermaids?*

Jalarm: Again, these are different physical beings that came to this planet as visitors and yes, they could swim in the water—they had a fish-like appearance—and yes, they did look like humans to a degree. And so, you could say that they were men or women that swam with a fin under the water, and they were a race. They helped to influence the energy that was being locked in on your planet to help stabilize it, for it did get out of alignment a number of times before the most recent time. And so, these people, again they are influenced from a Hierarchy from the Angelic Realms and were willing to work with them on a mission to help ground the Light into the seabeds, the ocean floor, and so that helped to stabilize the planet. Does that make some sense?

Jacq: *Yes. Here is another question. Where did the up-standing ape-like creatures come from?*

Jalarm: Up-standing ape-like creatures were of many different experiments created by the Old Empire, which I have spoken about to you before. They were of a reptilian nature and a Draconian nature. They were cold blooded. They varied, many because of experimentation—there was DNA material taken from many things, or genetic material taken from many things and many beings. If that makes sense. And so, if you are asking what the direct line for the man was that became the walking ape-like creature (and I say ape-like; I didn't say ape—this makes a difference) ... Does that make some sense to you?

What I am trying to say was there were many creations. Some failed and some did not. This was over (he laughed)—again, I am hesitating, about time ... millions of years.

There was a need by the Old Empire to create a being that would be like a slave to them and to work for them. And do jobs around the planet for them. And they wanted someone to be called when they were needed and released and left to their own devices until they were readily called again.

The one that was most successful and later became man, or a further development even later called a barbarian, was the ape-like creature that was developed by the reptilian/Draconian Empire, and genetic material was used by their own physical being. They also captured physical beings, such as the Leonine, and their DNA were all intermixed and implanted into an ancient historical being that was very like the dolphin. It was the manakee. It had breasts so when the little ones were born, they were more mammalian than reptilian. They were of slightly warmer blood because other genetic material was used from other extra-terrestrial beings such as the Leonine. They are warm blooded, and they are hairy, and the hair grew on the babies even though the birth mothers were hairless.

The babies were born into water and allowed to float to the surface of the water to embrace the air or the atmosphere that existed upon the Earth. They were suckled by these manakees who were already upon the Earth. They are very old. They are related to the whales and the dolphins, and they were well and truly here before the Old Empire ... before the reptilians and the draconian. They were on the planet first and swimming in the ocean to help connect to Creation of the Divine Light, a Divine Source of Life. *And they still do.* They still swim in the oceans to hold that energy here on this Earth and help it to maintain its balance.

Jacq: *Thank you. Another question is how does the human fit in with the myths about Hunaman and the race of Dravidians who are similar to the Australian Aborigines?*

Jalarm: Well, the evolvement of, shall we say man, when it became enchristed, which was later, it became a human that was a man of Light; also to help Earth, the Divine Source of Creation of All, which was Light, Love, and Compassion. These are the energies that come with that Source of Creation. These beings were later blessed with this enchristed Light and became God-like beings. Before that, all the experiments that took place were to create something that was standing up to act as a slave to the Draconian/Reptilian races, and these were created without permission from the Source. And these beings were created to become human. It is another play of words into Hunaman, which was well known to the people who lived in India. But of course, the Hunaman or the Light man came long before a lot of these races had come to this planet. Some came from an evolved source and knew and understood well what had taken place upon this place and wanted also to help Earth and ground the source of the Divine Light or Enchristed Light. And so, these roles were taking place by many races, which I have already told you came to visit this place. Some left and some stayed. The land you know as India was such a place. There is an evolvement of the energy of that point of the planet. Does this make sense? (Yes.)

We asked the Oracle about names of angels and were given '**BANLL**' *(?) for a 7th dimension angel. We still do not understand. But Jalarm has clarified that we are now communicating from an extra-terrestrial point of view and their names, numbers, time, and distance is measured differently.*

Note

I advised that after thinking about *manakees*, I realised that Jalarm was speaking about keys and giving me a key. Jalarm is referring to manatees or the dugong—a race of sea mammals that hold the 'key to Man.'

Jalarm usually refers to a dugong, but he wanted us to realise that the manakee (should be manatee) was the 'Key to Man'—or the original key to man—the experiment chosen by the Reptilian scientists to do their work.

There is a confirming entry in Wikipedia:

The Sirenia (commonly referred to as sea cows) are an order of fully aquatic, herbivorous mammals that inhabit swamps, rivers, estuaries, marine wetlands, and coastal marine waters. Four species are living, in two families and genera. These are the dugong (one species) and manatees (three species). Sirenia also include Steller's Sea cow, extinct since the 18th century, and a number of taxa known only from fossils. The order evolved during the Eocene, more than 50 million years ago.

The manatee appears to have an almost unlimited ability to produce new teeth as the anterior teeth wear down. They have only two teats, located under their forelimbs, like elephants. The elephants are thought to be the closest living relatives of the sirenians.

Thirty-Eight

Sacred Geometry

The inner sun, The pharaohs, and the cosmic number system

It is the ninth of the ninth month, and the Mystery School has reassembled with Jacqui, Jill, and myself, after our perambulations hither and thither. Human life is spread over a time, and Jalarm tells us again today that time is measured differently in the cosmos. Another important aspect of time is *in-tuition*; information must produce transformation, and transformation takes time. Hence, the Mystery School, from time to time, does not meet, so readers and those who seek to know the mysteries are able to digest information on multiple levels within.

While there is text on a page (as Jalarm tells in this transmission), names and places and people in the past still have influence in the present and may ignite this in-tuition process. In today's transmissions, Jalarm confirms that He is one and the same with Cosmic Sai Baba (hence the photograph of me with Sai Baba in white!). This day's transmissions and the messages of the Oracle, while focussed on the Pharaohs of Egypt and the Upper and Lower Nile, reveal surprising matters about number systems of the cosmos.

Jalarm: It is I, Jalarm, and I am pleased to be here. You ask questions and I am ready to answer them. I would like you to know also that the connection between Jalarm and Cosmic Sai Baba is the same.

Cosmic Sai Baba carries many, many names as he has said when he was here before in an Earth body. But he is not limited any more with that body and so he can move around and influence very easily.

The time for the frequency to rise has made it easier for everybody to connect to their inner sun. And I would like to call it their inner sun, although it has often been referred to as the soul. If you think about the soul, it is a word for *sol,* which is another word that is talking about the sun. It is all in the *sound*. The translation and spelling make them sound as if they are separated, but they are not. And the ancients knew and understood this. They connected with the Life Force and the Divine Light every day because they knew and understood that from the Source of Creation.

So, I would ask you now, my dear—have you any questions?

Jacqui: *Who was the first Pharaoh of ancient Egypt?*

Jalarm: The first Pharaoh has been recorded in ancient Egyptian times, but the Pharaohs existed long before Atlantis Fell and they have different names and there is confusion about their existence. But they are what you would call 'The Atlanteans', and so the Pharaohs did exist then. They were not dictators as they became later—they were people of 'high born', and by that I mean they were of an advanced knowledge and advanced understanding, and they came from Venus. I am glad you have asked this question because I have already sent the message to say how closely you are connected to Venus, for when they worked and lived on Venus, it was a different frequency, and it still is, where the physical aspects of Venusians still live. They influence those here on this Earth because they are connected to them.

Not everybody on this Earth is connected to the Venusians. The three of you all do come from that place. And so, there are different names. Yes, I would like you to know that the Pharaohs existed long before the Ice Age. Does that make sense?

Jacq: Yes, thank you. We didn't get a name for the first Pharaoh.

Jalarm: I would like to spell this out on the Oracle. I will take my leave and allow you to receive the spelling out on the Oracle. This is important because I want you to understand what a marvellous gift you have been given with this Oracle. It will spell out names and dates in its true sense and certainty.

What was the name of the first Pharaoh of Lower Egypt?

The Oracle: DB888 H7. (Jalarm said it will mean something to us later.)

Jalarm: I am here, and the numbers and the letters represent a signature. It means a lot to us—perhaps not to you yet, because you have not got the dictionary for the signatures—if that makes sense.

You asked for the name of the first Pharaoh, and we took that to mean the first being from Venus that came to help enlighten those upon this Earth. And so, the number is how that being is known because in the universe, mathematics and sacred geometry are very much a part of a measurement, if you like. To draw a measurement from one point to another does not mean all that much because there is no beginning or end. And so, this is why we use numbers. The numbers we use are not quite the same as those that you have in your rotation of numbers. And already, members of your different races have ways of expressing different numbers. They have different names. They even have different ways of writing them, and so this is why I am holding back a little in answering your question for it does not allow the whole dimension of what the numbering system is, but I can assure you there is a sacred numbering system. In fact, your Jesus mentioned this in saying that *'every hair upon your head is numbered.'* Do you understand? So, it is a little hard for me to explain something that I know you would not be (without being rude) able to get your head around. Only because you have not been exposed to the extra-terrestrial number system.

So, the being that came was this number. It did eventually have a name that fit and became known to other races that came with spirit. In fact, I would like to say it is another aspect of the word 'Jalarm'.

So, I hope you will accept this, and now we should move on, if that is alright? Is there another question?

Jacqui: *Val is asking about what date was that? ... But is that relevant?*

Jalarm: Not really because time is not measured in the cosmic worlds in the same way it is measured here. So perhaps in linear thinking, which does exist here on Earth, it does make it difficult to try and put a time on an event. We do attempt to do this, but understand that your planet has been in different frequencies. It has (been) and was in the 4th dimension and moved to the 3rd dimension when Atlantis Fell. It has also been in the 1st, 2nd, 3rd, and 4th dimensions.

But now you are moving to the 5th dimension, all this is changing. All this is difficult to talk about in the linear numbering system that exists on your Earth. Does that make sense? (*We all said yes.*)

It will cause confusion, I think, if I start to lay out time because, in addition to this, the time dating is used upon the Earth is not totally correct. Your scientists know this because they disagree.

Jacq: *Who was the Pharaoh who united the Upper and the Lower Nile?*

Jalarm: Understand this was time after the Ice Age when the Pharaohs became more Earthed and more involved with the human body, more caught up with their own thoughts rather than the bigger picture. Although many were influenced from their Higher Selves—their Soul Consciousness, their Sun Consciousness. Does that make sense? (*Yes.*)

So, there is also confusion with those names. Even the spelling differs again. I hesitate to give names because there are a few that were established upon the ancient Egyptian history. The history, at first, was a continuation of what existed before the Atlantean time, as I have already explained. And so, the Atlantean time is the true source of the evolvement of Ancient Egypt.

Understand that evolvement of Ancient Egypt also happened in other places around your planet. And so, the questions that are asked could influence and show that this was a major influence all around the Earth— such as the Atlanteans, the name **Jalarm,** and the numbers that were given to him, or who he is known as, which influenced many, many places around the planet before Atlantis Fell.

Thirty-Nine

The Extinct Vanara

Jacqui: There is one more question: Chris asks about an extinct intelligent monkey-like race called Vanara?

Jalarm: This is an important question, and I would like you to ask the Oracle. I would like to put thoughts into your head and hopefully you will come up with answers. (We all agreed.)

Group discussion and question: It looks like the Vanara brain was used to help the evolvement of the ape-like creatures with intelligence. Was that a separation from the animal ape to the

ape-like creature that man evolved into after many experiments?
The Oracle: (Big) YES.

Jill: My understanding is that when the reptilians were creating man, they were using some of their own DNA and also the DNA from dead warriors of the Leonine race, and the Leonines were very upset about that. Maybe they used their brain as well?
The Oracle: A BIG YES AGAIN.

Group discussion and question: The Draco created the reptilians and then the reptilians began experimenting themselves. The Draco were like the Gods to the reptilians. Draconians were never on this Earth. When you think about it, the Draconians would be linked with the dragons perhaps? Let's ask that!
The Oracle: A big YES.

Group discussion and question: So, we are told the dragons were eventually blessed by the Source—so does that mean the Dracos were blessed also? (We know that scientists link bird DNA with that of reptiles.)
The Oracle: A big YES.

Group discussion and question: How did the Draco, reptilians, and dragons gain the warmth? Did they misuse the divine fire blessing from the source?
The Oracle: A big YES.

Group discussion and question: Is this what is called the fallen angels?
The Oracle: A very big YES. (We felt we had hit the jackpot with that question!)

Group discussion and question: Is it helpful to work with dragons?
The Oracle: YES.

Group discussion and question: Is it to do with the pulling away from God (dragon) and now reconnecting to the Source?
The Oracle: YES.

Group discussion and question: Is this fiery dragon—is that another way of looking at the rainbow serpent?
The Oracle: YES.

Group discussion and question: Are they the same race?
The Oracle: YES.

Indigenous artwork shows relation between dragon and rainbow serpent

Jacqui: When you have a dream about snakes, it's always spiritual.

Observations: Physiologically, the base of the brain (which is linked to the spine) is reptilian and that is overlaid with mammalian (animal). Of course, the junk DNA from the Star People is yet to be realised—it is this that gives us our advanced psychic abilities.

Jacqui said when she visited the Ashram in India, Puttaparthi, she also visited the Super Speciality Hospital that Sai Baba had built. When she walked into the main entrance she was overwhelmed when she stood under the huge chandelier with how bright and peaceful the Divine Light was standing underneath it. She still has dreams of Sai Baba, and it is well known that he is there in the dream. It is not one's imagination.

Valérie: What shall we call the Beings of Light ... or Ascended Ones? What is the best word to use for the mainstream audience?
The Oracle: FOHDE

Valérie: Is that like God?
The Oracle: YES

Valerie: Is that Star People's language?
The Oracle: YES. (And then spelt out FOCA.)

Valérie: The letters are so like a Scandinavian language!
The Oracle: YES.

Valérie: I know in Pagan times they offered prayers to Skanda who is the son of the Lord Shiva. That is why they are still known as Scandinavians. We are told of the tall, blond, blue-eyed Star People that used to come and go in the northern hemisphere. All that was before recorded history.

The Oracle signalled Jalarm wanted to speak through Val again by moving around in tight circles.

Jalarm has given an account from time out of any memory about the bird-like beings and their role here on Earth, and how the DNA was shared across many species. The Earth was in a different orbit then, and only cold-blooded creatures survived. The group has asked Jalarm a question about the so-called legendary griffin and Jalarm has asked that some research be undertaken. Meanwhile, the trio ask the Oracle questions about the relation between the griffin and the reptilians. The replies and further questions about dragons have an important part to play in understanding how warm-blooded beings came about and led to the human, the one who is filled with the hue of Light from the Source.

The griffin has wings, claws, paws, feather-like skin with softness of fur and animal tail.

We asked the Oracle about the DNA from the bird race.

Us: Was it taken without permission to create the griffin?
The Oracle: (swinging into action and moving the wine glass very quickly to knock the label) YES (and kept pushing the label so it nearly went off the table. That meant to us, a very definite yes.)
   Valérie said that when it is taken without permission from the Source, it hasn't received a blessing. But as Valérie spoke the wine glass moved by itself and said 'NO'. So, we explored a little more.

Jacqui: The griffin was once revered by people (then the Oracle made it clear by going around and around in circles that it wanted to have a BIG chat through Val).

Jalarm: It is I again, and I am very pleased that you have had this conversation about the griffin. Valérie was thinking it was created without permission from the race of the birds and that is very true. However, it was eventually blessed by the Source from the Creation of All.
   There have been many happenings through the ages—through the universe and your galaxy—of different races that have interblended their DNA or their genetic material to create another race. A bit like what has happened with you when you were first created as human.
   So, with the griffin, it was developed, and a race was formed to go on to find the blessing from the Source, which was given by the Hierarchy, and from that place the race of the griffin (because there was a race, not just a being itself) was able to enter into the foray of helping to spread the Light throughout this corner of your galaxy. Does that make some sense? (We all agreed it does.)

Jacqui: I was going to ask a question and I find thoughts running madly interblended—are you putting thoughts into my head? (Much laughter.)

Jalarm: (laughing) Indeed, this is what I have said before, I am putting thoughts into your head (and I do this on purpose) so that you can discuss it. When you come together it becomes a sort of melding from different points of view and this will help many people—because there are many, many people who are reading this information and they come from different points of view also and you, and you, and you (pointing to the three of us individually) will be able to put out the information so it reaches many more than just one point of view, or a similar one. Does that make some sense? (We agreed.)

Jalarm: Good—because a griffin comes from many races. It has wings, which is a bird-like being. It has claws, which is again a bird-like being but also reptilian, and it has a feather-like skin, which also links with the softness of fur that comes from the Lion People, as you can see. The Lion People exist in another corner of your galaxy. In fact, you have been given much information about their role in society. When I say society, I mean the collection of races that exists within your universe, your cosmos. And this is helping people (I hope) to realise that this Earth and the people on it are not the only universe. I want to help people to come to realise that there is much more within your universe, your cosmos. They all interact.

There are also the ones who are waiting, in a soul form, to come into a human body to experience the life of what you do here on Earth as a human. For that is a much later stage in evolvement. So, getting back to the Leonines (the Lion People) they are, of course, part of the griffin. Does that make some sense?' (We all agreed.)

And the Leonine People are very warm, loving beings—and there is much of the lion family, the cat family, that exists upon this Earth and you know the kind of energy that comes with them. For they can be very loving and very gentle, but of course, if angry or hungry there is a twist to their tail in how they treat other things around them. I will not go into this for the moment.

Okay, so, the Leonine People have also considered themselves to be like the policemen of the cosmos and this has been written about in books. So, is there another question?

Jacqui: Another question from Chris … When visiting Wales, people will encounter images of dragons everywhere. Do dragons still exist?

Valérie: We saw a lot of images of dragons in Denmark also!

Jalarm: As I have just explained, there have been many races formed and created. And when you think about the dragon, it is very reptilian—but it has wings and that, of course, immediately connects it to the bird race. It also has fire. And I would like to remind people that the fire exists in your sun and many places within your Universe, but there are two aspects to the sun—one is to destroy, to break down the unwanted, but also there is fire that gives warmth and heat to life, to the warm-blooded creatures that have been created. And this is a raising of energy, a raising of consciousness, and it is what is leading to universal love. For love is an energy of warmth, caring, consideration, humility. But also, one to understand what it feels like to have suffered in some way; and also a feeling of being hurt. Some of those feelings are totally foreign to a cold-blooded being. And so that is another reason why there is a queue for people to come in a soul into a body of a human. That again is a much later development in the universe. Does that make some sense? Is there something there that you would like me to qualify?

Jacqui: The only thing I think about is why do we incarnate into this physical world? Why do we have to take on a human body?

Jalarm: Well, I have just explained: A human has family that immediately comes into the creation of a child with family—because it doesn't come alone; it has to come through beings upon this Earth. And they are immediately connected in energy to that family and from that, hopefully, there is a bond with that family. And they begin to learn and understand about the warmth of love, of caring, of interaction, of marrying—to perhaps marrying another to experience a life together from which they learn from each other and produce more children to give opportunity for more souls to come into this world. It is an ongoing thing. As I have said, a lot have come from cold-blooded races, and they have not experienced these things at all. Those emotions—the warmth of a sentient feeling of a human. Does that make sense? This is the reason they come and there are many waiting to come to experience this.

I would like to add also that the dragons (for want of a better word) were created much like the former ones mentioned—the griffins—but were a different race again and also, they were accepted by the Hierarchy and blessed from the World of Light. There is a similarity I would like to say, in a way, about the spine that exists in the human and the spine that exists within the reptilian races and the dragon. The dragon is very much connected to a snake-like being, but there is a spine and there is a tail. And of course, the human shows evidence of once having a tail. The human is an evolved creation, and it is very interesting from many, many, many different races from around the universe. And so, the dragon is held as a sentient being but one that can embrace both the cold-blooded and the warm-blooded beings. The warm races exist. They have the fire within and the leathery skin and wings. There is much within the dragon that represents the human and its beginning. Does that make sense? Because the human in its beginnings was from a race known as 'man'—it was very experimental and was not always blessed from the Source. Humans have gone on to being a 'Lightman' and it has been blessed from the Source. The Source of Love and Light. Does that help you?

(It does, thank you.)

Jalarm: Sometimes there is a story of, shall we say, 'Saint George and the Dragon.' And there is a winning over, or mastering of, the heavy energy represented in the heavy skin that is leathery like and the fire that can destroy. Anger if you like. Or the fire that just destroys

without any feeling, any emotion. If you can take your imagination just a little further you can see that story is symbolic of you as a human and what you are doing is you are overcoming those influences from the dragon—the fire, the anger, the cold-bloodedness without feeling.

All those things need to be mastered to become a God Being from the Source from which you come. Does that make sense? (We all agreed.)

Saint George and the Dragon

Forty

Good Living, Food, and Common Sense

An important teaching is 'you are what you eat.' In a previous transmission, Jalarm told that a wellbalanced diet and taking appropriate supplements can aid the reactivation of the ten strands of inactive DNA within the human. In this session with the Oracle and Jalarm, we take up this earlier issue briefly.

Jacqui: We were told that a good diet (eating and drinking well) and taking supplements that improve physical and immune systems would influence the reactivation of the inactive Star People strands of DNA within.

Jalarm: It is I again. Valérie is right to point out that some beings have a physical body that has a blood group that is more ancient than, shall we say, the newer blood groups—and it really does depend upon the blood group as to the best food that one can eat. There has been a lot of study and written work done about this. So, it is important that people know their blood group.

The indigenous races have the oldest blood group and that is written in the way they look—they are dark haired and brown eyed, with dark skin. And so, the blood group O is connected to the older blood group. I mention this because it is rather important that they eat some meat. Not a lot, but a little. And for the others they can eat a very balanced diet of protein and recognise how they feel when they eat, and if they feel uplifted and healthy, then continue to eat that way. It is a lot to do with individual choices of the individual DNA, because the consciousness of each cell in the body holds a consciousness also that links into other lives.

So, the diet of what humans eat or drink should be based on what they feel and how they react. If people 'tune into' their body and how they feel when they have eaten, they will know whether something feels good for them, or not so good. They could even experiment by eating just one food source alone and see how that is and then try another source alone and see how that reacts to their body—this type of thing. I am not suggesting that you only eat one source of food all the time, but just to see how the body feels and reacts because you are serving your body in taking care of it, looking after it, because it does have a consciousness of its own.

It is important to give thanks and a gratifying feeling to Mother Earth for growing the food, nurturing the food, and sharing the food that you eat. And the liquid that you drink. So, if all that is done in harmony with the Source and thanks is given, it really doesn't matter what you eat if you feel healthy and good. And as long as you do not overeat. *This is important.*

Jalarm: So, does this answer your question?

Jacqui: I think it does. One other question he has here: *Is Vitamin K an appropriate supplement to enhance the activation of strands of DNA?*

Jalarm: This is something that you would find for yourself. You could try it, and if it feels good, then by all means take it. I would hesitate to suggest that you eat vitamin supplements ALL the time, or to eat something ALL the time. There is an old-fashioned saying about *'a little bit of what you fancy does you good,'* and there is truth in that. So please be easy with yourself, not so strict that the fun or enjoyment of what you eat goes out the door. It is important to be able to sit down and enjoy your meal and your drink, and the sharing with others at a dinner table. And make the most of that, but do not overdo it.

Because you are in the world of eating food, and it is important to nourish the physical body—you understand that.

So, thank you my children, I think this is enough for today. I shall look forward to meeting with you again. Of course, you are never alone. And you can always call upon me whenever you care to. My love is with you.

Thank you. Thank you. Thank you.

Forty-One

Names and Forms

We have all emerged from the Source of All, and when we take up our bodies, we form a relation with whom we feel the strongest connection—to the All, to Boundless Love, to that name and form we feel affinity for. Now is the time for planetary healing, now is the time to understand and experience, all is ONE. Read on as Jalarm unfolds the journey of the soul.

Jacqui said she felt like she was butting in, asking about souls residing in the constellation of Pleiades, instead of taking up the opportunity offered by Jalarm. I added that when that question was asked of Yalum—while he was answering—I (Valérie) immediately saw lots of souls connected to that story from the Pleiades. They seemed to go out as aspects to join with planetary beings from other places.

Jacqui said she had met a famous person's wife at a dinner, and she was delighted to find that she was open to talking about White Eagle and other like-minded matters. I said I had always thought that White Eagle was another aspect of Sai Baba, perhaps a different level of frequency but the same energy. I suggested we ask the Oracle.

The Oracle took off by itself and then we asked our question. It made it clear that Jalarm wanted to speak through me. (The glass moved almost before we put our hands on it; in fact, I hadn't put my hand on it.)

Jalarm: It is Jalarm, and yes, it is, my dear. There is a string of different beings that have been named from Sai Baba. He did say that he was all names and all forms—and so, if you think of it like a bigger picture, you will know that he is overviewing everything that is taking place upon this Earth, your galaxy, and your universe—which is the reason that Sai Baba is much, much more than what it would seem to many. Sai means 'mother', Baba means 'father', and I will say it means **Mother–Father God,** and that is the energy that you connect to every time you sit here at your sanctified Oracle.

L-R: Ramana Maharshi, Archangel Mikael, White Eagle, Sanat Kumara, Lady Venus (who is also Archangel Maria), Quan Yin, Mother Mary, and Mary Magdalene

But getting back to your question, '*Is White Eagle connected to Sai Baba?*' ... I would say yes, very much so. And so, my dear, you have connection to this energy—the same as Valérie has and the same as Jill has, and so many others that connect to me as Sai Baba in the way that I want them to connect. For different paths mean many different things to many different people and so many have written a contract to come on Earth and help raise the consciousness for the people that follow a certain path, or another path, or similar paths! Either way you are all Light Workers, and you are doing the work beautifully and I thank you for that. Thank you, my children. Thank you. (He left again.)

We chatted among ourselves about different questions and then Jalarm made it clear, with the wine glass going around in tight circles, that he wished to speak through me again.

Jalarm: I would like to just talk to you on the matter of the meditation that you are going to hold on the full moon at Satori Springs in Canyonleigh; you will be meditating with focus on planetary healing. I would like the three of you to sit quietly, not together, and come up with the different aspects that you would like to focus on for that mediation. Then pool your ideas, if that is alright.

It is important that you start trusting the information that I send to you. I will send different information to each of you. Does that make some sense? (*We agreed.*)

I have already sent the focus of Fukushima upon Valérie's mind and she has picked it up, along with promptings from others, including Chris, whom you know, and the water very much so—the Earth's water needs healing.

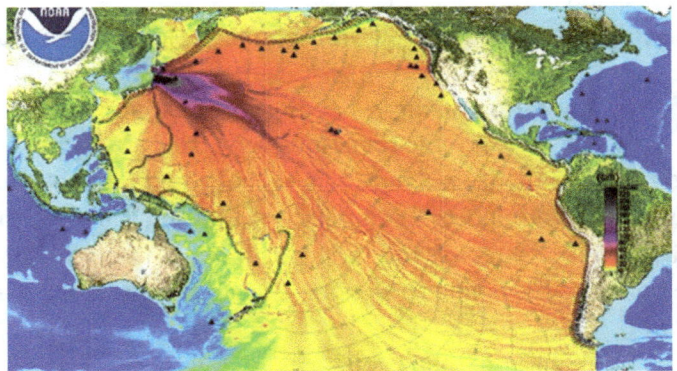

Radiation from Fukushima flowing into the Pacific Basin; Jalarm tells that ALL WATER on this planet needs cleansing

It is losing its energy field of Light and Love, and this needs to be raised so a focus on water, *all* water upon the Earth, this planet, is important. And of course, in a secondary sense, although it is not meant to be a separation, the water also exists in every form of life that has fluid in its body—this needs to be cleared as well. Does that make sense? (*We all agreed.*)

After a group discussion, we decided to ask if Jalarm has anything else he wanted to speak with us about—he suggested that when he first came into the meeting.

Jalarm: I am here, and you are wondering if there is anything I would like to say because I did introduce myself in this way. In fact, we have said a lot more than you realise. It is not always spelled out in words, or in language, but in the reaction as it happens! You will see. It is not something you say like 'it *just happens to be.*' In fact, we are always helping you to come to understand. We advise in different ways, and it is not always by language.

Everything is energy. I would like you to think about that. **Everything** *is energy.*

And there are different frequencies and vibrations of energy and so if you think about energy you could go on to think it can take a form, which is what happens in the world of Light. And then from all forms there to create life and from the life, a story, and from the story, enlightenment. And from enlightenment it goes back to energy and from the Source. So, it is *one huge cycle* that is happening upon this world of life—from this planet, if you like. This galaxy, this universe. And other universes where there is form and life.

When you refer to darkness, we talk about the form that is altogether and One.

This is the mystery and there needs to be talk about this mystery. There is a balance between the two. However, I have not come to lecture, I have come to say thank you, my dears—all of you. I sincerely thank you for the work you do and the commitment that you have given to this circle. I thank you, my dears, and I will look forward to our next meeting. Because Valérie is beginning to wonder if this is the last. *I can assure her that it is not.*

Thank you, thank you, thank you.

I am the one channelling, and I remark (with a laugh) that *I cannot think anything without Jalarm telling everybody what I think!*

Forty-Two

The Dark-haired, Dark-eyed Peoples

In order that we, the hue-man (the being that is filled with the Hue of Light), might 'see the light' and take our place in the 4th and 5th dimensions—among the Star Peoples of our universe—Jalarm and the Oracle pass through information on the multifaceted history of the hueman. In this session with Jalarm, we learn of the origins of the darkhaired and darkeyed peoples. We hear about different races, different Star Peoples, and different times of genetic engineering.

Jacqui: Val has a question here: Who are the dark-haired and dark-eyed Star People from whom some humans have inherited genes?

Jalarm: Now this is an interesting question. And I would like you to work with the Oracle here. Because there is too much talk coming from me and we want to use the Oracle as well. So please stay with that question. Talk amongst yourselves, find a question, and the answer will be given. Is that alright?

Us: Where did the dark-haired and dark-eyed (white skinned?) Star People come from?
The Oracle BOFO.
Us: Is it in our galaxy?
The Oracle: YES. (The Oracle indicated that Jalarm wanted to speak.)

Jalarm: It is I, Jalarm. Yes, indeed, I think it is time for me to talk again. Yes, the people who have the dark hair and dark eyes and white skin do come from within your galaxy. It is not a planet that is often spoken of amongst the people here on Earth, but those people did come here, and they did live here, and they did undertake some genetic engineering. And this was done at a much earlier—shall we say, more Lemurian time—and this was after the evolvement of man to human from the Pleiadean story. And so it was, as I would say, Lemurian time.

The dark hair and the dark eyes are evident in many of the so-called Melanesian or Polynesian, even Australian Aboriginal (Australoid), beings that live in this corner of the Earth which was ancient Lemuria. The skin became slightly lighter because of the genetic engineering from the Star People who had white skin.

The ones who we were speaking about, with blonde hair and blue eyes, came later. And so, your question was about an earlier time, and I wanted to mention this because of the influence and the uplifting of the human consciousness that began after the genetic engineering and the blessings; the Christ energy to the first humans on this Earth, who were the Australian Aborigine.

So, you can see a pattern here, can you not? Of the beings that progressed from this land you call Australia and then reached out to many of the islands and the lands that existed in the time of Lemuria but have since sunk under the water. You will find there is evidence of it under the water and certainly it (Lemuria) exists within the many legends or myths in all these people that live in this area, that have survived going under the water. And then of course, later we would say in a 'round term' Atlantean time, which is when the blonde-haired, blue-eyed people came. But there were other Star People as well.

The Chamorro People of Micronesia, circa 1915

The Untouchables of Malabar; Dravidian Australoid

I am speaking from an overview point of view to help you to understand that genetic engineering took place many times, at many places around the Earth. There was also much travelling by the indigenous peoples. Some of the people that were human and did move around the Earth moved by water; some moved by airship; and others intermingled with those that visited them. And so, there was a cosmopolitan interaction with one another upon this Earth. As, I might say, it is being interacted and played out now. If you think about that.

Is there a question you would like to ask about that?

Jacqui: No question there, but I do want to ask how many souls reside in the Pleiadean constellation?

Jalarm: It is true. The World of Light, where the souls are created, and the energies that move into those creations, come from other places. Other worlds, other dimensions. Does that make sense? It then becomes very complicated because we are dividing things by asking different questions and focusing on different points. In fact, as I have said, they are all at the same time—it depends on the focus. And so, your life as a human, right at this time, is focused right here on Earth in a $3^{rd}/4^{th}$ dimension now. But you are capable of reaching into another dimension, another place on Earth or in the galaxy at the same time.

And you can be influenced by these different focuses or different existences that you have had altogether. If you had them all at once it would be confusing ... and so there is a safety net in some ways, in not being able to fully go into all the different points at once—otherwise, you would be totally confused.

However, with evolvement of the soul and the Being of Light, you can reach a point of Light where you can reach into all of those lives—all of that infinity that is part of you—and not become confused.

The Dark-haired, Dark-eyed Peoples

"We are all visitors to this time, this place. We are just passing through. Our purpose here is to observe, to learn, to grow, to love... and then we return home."
— Australian Aboriginal Proverb

But that is an evolvement that takes place, and that is nirvana if you like. It is a place of enlightenment that you would evolve to that makes you a God Being.

Does that make sense? I hope it makes some sense, because there have been visitors on your Earth as God Beings (looking aside from the fact that you are all part of God) and who are able to help and work to raise the consciousness on Earth, but it is done in a way that each octave that is raised is always at a levelling out, so that all may raise together.

Which means that when you come as a soul, you are part of who you really are and you are here to help one another and to find a level playing ground, if I can use that word, for that is what is meant to be. That is part of the Greater Plan.

Am I making myself understood? (All agreed.) Is there another question? (He left.)

Forty-Three

Sacred Dance

It was the New Year of 2014, which came, as many observed, with a new moon. While the moon was weak, it augured brightly for a year of love, expanding and filling many hearts. A new moon is always a conjunction of the sun and moon, and Jalarm explains, below, the balance of energies flowing to the Earth from both the sun and moon.

Jalarm: It is I, Jalarm, and I am very pleased to be here and to know that I am welcomed. I know you are wondering about questions today, but do not worry for I have some stories to tell you also. So shall we move on? Are there any questions I can answer for you?

Jacqui: One question is, we are wondering if there are any celebrations held from where you come from, if any?

Jalarm: You are meaning 'in the star worlds,' I guess? (Yes!) Indeed, we do have celebrations. We have dancing, we gather, and we give our gratitude to the Source of All. To the Source of All Creation. That is always uppermost in our minds.

Now, I am speaking from a certain level, or frequency, of dimensions—there are others that have different ways of making subservience to the World of Light, but I am speaking from where I am coming from. And so, there are different levels of thinking, of knowledge, that exists at different levels of frequency. I think you understand this (I have explained this before). And so, it is a little like climbing a ladder and yet I do not like to concentrate on that so much because everything is interwoven, and it is possible to jump from one place to another. And from the frequency where you are now, you can jump to where I am now. And in a way you are, and that is why you sometimes feel confusion because you are not readily able to jump into where I come from now in that sense and imbue the frequency totally. But at another time you have come from here—so does that confuse you altogether? (We all laughed.)

I joke with you, of course, and so what I am saying is that everything happens at once. It really is a matter of where you are focussed. Does that make some sense? (All agreed.) And so is there another question you would like to ask?

Jacqui: Val is asking for a friend if Nibiru is a comet or the moon?

Jalarm: Indeed, it has been said that Niburu is a comet, but in some ways, yes, the moon is, and was, a comet that has been anchored around the Earth. I think we have spoken before about there being two moons around the Earth at another time and yes, the Hierarchy did have a comet that was anchored as your moon. That is true.

And I know that the gentleman who asked this question is of the belief that the moon is inhabited by negative energies, and I would like to add that it is not.

I would like that to be said. It is occupied, that is true, but not by negative energies. In fact, the energies from the moon assist the energies from the Earth in finding balance at all times because the moon reflects the sun, and the energy from the sun comes from the Light of the Divine, which is also reflected in the moon. And so, I can clarify that by saying that the energy always coming on to the Earth from the divine aspect of the Light is in balance and influencing the Earth for its better good. And that was designed by the Hierarchy thousands and thousands of years ago.

And so, do you have a question?

Jacqui: What can you tell us about the Occitans from the south of France? Is there anything you can tell us about them?

Jalarm: The Occitans, yes. They are a race and have been living in the south of France for a long, long time. They existed there long before the so-called time of the Ice Age and the fall of Atlantis. So, they have been around for a long time, yes. They are a race of human and so I would like you to reflect upon that. Is there a question?

Jill: We do need to know more about them ... well, Valérie felt that she was one of them!

Jalarm: It is true, the cells that are in Valérie's human body have a direct descent—and I say a direct descent—from the Occitans. That is true. And we gave her insight to that when she was travelling through the area. There is also a link with the country known as Scotland, but before it was known as Scota. It was a time—a long time before that. Understand that the borders that exist now, of course, did not exist before Atlantis Fell. But there was a lot of activity and a lot of different races, and we have spoken about that. There were some that were Star People and there were some who were an evolvement of the original human.

And so, in that evolvement there are many, many different races that came about on this Earth. That is a long story, but it is also contributing to confusion among archaeologists when they find a bone that seems to connect to one race, and then another, and they differ with some and not with others, and so this is where the confusion is, in that there were many different genetic experiments by the Star People and so each race that developed with a change became another aspect of the human. I am talking about the human that was created in the earlier days of Lemuria or Mu when the Pleiadeans came and first created the human from man, as we went through before. Does that make sense? (They agreed.)

Occitans flying the flag

Forty-Four

The Role of Trees

Amid the extreme heat of an Australian summer, The Mystery School met. With humility, they asked for a message from Jalarm and received a surprising answer about how Oracles operated in the times before the fall of Atlantis.

Jalarm: I am here, and I am very pleased to be here, and to know that I am welcomed and given an opportunity to communicate through you three girls because the work that you are doing is very important, more so than you realise at this time. I am grateful that you only want to flow with your feelings because that is what I am encouraging you to do. So, asking me if I have a message, rather than coming up with questions—that is good. However, there is really no message I would like to make today except that we from the World of Light are very, very happy with the work you do with us.

You are an *oracle* because in ancient times, that is much the same as the Oracle often given there are various recordings made of Oracles—and messages from ancient times and this is what in how it was received. Not exactly with the wine glass, but rather through a crystal. And this message was very similar, more like dowsing if you like. But it was similar and it still operates the same way. So, if you go ahead now, this day, I am ready to answer any questions that you may have.

The role of trees in our creation

Jacqui: A question from Chris is, can a tree transform energy? And can humans obtain a positive healing energy from trees—i.e., the older trees?

Jalarm: Well, everything is connected, you know this. Everything is a consciousness and so it is very easy to share a consciousness and I am not necessarily a voice with words ... or hearing words ... I am meaning a consciousness with a knowing and it is also a force that comes from the Source of All Creation. I might say that is a consciousness also. And so, you ask me about the trees—and yes, of course, they have a consciousness. They are living beings. You have in mind living beings such as humans, but the trees are also living beings. Just as a rock is, and a flower, and animals, birds, and insects. You are understanding, I think, even above the Earth and the planetary connections around Earth.

Everything has a consciousness and so yes, you can relate to the trees, which connect to the Earth—and that doubles the consciousness—and it is possible to receive an understanding that would then be translated into your brain, or through your brain, into knowledge.

Everything has a consciousness ...

Does that make some sense? (We all agreed.)
Does that answer your question? (I think so, yes.)

Jacqui: The second part of Chris's question is did trees originally have a role to bring balance to the Earth's ionosphere and magnetic field?

Jalarm: As I have already said, everything is connected. So, I have already answered that question. But if you are asking if a tree, if its form, has come from another place within your galaxy, there is no need to go there. I would like to add that everything that is in a physical form, and by that, I mean in a form which is physics and chemistry, which is what your human body is also, but so is everything else upon your planet—and your planet itself is physics (energy) and chemistry.

And so, it was created, that is for sure, and everything that is needed to grow upon this planet was brought here. Is that enough for you?

Jacqui: Agreed.

Jalarm: I would like to add here also that there is a signature for everything that has a form and so the signature was brought here to allow a form to take place and grow, interacting with the energy that exists in this planet. And you ask about the tree, and the tree is one of them. And so, it is having a direct connection to the Creative Source of All. It has a role to play, you know, with the interaction of oxygen and carbon. And this is a very important role that is played on this Earth.

Is there another question?

The Role of Group Minds

Jacqui: Another question from Chris. Recently, the Canadian sardine fleet returned to shore with no catch. The sardines had disappeared. Is this evidence that species have group minds? Can group minds of different species collaborate?

Jalarm: Yes, in a way that is true. I think we have just already explained about everything being connected. The group mind, if you like to describe it as that, is a consciousness. It does not operate the same as in thoughts and words, but in some ways it does. There is an energy that flows, and it is immediately connected to, shall we say, 'the school' of fish. The same as the birds in the sky when they flow in unison. You look at them and the pattern is formed, and you can see that there seems to be some sort of connection in the way they move together, totally in unison. So, is that not evidence of a group mind? If you like to put it that way?

The same as the birds in the sky when they flow in unison

Jacqui: Well, talking about the group mind, one of the questions Chris has is how do you change a destructive group mind?

Jalarm: If I may intrude here. If there is a group mind that is not necessarily the fish or bird, but in the human—if you feel that there is a 'destruction' afoot amongst that group mind, then that can be changed or influenced, but one has to be careful about what one can influence.

You are all creators. When you connect to the World of Creation and work from that point, you can put it to the consciousness that exists there and ask if this is right for humanity or the Earth, and if it is not. Then just leave it alone. But if it is not then just pray and ask how you can help to change or influence it. And you will be told, I know, that energy by thought and prayer, everything that connects to that consciousness of Universal Love, will be sent to that place that you feel is influenced by a destructive force. And that is all you need to do.

(We all agree.)

Jalarm left for the time being. There was conversation amongst us.

Jill said that on the radio in the early hours of the morning there was a group of up to five tribes in central Australia who have a spiritual uprising together, in that they are wanting to erect a huge cross. The cross is going to be on a hill. Engineers are working on the construction, and it is so high they are concerned about low flying aircraft. And they believe it will be the absolute beginning of a spiritual uprising throughout Australia and beyond.

She said she heard a little about that in inland Australia and thought, *well that is a little bit of a 'group mind' working in a constructive way.* It sounded so interesting, a total collective thinking of the elders, and they are basing the idea on the huge statue of Jesus on top of a high mountain in Brazil.

Valli: I feel that this is not representing just Christian teachings but a more universal spiritual thinking.

Jacqui: In the 1990s, a tall being woke me and showed me a very huge cross. Later at the annual Mind, Body, and Spirit Festival, I saw photos of hundreds of people around the world reporting seeing this same cross.

An artist's impression of Hat Hill with a 20-metre tall lit cross as planned by photographer Ken Duncan for the Australian outback

Forty-Five

The Phoenix

The meetings and the discussion topics of the ladies who come together and comprise the Mystery School are never idle speculation. Beings from many worlds attend and the air is thick with energies from the higher dimensions—other beings from other worlds are present and learning, as Jalarm has told. In this transmission, Jalarm takes up a discussion about the myths and patterns of the sometimes-called fabulous bird, the phoenix.

The human body has many sheaths; fire, earth, space, air, and water all exist within the various sheaths of the human. Air is present as oxygen, and one of the ladies asks about depriving cancerous cells within the body of oxygen. Jalarm confirms this is correct as a technique of healing. It remains to be seen when science will catch up with spirituality, its long-lost cousin in research, about the truth of life on Earth and life in the universe.

Jalarm: Yes, it is I, Jalarm. You were talking about the phoenix and rising from the ashes.

It is symbolic. We used the bird as phoenix because it was the bird that helped to create this planet in the first place. And so going back to the phoenix and the rising from the ashes, it is symbolic but very real in some way because as we have already said, there is a signature for everything.

So, if you think about it, a bird dying is at the end; only, no—it is not the end, and so it rises from the ashes. And it can keep doing that. And if you think about it, your life is like that here on this Earth. You come, you die, and from the ashes you rise again. So, each being is a phoenix—a being who has risen from the dead but then some strange stories can be created about that and, in fact, it is not strange or weird. It is a fact. That you come and you go, you rise again, and you fall back, but in each rising and falling back you raise in consciousness. You understand this and this is what is happening to everything upon this Earth that was first created by, shall we say, the phoenix.

The Earth was forged by fire; the cycle continues without end ...

...because fire had to be introduced into the planet when it was forming as gasses and forming water and a solidness, which eventually created the Earth; fire had to be introduced. That is the signature and that is when, shall we say, in allegorical terms, the birds were thrust into the

fire. They became mulch that nourished the Earth, and from the Earth they rose again. Again, I have said just recently on this day that everything is consciousness, and the ash holds consciousness, the Earth holds consciousness, the fire holds consciousness, the birds hold consciousness ... and you can see it as ONE in the story. But it is everything on this planet. So, am I explaining myself? You need to learn to flow with your imagination and see how it fits within yourself and within your understanding. Does that make some sense?

Leela, the sport and play of the ONE

Jacqui: The only thing I would like to ask is that you seem to take over my hand when drawing this circle. Can you tell me about that?

Jalarm: Well, my dear, my energy is here and it is encompassing all of you and so I took the liberty of using the energy of myself to help you to use your pencil to flow in a way that would give understanding and also prompt you to ask. So, I may have played a little Leela (Sanskrit for 'sport', play) and I hope you are not offended. Did you mind my taking your hand to create the drawing?

Jacqui: No, I quite enjoyed it.

Jalarm: That is good, that is good. Well, that will allow me to do it more often with the three of you, if that is alright. (We all agreed.)
    Jalarm left again. And we all laughed.

Cancer and Oxygen

A meditation took place. After the meditation, Jalarm returned.

Jacqui: We just had a little meditation, as you know. What Valérie is asking is about the cancer issue. What are your thoughts about isolating cancer in the body and depriving it of oxygen?

Jalarm: Well, it is not that simple, but it is the answer. For cancer cells exist in everybody and it is only in weakened areas or where it is vulnerable in a physical body that the cancer can take over and cause serious problems. But yes, that is the answer, and it can happen and assist people if they can isolate the area and deprive it of oxygen. It will just die off. The important issue, of course, is finding the physical problem within the physical body at a very early time and then it can be deprived of oxygen very easily and very quickly. If it spreads too far it makes it more difficult. But it is possible ... and so have I answered your question? (Thank you.)

Jalarm then decided to leave with the message, was it enough for today? The Oracle confirmed by spelling out it was the finish. We were all very grateful for information given to us.

We were also given a lot of information about infinity and the expanding universe, but the recording was lost(?) We believe it has been held back for the time being.

God is everything, God is nothing, God is absolute. (Quote from Sai Baba.)

Forty-Six

Hanuman

The Mystery School chats on—for learning in the higher dimensions is cyclic and not linear, nor rote repetition like the 3R's of reading, writing, and arithmetic ... gathering and expanding information when working with the higher energies is like the double helix spinning, slowing down, gathering speed, and churning with similar, like ideas. Man and woman must play the game of discovery and self-discovery.

Our group reflected on the history of our Earth. There were discussions about conflicts and fighting, and evidence of atomic or nuclear weapons being used in ancient times. There is evidence of high levels of radiation and grains of sand turning into blue crystal at some places on Earth.

We asked through the Oracle, *was there atomic or nuclear conflict in pre-historic times before the fall of Atlantis?*

The wine glass moved quickly by itself, confirming that conflict did take place in the Indus Valley.

We asked the Oracle: how long ago?

The Oracle advised quite strongly that this took place 800,000,000 million years ago. This response was very strong.

Jacqui: *(after saying she had a strong feeling about that war) Was it connected to a monkey god?*

The Oracle indicated that Jalarm wanted to speak through Valérie.

Jacqui: *I have a feeling it is Swami (meaning Sai Baba) because the energy is so strong today.*

Valérie: *Well, Jalarm has said he is an aspect of Cosmic Sai Baba.*

Jalarm: "It is I, Jalarm, and you are asking about the fighting that took place above the planet, and yes, there was fighting that took place. Yes, because there was a disagreement as to who the planet belonged to. And so that was what the fight was about. It was between the Dracos and Hanuman. Hanuman was/is like a Leonine and he went on to be the first human. At least that was the DNA and the first image that became the first human. He was the one who loved God the most. But going back in time, there was a Star Being that was known as Hanuman. It (the fighting) was over, as I said, who had the ownership of the planet.

The Star Being, Hanuman, was the over-sighting spirit of our planet ... and also the Monkey God, Hanuman

Now I would like to say here, the planet was being formed in this very early time, and I would not say one side or the other *won* a war because in war there are no actual winners. There are only those that appear to have won. And so, it was agreed by the Hierarchy that the Draco or its eventual ... hmm what can I say, light form, that were created by them ... could live on this planet. You will find also that there are stories about these wars about the reptilian beings, and the snake-like beings that had wars with each other—that is recorded in the Australian Indigenous Dreaming stories. There is similarity there.

But for those that were fighting with technology (which, by the way, is still more advanced than what exists on this Earth planet), there was fire; there was energy released like an atomic bomb. And the evidence of that exists now in the Indus Valley. There is some recording of radiation activity, and it shows just how severe and how dangerous this activity with wars using atomic and nuclear bombs can be. It is very dangerous, and there is no future in it in the long term.

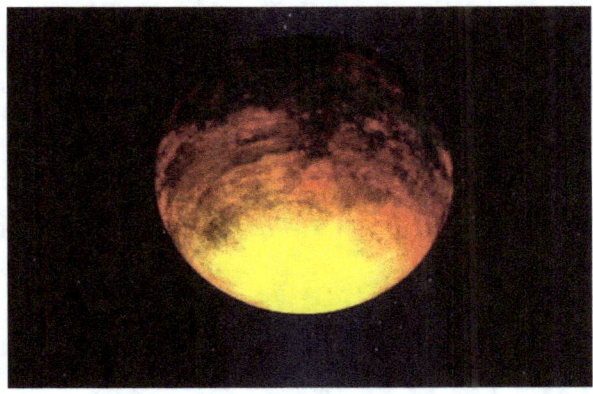

There was radiation activity, which turned sand to blue crystals

These are other reasons why the Star People have decided to come:

- to announce themselves and to inform the peoples upon this Earth of the history of what has taken place upon this planet.
- to announce what is important regarding what will take place upon this planet.

Any attempt to 'fire' (weapons) at the Star People will be stopped. Very easily. But it is dangerous! There will be an announcement made by the

Star People giving opportunity for the Earth people to think before they start pointing their weapons at our starships. Because they will never be able to hurt them—they (the Star People, their vessels) will just merely move into another dimension, but they will come back again. And so, it is fruitless firing weapons, and they (the Earthlings) will soon realise that, and stop it, if they are wise. And I hope they will be.

But there is no war plan (by us), I can assure you. That has been and gone. There is no future in it (war) and we are hoping that the Earth people will rise to the occasion and welcome us.

Thank you, my children, thank you. I would like to end here. Thank you.

(Jalarm ended at 12.12.)

Forty-Seven

Yowies

I would like to take this opportunity to share a recent experience a friend, Jeremy Buddle, has shared with us. It tells of the up-standing ape-like creature that still exists on our planet in the next world. The astral world, you might say. This relates to Jalarm's information above regarding Hanuman, the Star Being, who was the over-sighting spirit of our planet ... and also the Monkey God, Hanuman.

Where we are today with the yowie (a separation took place)

Up until mid-2015, my take on the Yowie phenomenon was based on what others saw, like a mystical creature in a fleeting moment rushing across a road only to disappear. The media always described them in a fearful moment, generally perceived as a threat to humans. In recent years, increased reports of sightings and videos online purporting to have an actual recording has only played into the uncertainty of them.

However, in a remote place of Megalong Valley, NSW, I stood on a track not wanting to return to the cabin where I was staying. It was dusk and I feared the track through a swampy forest. Suddenly I felt a person behind me. I had not expected anyone. I had been alone on this property for ten days.

'You can look back or you can keep walking,' I heard.

I looked back.

And standing twenty feet from me was a seven-foot tall ape-like being covered by ginger brown hair and only interrupted by a distinct heavy dark brown face, dark eyes, a thick mouth, and a wide nose.

I was about to run back to the cabin in a childlike fear, but I felt a light energy around my feet that rose through me. The fear left me, and I was captivated by the face that smiled, though I did not see the mouth move. And it had such an alluring energy. There was a communication from its face to mine, which I did not understand. It was too mature, too wise, too human-like to be an ape-like being. I did not want to associate it as a Yowie—it did not seem fitting—but I did acknowledge others would see it as one. I did not feel threatened by this being. It turned around, moved along the track, and disappeared.

The Aboriginal people would say if one saw a big hairy fella, it would herald big change for that person. The following year, I was hospitalized for a serious infection and an accident involving my right hand where I needed two surgeries and was off work for six months. And in 2017, I was hospitalized for a rare blood disorder; my platelets had disappeared after an influenza vaccine. It took months to regain strength and a year for my immune system to recover. To lose the use of my right hand as a right-handed person meant I had to redesign myself. My left hand had only been a supporter to my right hand; now it had to lead. It shook my thinking up completely by rewriting a belief system of who I had become.

A healthy immune system is about self-protection and my decision to have an influenza vaccine was an attempt to protect me in an epidemic, but it had, in fact, done the opposite. The vaccine turned my immune system against my platelets. I had allowed a foreign substance to enter my body out of fear, rather than trust my feeling that I did not need it and I was not going to get influenza.

These traumatic events I saw as change and had happened to prepare me, to strengthen me physically and mentally, as an adjustment to a higher consciousness, the fifth dimension.

In March 2016, Earth entered the fifth dimension—a momentous moment considering Earth had been in the third dimension approximately 4.3 million days since the fall of Atlantis, and on leaving this dimension in December 2012, Earth rushed through the fourth dimension in just 1,184 days. One significant and most discerning symptom was the perception of time speeding up. Most of us felt it, to keep us on course and make us think about change. The changes affected all of us regardless of if we were conscious of it.

This arrival has enabled a differential relationship for humans to another race of people on Earth. The Animal People. In some countries, humans lay claim to a race of the Animal People and some of the least known are Am Fear Liath Mor in Scotland, Almasty in Russia, Maeroero in New Zealand, Hibagon in Japan, and of course, Big Foot in U.S.A.

In Australia, the collective view of humans has changed toward believing in the Yowies but not knowing much about them. Humans are more open minded now and many want to know more. And the Yowies know this. They are deliberately increasing a visible presence to awaken humans. No longer can we be the centre of our own attention as the only people and treat the mystical being as an appendage to that existence.

A national park north of Sydney was once the land of dense bushland, rock platforms, tall cliffs, and creeks through deep valleys. However, things began to change in late 2018. Regularly walking a particular bush track, I noticed things being made from wood and rocks placed at the edge of the track: a tepee, a large standing cross, small rock cairns. After online research comparing these unnatural items, I saw comparisons to what others had found in other bushland settings in Australia related to the Yowies. Once I accepted that these unnatural items I found were of Yowie origin my awakening to them began. I had connected to them.

As an intuitive person, I connected to the energy of wood and rock markers as guidance to learn about them; for example, a five-level rock cairn represented the fifth dimension. These markers were made by hand and the energy attached told me it was in fact by a Yowie. As more markers were placed, I accepted they were made by other Yowies. At this time, I became aware of a transparent black figure engaging me in a social way, allowing me to learn (through listening to this being's energy) that he was a male Yowie, about fifteen years old, and his name. In a vision he showed me the spelling of his name. (Out of respect to this person, I have not provided his name and the reason why.)

This person walked short distances with me, allowing me to see him walk on all fours then walk like me. He wanted me to play with him; I could hear his voice speak in English. Their energy translates their own spoken language into English. Eventually we co-created a large tepee, a symbol of a pyramid that represented energy, and a symbol of them that announced their presence on this land. Their technology is energy.

What we did was to announce *our* presence and by learning from them, and respecting them, they chose to include me into their life. It was at this time that I received an intuitive verbal message, 'The Yowie will look after you.'

Days later, this young Yowie stood at the last bend in the track before reaching my vehicle. He was with his family: his mother, father, and younger brother. They were transparent but clearly defined, making me understand the true nature of them, all of us: we are beings of energy and light.

Through intuition and observing the clan, and this has increased to members of other clans, I have learnt how they live in the forests, maintaining and adjusting to the balanced energy of Earth. It is a needful approach to the land of abundance, without hurting it. The Animal People are the protectors of Earth, the planet we share.

This national park I walk through regularly is not a national park to them. It is their land.

Humans lock up large tracts of land to protect it against the possibility of harmful use by other humans, but we exclude something about the land through an unconscious mind.

During the early days of the ninety-day lockdown in NSW, with the planet in a viral pandemic, I used my right of essential exercise to leave the property and walk my regular track. I was stressed by the unfathomable event. At a place I called Balance Site, a vortex of Earth's spiralling, healing energy, I focused on a transparent ginger-coloured Yowie standing off track. I recognised his energy as familiar. He was the younger brother of the father of the clan. Around him was the collective energy of many Yowies, in varying levels of transparency. I could make out their distinct shapes. There was another whom I saw almost as clearly. His hair colour was a sandy brown; he was shorter and stockier.

'Hello,' I said.

And what also became clearer was the distinct awareness of many clans gathered at least ten wide and four deep. I heard from the sandy brown Yowie, 'If you die, we die.'

I was slightly hurt by this. I was the symbol of the human race. Then the sandy brown Yowie said, 'We didn't create this pandemic, but we do support it. It is about helping you (humans) to learn. Do you understand?'

'Yes,' I said.

I thought about the harm humans were doing on Earth, polluting the atmosphere, the oceans, mining, and deforestation. Gradually, the Yowie gathering disappeared—from the rear first.

I held an intuitive feeling Covid-19 would stay infecting humans until we got this message. I am not sure if it was given to me by the young Yowie, but it has stayed with me. A year after this, I asked the father of the clan in a sit-down meeting:

'For the virus to spread, does this mean we are not understanding, that humans need help putting this planet in harmony?'

He answered, 'Yes.'

And what we experienced during 2020, seemingly as a gift from the pandemic, was how Earth could recover quickly from the actions of a collective unconscious mind. The polluted atmosphere and waterways cleared. And I saw frogs and the funnel web spider return to the suburb I lived in after being missing for decades.

This pandemic also harmonized the last shift into the final frequency setting of the fifth dimension, a higher level of truth. And to be in this consciousness, we must be truthful to ourselves. This is what the Yowies are showing me and all of us.

Article shared by Jeremy Buddle, Sydney. A big thank you. jeremyasher07@hotmail.com

I, Valérie, took this photo at the entrance to Kariong Glyphs. I thought it was a cut into the tree trunk, but when you look at the feet they seem to be outside the tree, not part of it. The tree should have fallen over?

Forty-Eight

Frustrations and Knowing your Purpose

In this session of the Mystery School, we remarked that the energies were very strong indeed that day, and recalled other occasions and members of the Hierarchy, when they had been present.

Jalarm: Do you have any questions?

Jill: Like Jacqui, I also overheard on overnight radio that Aboriginal elders from five different tribes … they want to build a huge cross in central Australia on a high hill, and that is going to be the spiritual centre in Australia and go on further with energy flowing out to the rest of the world. Is that really happening? (**Jacqui** *interjected and said that was Ken Duncan the artist*).

Jalarm: Because this is man-made and was inspired by us, we encourage anything that helps with change; change in thinking—or attracting people to an area where the energy is very high and will influence people, whether they realise it or not. And so, it would not be focused so much on religion but rather just a cross. This is what we hope—but this will happen.

Jacqui: Jalarm, there is a question here: *does middle earth contain a giant reservoir of water? I think it has just been announced on the news that there is five or six kilometres of water in the centre of the Earth?*

Jalarm: There are many reserves of water beneath the Earth's surface—you know this. And they are at different levels. And some of the levels, as they get deeper, are ... the water is quite hot because of the centre of the Earth. The centre of the Earth is fire. And so, there is fire, and water, earth, and air—you understand? (Yes.) That is the symbol of the simplicity of what the Earth is made up of.

There is water—yes. There are caves—yes, and there are problems with mining the Earth.

The imagination could get carried away because books have been written about this in the past, shall we say, science books or fiction books, and so one (and I don't just mean you) might imagine places where you could sail a boat, but it is not necessarily like this. It is reservoirs—yes, caves; yes, water; yes—so the Earth herself is not totally solid ... and this is the reason why we are always encouraging the little Earthling not to mine the Earth because it can help—and does—put the balance of the Earth into an uneven state. Does that make some sense? (*We agreed*). This is something that needs to be considered very carefully.

Frustration—Soul walk-ins

Jacqui: *Jalarm, is there something you would like to say to us?*

Jalarm: I would like to say that I understand and know that:

- there is a lot of frustration upon this Earth, and the Hierarchy (from the Star People's point of view) is aware of the frustration that is being felt.
- there are many people (who are Star People) who have come into the Earth body. There are Star People born into an Earth body when they did not have to come. And there are Star People who have exchanged souls with Earth People and continue to live in the Earth body with agreement of the Karmic Board. (Star People) walk amongst you, who are not easily recognised as Star People.
- there is quite a contingent of visitors upon this Earth to help the little Earthling to raise in consciousness.
- Star People have come to hold the new energy that is coming onto the Earth and affecting everything upon this planet (including the planet itself). That is why there is a decision for the Star People to come and show themselves.

For it must be known exactly who you are and where you have come from. *It is that simple.* Is there anything else you would like to ask?

Jacqui: Just one little question I have. *If you are a Star Person that has been sent to Earth to help people, do you consciously know that you are one? Oh, No! That is not the right question?*

Jalarm: Actually, it will do, because not everybody does know, but many do. Because they have come like Valérie—

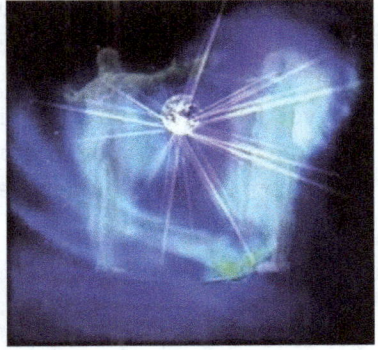

and she is one of many—as she has walked into a physical body. In fact, there is an agreement to an exchange of souls. You understand that process.

It can be very complicated ... the soul thing. But we give answers to any question you have about the soul. The soul is often referred to by man, in classic writing, about a human being as being 'a good soul'. In fact, everybody on Earth is a good soul. But some make wrong choices, and they also live their lives influenced by other things that do not allow them to be strong and be exactly who they are from the Source of All Creation.

They digress or are influenced by entities, also. So, it can be very complicated. *Would you like to ask something about that?* (We said we were happy with that but were sure there was more.)

Jacqui: *It worries me about those people who are starving to death or are in such terrible conditions ... uh, with cruelty and war ...* **I just find that so distressing**.

Jalarm: Indeed. This is a world of opposites, of conflict, so that you can make choices. Those that live in these dire situations have come in agreement to live that way because it does help others to develop humbleness and to realise how well off they are when they are not in that situation. It gives opportunity for people to help one another. Do you understand? (*We agreed*.) So do not fret or worry, because I have said before, as a soul in a human body, it is not everything.

You are here for a while, say as a child, a baby, until about eighty or ninety years old, maybe longer, but that's it. You return to the Source. You return to who you really are, but that is another story.

What happens here is not everything. It is not the reality as Cosmic Sai Baba has often said. The reality, my children, is who you are as a soul. And how you live your life here on this Earth. This planet can be very difficult, but it gives opportunity to grow in character and this is what you are doing from the way you behave. *Does that make sense?* I will leave for a while...

Forty-Nine

Sister Planets

As the Earth approaches the autumn equinox, we, who do global service bringing skills and energies together to form the Mystery School, meet once again, after a long summer and amid global challenges. Jalarm has come and reassured all present that all things shall be well if we learn who we are and why we are here. True to our task, we ask questions about the history of the Earth and the presence of Star Peoples.

The wine glass spelt out that Jalarm was present and wished to speak through Valérie.

Jalarm: It is I, Jalarm, and I am very pleased to be here and to know that I am welcomed. We have a lot of work to do today and so I have just come to announce my presence and to let you know that I am here, ready and willing, to answer any questions that you may have this day.

I have just told Valérie (telepathically) that I will also lift away any pain and regret or sorrow that she has in her mind so that she will feel much better as the Oracle goes on. So, over to you, my dears.

Jacqui: Jalarm, does our Earth have a twin planet? So that there might be similar attributes in the landscape and people who are not unlike the people we have on Earth? And flora, and fauna? I just thought when they were setting up this planet that they might have sent people's genetic codes from a similar planet. I am sure you know what I mean.

Jalarm: Yes, my dear, I do understand, and I know what you mean and of course I have said before that everything upon this planet has come from somewhere else. And so, **yes**, there are planets such as this one that are very similar to the Earth. And there are people, also, that are very similar to the human, not quite the same, but very similar. Certainly, their emotions are the same.

There are different levels of consciousness that exist in various races in the Cosmic Worlds, and by that I mean different frequencies also, so they are not readily seen with the physical eye, or with a telescope, if you understand what I am saying. But rather, they live in a different frequency altogether. However, they are aware of what takes place here upon this earth. This planet and, er, all that has been created upon this Earth, has come from another place. So, is this what you want to hear—or is there something else you wish to ask?

The Earth has planetary sisters elsewhere in the universes ...

Jacqui: Yes, do you think physicists and people working in that field will find this planet in maybe ten or twenty years?

Jalarm: I am not saying that there is just one planet, my dear. But yes indeed. The existence of Star People will be very well known and accepted by this planet, this Earth, very soon. Very soon indeed. For it has gone on long enough now that we have been presenting our presence, and in fact we have always been here, in ancient times until now.

In fact, we created this planet, and it is time that the Earthlings know this and accept it, without seeing something as strange or weird but rather accepting the knowledge so that they can move on and begin to realise who they are and why they are here.

Jacqui: So, entering the Age of Aquarius, is that what you are saying? And entering a new dimension of thinking and being?

Jalarm: Indeed, it is, yes. It has been for quite some time now that you are in the process of moving into the 'Golden Age' as we have put it. This is the time. This is the time that people need to 'wake up'. Does that make some sense? (*It certainly does*.) And if I can add here, as Star People, and I speak on their behalf, I am hearing the message from my superiors, in that it is ready to announce that our presence will be made here very soon upon this planet, worldwide. So, does that make you happy?

Group: *Yes*

The Star People will come forth and announce their presence

Jalarm: We have a plan. And if you would like to leave that just for the moment, because we do not want to put out the message because even though it seems like it is just between the three of you, it goes into a recording that happens around the world and around the Earth. And it is very easy to pick up other messages from other people who are on this Earth—some are fantasy, some are real. So, we are not ready to say how we are going to present ourselves … but we are. Is that alright? (*We agreed and said we will look forward to it.)*

Valérie: *Since this article was given above, we have had several recorded YouTube videos in 2022, where Alcheringa and his team have invited requests for an interview with your leaders. E.g.,* https://www.valeriebarrow.com/?p=5431#more-5431

Fifty

The Opening of Star Gates

It was a time between lunar and solar eclipses. The Mystery School assembled, and we were guided to understand that we are lightworkers and the thoughts and questions are seeded within them.

Jalarm *makes it known that he would begin by speaking through Valérie.*

Jalarm: It is I, Jalarm, and I have been listening and putting thoughts around you and you have been picking them up. This is something I have said we do, from the world that I come from. Once you pick up the thought it becomes your own. And so, we are not interfering in a karmic way, if you understand what I am saying. So now do you have a question?

Chris: *Is this period between eclipses a time when activation of the 4th and 5th dimensions within will be 'brought into the light' or accelerated, or a lifting of the frequency of the human?*

Jalarm: It is all those things; of course, with the new energy that is coming onto this Earth, it has been coming for quite some time—I have explained in the past that there is a net around this Earth that is slowly opening in crossover points that have been known as *Star Gates*. The Star Gates are widening and there are many places around the earth that are experiencing the new energy.

We are careful to monitor the energy in places around the Earth because we do not want it to be too much for the life forms on your planet. You understand, you are combining the Old Empire with the New Empire, and this is a group of many, many races that come from around the cosmos, from other worlds, from other universes.

They are all coming in a soul form and there is a need for them to raise in light gradually together. There are some in a darker, heavier energy; *this is not to be judged, for you are all here to help one another*. And I would like all to remember that. For it is not a time to compete with one another—it is a time to blend, understand, and raise in consciousness where the upliftment of arms does not exist in the thinking.

It is a time for people to understand each other, realise their differences, accept the differences, and find consensus with each other. If you look at what seems to be a 'mess in society' in certain places, you will see that changes are happening in the way things have been handled and dealt with.

There is more willingness, in the United Nations, and I do not mean just the body of the United Nations, but I mean the different nations around the world that are more ready to discuss issues and problems that have arisen, and matters that need to be resolved. You will see that, and we from the World of Light are very happy to see this. Because nothing can be gained from firing at people, killing people, maiming people—nobody wins; all lose. *So, is there another question you would like to ask*?

Chris: You have recommended to us that we conduct meditation circles at the time of the full moon. This full moon falls on a day of lunar eclipse. It is taught that that prayer, chants, and meditation during eclipses are magnified, multiplied, up to the power of 100. However, this should be done in a pure, protected setting indoors. The question is *what is the best way to observe the full moon ceremony during an eclipse?*

The Star Gates widen and the energy flowing from deep space to the central sun of our universe, and the Sun of our Solar System is guided gently that we may all raise in consciousness together

Jalarm: I would encourage everybody to follow what they feel is right in their hearts. Because there are so many individuals upon this Earth: *it is important for them to know what feels right for them*—so it is not a good idea to say, 'You must do this, or you must do that!' It is important that everybody follow, indeed in a way of uniting, that does not have to be divided by a wall, or a house, or even a temple or a church. It can be inside or outside. It is a choice, but it is important that the intent goes out and joins at a level of consciousness that it will achieve what everybody is aiming at, at this time. And I say **everybody** because even though there are many who are conscious of what they are doing, there are many who are not readily conscious of it but still desire peace on Earth.

Everyone does not want to see their children destroyed—everyone has an innate feeling of wanting to protect and to live, and that is born into everyone on this Earth. So, I think if you concentrate upon that, you will understand that it is not important to separate this or that, but rather for the intent to go out. For even the indigenous peoples for aeons of time have lived without walls, but they still are able to relate to the Source of All Creation. You understand. (*We agreed.*)

The indigenous peoples lived without walls and related to the Source of All Creation

Fifty-One

What World Will We Create?

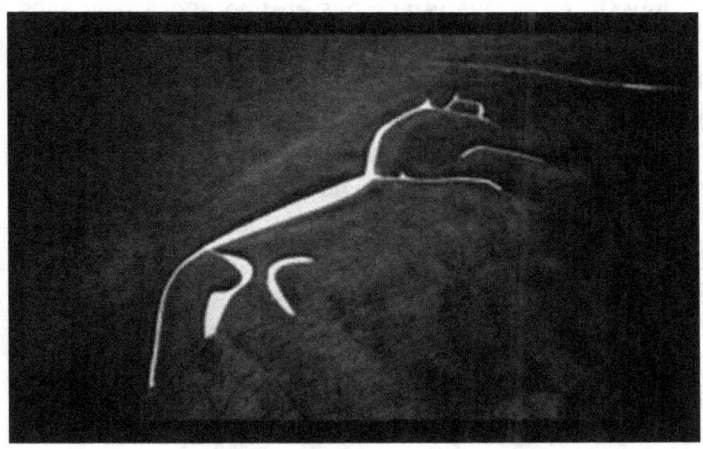

Jalarm: So, is there something you would like to ask?

Jacqui: Well, I do have a question from Chris. It is about the Hierarchy coming and helping the humans and I am asking if there is a being in the Hierarchy who has a horse head and a human form; is this the one who came to teach the up-standing ape-like creature how to make fire?

Jalarm: This question about image is something I would like all of you to consider yourselves to some degree. You can ask the Oracle if you like. The reason I am hesitating is because imagination is a 'nation of images' and that is what belongs to the World of Light. So, there are *many* images—it is innumerous as to the images that exist. The Star People who work to help the human to evolve, to understand who they really are, use images to assist that, but it is not the same for every being on Earth. One has a path. Another has a path. Each soul is totally different from the next soul. And so, an understanding of an image may be lost with some and not with others. Do you understand?

And so, images have been used to help some understand more of other worlds—and for a question such as the Hierarchy with an image of a horse's head, I could readily say 'Yes.' But then it would not be accepted by others because they would not understand at all. But Valérie has said about a signature that exist on Earth and everything that has an image on this Earth is the creation, shall we say the pattern, that is needed for it to continue to grow. Everything has an end and a beginning on this planet. This is not the same in other worlds. But on this planet, it has a beginning and an end. And so, with each signature it also holds a pattern of an image and that continues to grow and to evolve, but it dies back and then it grows again with the same image. Otherwise, it would become something else. So, are you understanding? (Yes, thank you.)

The image of the white horse, when people think of it or speak of it, it is poetic, they like it, they smile, so it is one of a beautiful energy—so may I leave you with that.

The white horse elicits a beautiful energy

Again, Jalarm jumps in and borrows my voice box.

Jalarm: I am here, and it is Jalarm—and do you know that right through early times it has been recorded that Plato and some other philosophers worried about their children and what was going to happen in the future, and it is still a subject brought up in these times by parents?

People can only be encouraged to be good citizens, good humans if you like, good people. And of course, from the laws that you have in the land, if they misbehave or do things that are dangerous to society, then they are brought to account. So it is that easy for people to just run wild, shall we say. Because I can assure you there was a time, on Earth, when people did live in caves, and they did run wild, and there were no laws. And there were no ways of expected behaviour—they were just left to their own devices. They developed weapons and they just used them, without any consideration of hurting one another. This evolved and people did learn and start to move out into the sun—after the period of the Ice Age, which is what you would call your ancient times now, and I am not talking about Atlantean times; from there, many things happened. Religions were created, also language and people divided, some of them, and joined together and became different countries. They became different races—they interacted with some of them and so more races came.

So, if you look at the big picture, they have evolved. Humanity has evolved. And we talked earlier about the indigenous races—or at least Sai Baba talked about the indigenous races, and they were readily evolved in that they were connecting to the aspect of themselves who are Star People and so they had that extra consciousness, and they knew how to telepathically communicate with each other, so they were quite evolved in the beginning and aeons of time later. They went through that change that was the recent Ice Age and came out still very evolved. They didn't have the problems of ice and snow that existed elsewhere.

The Rainbow Children will not have the problems of earlier times...

Jalarm: It is I, Jalarm. What I was worried about in ancient times was how the younger people worried the older people in their behaviour, etc. Understand, of course, that young people bring in new energy and new ways of thinking and this can be interacted with old ways and so it finds a better balance, as life goes on and as centuries go on.

And so, now, there is still concern about the young and their behaviour and this is understandable because a lot of the behaviour is not acceptable. However, they do come in with new ideas and new ways of thinking so, I would encourage the older—the elders—to listen to the young and ask why it is that they want to break away from and change things. Because they are not happy—and from that point, they can be guided to living a life and making changes where there is help for many people, which will be helpful to younger people who will be coming up behind them. That sort of thing.

Jalarm tells take time to listen to young people ...

And also, with the different levels of light that I have spoken about before, it carries different consciousness and you all know that you are moving into a higher level of consciousness, and once you get to a certain level then the influence and the knowledge and the wisdom that is sitting there waiting to be exercised into the consciousness is coming from the knowledge that has been inherited from the Star People that helped create the human in the first place.

From that point of view, they will be able to speak telepathically. They do to some degree even now. But psychic abilities will be developed more—their sixth sense will develop so that they will be able to handle many things much easier and even develop the abilities to manifest what

What World Will We Create?

they need. And so, the money issues would go away, but that will be some time off.

Are you understanding? And so, I will take my leave. The day has ended now, and I thank you for the interaction that has taken place. It has been my pleasure to have been here. Thank you, my children, thank you.

A New World is coming. What place will young people have?

Fifty-Two

The Earth Mother as a Live Being

Chris: (Asking about the Indigenous people) How important is it for them to regain their knowledge and their ancient ways?

Jalarm: It is I, and it is I as Jalarm, because we are focusing on this for a reason, and you will come to understand that more as time progresses.

The Indigenous people had a very, very strict way of living. And they also honoured the consciousness of God the Creator in everything. There was not really anything considered sacred and separate or non-sacred. They considered everything sacred. So, there is a big difference in how, shall we say, the westerners, or other races think. But when the white man came to Australia, unfortunately, they intruded into their way of living and the way the Indigenous people honoured everything. There was a lack of understanding from where the white man came from—and I need not spell it out—it is well known, I believe, in how the Indigenous people have been torn apart. And torn apart is correct and even from their totemic understanding that has been lost, for many just have no idea who their parents were and who their tribal ancestors were.

Unfortunately, I would have to say that the Indigenous people are suffering deeply because, yes, they do need to hold onto their beginnings and who they really are. But unfortunately, so much ritual, ceremony, and knowledge has been lost. They understand this deep down, and they know; and they do now actually realise that they all need to join to become ONE and share what they do know because it hasn't been lost completely. There still is a lot of information and knowledge available and they have agreed, certainly at a soul level to share this knowledge now, and share it with the white people of the east, so that there is a true understanding of who humans are. Because, of course they are, in Australia, the first humans.

And they did go out and spread out amongst many around the world. This is not proven yet, although there have been many studies made about the possibility of that. And I can assure you it is real.

Jalarm: So, is there something else you would like to ask?

Chris: Yes, the women? The tribes were often led by women. Is this going to return in some form? Is this going to spill over in some way from the Aboriginal people to the people of the west?

Jalarm: This matriarchal aspect of most tribes existed, and still does to some degree, because even though they may not be appointed, it is the women who speak up and insist that, shall we say, the men behave themselves. Because the strict laws they had did not allow any to break the law—they were so severe that they would be dealt with, and they were put in a place that they would not dare break the law. Unfortunately, they have been lost in the western world, and without ritual and ceremony and their own law, they have been lost. But then I speak of some, not very many; most still behave well and do their best to help their families.

The Earth Mother as a Live Being

So, this is something that has to evolve, maybe change, that is happening all the time. Everything is changing. Everything has movement; nothing stands still. And the Indigenous people, their role now is to teach as much as they can of their old ways and to influence, if they can, about obvious mistakes that the western world is making regarding nature. And I mean Mother Earth—for she is the one who nourishes you and is looking after you—growing things so that you can live. It is important that everyone respect that and take care of the planet. For it is a live being. And when I say a live being, I mean it has a consciousness, and consciousness is not necessarily a language. It is energy and a vibration, and the Mother Earth does have this.

So, with the planet herself, she can survive, she adjusts in many ways—and she receives help from other worlds at times. But she cannot go on being torn at without losing her balance in some way, and that will upset the interaction with other planets in your solar system. This needs to be considered carefully if the planet is to survive and be a place of beauty, which it is still—a place that people will want to come to live and to visit because I am saying the Star People do visit even now, even so as a human that comes with a soul into an Earth body and experiences it here.

Star People visit the Earth

Fifty-Three

Atlantean and Light Societies

The Mystery School assembles and Jalarm, the Atlantean, tells it is an important day and understanding of this will come later. The Mystery School seeks to uncover many aspects of life before the fall of Atlantis, in order that many will understand the many stories of human life before our recorded history and the research of archaeologists, geneticists, scientists, and anthropologists. While many have pieces of the story, the pieces are incomplete. Pooling different points of view and coming to broad understanding of the mysteries of human life and its origins from multiple sources is one of the important tasks of the Mystery School.

First, we chanted the OM together to bring harmony; and then we called upon Jalarm to bless our meeting and we welcomed his presence. The wine glass moved strongly to show he was present, then made anti-clockwise circles, which we have come to recognise as meaning he wishes to speak through Valérie.

Jalarm: It is I, and I am very pleased to be here and to welcome our guest. I am very pleased to see that the four of you have come together this day. It is an important one; you may not realise it just yet, but the understanding will come.

So now, if we can proceed, I would be very pleased to answer if there is any question that you may have.

Jacqui: We were talking about the civilization and the societies that existed before the fall of Atlantis, and did they use barter or money as a means of exchange?

Jalarm: You were speaking of the so-called migration before the so-called fall of Atlantis that went down, and the Ice Age was around that time also. You are talking about civilizations that existed before that time and which I know you refer to as a time when records were lost. I would say that yes, there were races that used money in the sense of coins to barter and to pay for or to receive. So, is there anything you would like to ask about that?

Jacqui: Do you have a question, Chris, that you might like to ask?

Chris: How did the community care for one another and ensure that they were always supported?

Jalarm: We are talking about beings, shall we say, that are races that were living upon this Earth in previous times, and they had gifts and abilities that were lost by the so-called humans. And I say human, because you understand about the Light Man who went on to be created from Man. All coming from Earth. So, you could say the 'Earthman.'

Now I am referring to the Star People that also lived upon this planet and this is what you are asking—did they have money for exchange, is this right? (Yes.)

Then, it depended upon them as to which Star People, or race, we are speaking of. The ones that have abilities to create, or how can I put it? If I can remind you in the way that Sai Baba created his life on this Earth. Sai Baba did not really need anything. He said so. And this is what he was meaning—he did not need money, because he could just manifest anything he needed. Do you understand? (Yes.) And so, the Star People from a certain level of wisdom, knowledge, and Light can do this. And so, there was no need for money—does that make some sense? (Yes, thank you.)

Is anything else you would like to ask?

Jacqui: Okay. The next question that Chris has is about the role of Hanuman. Is he still continuing today, i.e., the protector of the Earth?

Jalarm: Indeed so, indeed so. Again, I would refer to Sai Baba; Cosmic Sai Baba is here—you know that—because Jalarm is part of an aspect of Him and is focusing mainly on Atlantean times.

And so, this is what has happened with, shall we say, in the age of Sai Baba and the age of Hanuman, and many other aspects from different ages, like Jalarm if you like. But that is a very limited aspect of Sai Baba. And so, what I am trying to say is that Sai Baba is, if you remember, the words mean Mother–Father. Mother-Father-God from the Source of all Creation, and I would like you to think about that when I say the words 'Sai Baba' because I am talking about Creation—and the difference in the images is what is right for your understanding or some other person's understanding on their path of Enlightenment.

Am I explaining myself? (Yes, thank you.)

Fifty-Four

Ice Ages

The Mystery School continues to work with The Oracle as guided by Jalarm. Guidance is needed, for at times, Jalarm has to withdraw in order that the lightworkers of the Mystery School might even *think*. This is challenging service to humanity, for be that as it may, many have never been in the presence of one who is a member of the Hierarchy, and the vibration and energy is so strong, so high, that it is nigh impossible to think of a new question or to go off on a tangent.

The purpose of the Mystery School (among many others on the Earth at this time) is to recover the lost history of humankind, and its origins, along with a history of the Earth that helps us to understand how we got to today. Jalarm has shared that the Earth's moon was brought here from elsewhere, and that the Earth was moved from another orbit around our sun to its present place and orbit between Venus and Mars. Moreover, Jalarm and the Oracle have revealed that everything, every form of life, was brought here from another place. Think of that! The flowers, the grasses, the trees, the birds, and the bees! We do live in a wonderworld of creation and human flourishing.

We return to Jalarm and the discussion about the 144,000. **The Oracle** *signalled that Jalarm wished to speak.*

Jalarm: I am here. I am here, and I would like to explain, you have clarified amongst yourselves that the contingent of 144,000 came from Venus and they were Star People—yes—and the occupied different places around the Earth. And that was all after a time that the Pleiadean humans had already began to multiply, and so they were multiplying even more by then. And you can ask the Oracle how long ago that was, in your time. For that is the time that there was a very real upliftment of energy and light and universal love and from that the Earth people started to really multiply and began thinking with more understanding and more wisdom.

However, they still were limited and there has been growth ever since. A gradual upgrading as the planet, your Earth, comes into alignment with the galactic sun—and the core of suns that goes back to the Source of All Creation.

Jalarm: I am here, and you ask if there was something major that happened to the planet Earth to enable the Venusians people and successfully upgrade the animal man/part human then into a light man, more as the humans are this day. And yes, there was.

There have been many ice ages on this planet, and you will find there was an ice age that took place around that time 50,000 years ago. And with it there was a change in the Cosmic Order and the amount of Light or sun that was on this planet, but it enabled the human to still live on this Earth, to take refuge in caves, and you will find that there are a lot of recordings in the caves of the existence of the Earth human.

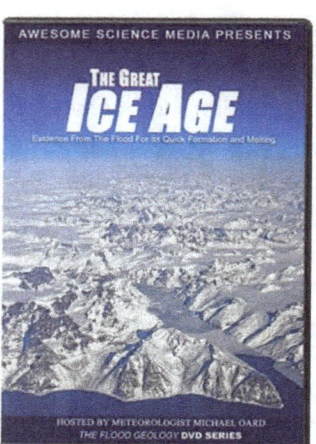

So, you will find if you do some research it will equate with scientific research. And I would like you to do some research because information needs to coincide with what is written by science. Sometimes science has it incorrectly, but you will find that information I am giving to you will coincide. You can always ask me more questions. So, I hope that answers your question. *Thank you.*

Science makes its discoveries, and Jalarm advises that information needs to be presented correctly.

Fifty-Five

Sanat Kumara and the 144,000

Many think that the universe ticks along like clockwork, until they read what our scientists and astronomers discover in the outer regions of our universe billions of light years away. Our lives are sourced from the stars and our story of human life is gifted from those who came from other worlds, other galaxies, other dimensions, to make this corner of the Orion Arm of our galaxy a Garden of Eden. Eden, of course, is a word that comes from the Star People; it carries a vibration, the vibration of 'creation of a beautiful place, garden, place of harmony and peace.'

After travels, adventures, and trials, the Mystery School reconvenes with love—for one another and for all humankind. Loving kindness is their goal. Loving kindness for all, as they explore the story of the human, and life before the fall of Atlantis. **Jalarm, the Atlantean,** is present.

Jalarm: I am here, and I am very pleased to be here, and to know that I am welcomed, as I always welcome the opportunity to speak to you or to work with the Oracle. I would encourage you to use the Oracle more often when you feel the need. It is very good for dates and names. So, I would like to ask, *do you have any questions today*?

Jacqui: On the internet, it is recorded that Sanat Kumara, along with 144 volunteer Star People, has come from Venus to assist in bringing out the divine light in animal man. We thought that the people from the Pleiades came first—we are not quite clear. *Can you help*?

The purpose of the Star People

Jalarm: It is true. It is true that the intention of Star People who came to lift the Earth in this corner of the galaxy into a higher dimension of Light were the first ones (sigh) when the ancestors were created, which was 900,000 years ago. And later, we have talked about this before, there was an upgrading of the amount of Light that was able to be accepted by the animal man, who had been embraced with divine energy—so these are the ones when first created by the expedition from the Pleiades.

And later, in what is known as the Lemurian times, the Venusians came. They came to influence the peoples and to help raise the energy again. They taught them more. They taught them many things, such as symbols that developed into a kind of writing or images. And this is what the Indigenous people still do to this day. In communicating a story, they use pictures.

So, is there anything else you would like to ask about that?

The number of 144,000, by the way, is represented by the number of people who came from Venus under the command of Sanat Kumara, and this was a very, very good time to remember in the upraising of the intelligence, wisdom, and understanding of the animal man or at least the first humans, and so they developed very quickly from that place on. The number of 144,000 was spread over the Lemurian times and so perhaps you would like to ask more about that?

Jill: *Maybe we should ask more about that—what would be the question?*

(Jalarm pulled aside for a while to allow the three of us to discuss the subject.)

Jalarm *confirmed via the Oracle that Sanat Kumara had never incarnated into an Earth body and that he was a Star Person on Earth. He also confirmed that the 144,000 people were Star People that worked with* *him to teach the new humans. They came en masse and spread all over the world.*

Questions through The Oracle

The group: Did *the 144,000 come after the Pleiadean mission?*
The Oracle: Yes, the 144,000 came en masse after the Pleiadean mission.
The group: What *dimension is the Earth now in?*
The Oracle: Yes, we are now in the 4th dimension!
The group: Will *there be peace on Earth? When will this come? Will peace all over Earth happen within the next seven or eight years when Cosmic Sai Baba is appearing in his Light Body?*
The Oracle: Yes.
Note: This message was received in 2014.

Fifty-Six

The Dingo

In many sessions of the Mystery School, we have been taught that *everything on Earth has been brought here from somewhere else*. The great sea beings, the whales, and other cetaceans, came very early to hold a vibration of peace  and harmony in the waters. The Earth was moved into its present orbit (to allow for warm-blooded creatures) and the moon was brought here to be our satellite. Jalarm and the Oracle have often spoken about creatures from the past and how they were brought here.

In this session, we learn of the dingo, which does not share any of its DNA with other species of canines. We also learn of the perpetual presence of high beings, angels, and possible mass vision of Sai Baba, who is still here in the next dimension.

Valérie: The dingo is not related to the wolf or dog in the DNA. Where does it come from?

Jalarm: The dingo came from the Star Worlds—the same as in the beginning of the human. It did not inherit a body that already existed upon this Earth. It just came here and evolved from that! Can you accept that? Can you accept that it is possible? For an energy to come here in a form without being interacted in some genetic way with something already existing upon this planet. Well, indeed, that is how the dingo came. And you will find that the tribal Australian Aboriginal people understand and know that and hold their dingo in high regard. However, it is an animal, and by that I mean it does feed upon flesh and so it can be dangerous, but left on its own it does not really interfere with humans.

In some ways the ancient Egyptians have adapted the, shall we say, the image of the dingo and they have made it into a God because it comes from other worlds. And so, everything that comes from other worlds is a God in races such as the Greeks and I could go on and on—but you understand that.

Jacqui: Is it possible to incarnate as, say, a dog?

Jalarm: I would say no. But this is part of evolvement of a race—and rather than say it could be the other way around, that the beginnings of the dingo, for instance, could evolve into a human. This is not quite the same of what you have just asked me. You understand that?

Jacqui: Yes.

Jalarm: And that applies to many of the animals, but you do not return to that. That is a different dimension, and it is not going down the ladder—in ascension, it is going up the ladder.

Dingo in the Flinders Ranges, Australia. The DNA of this species is not shared with other canines

Jacqui: Will Sai Baba manifest to a very, very large group of people in the next few years? Maybe even in the sky or something?

Jalarm: This is something I know Valérie is praying for and would like to see and hear very much, and many people ask it. For me I could say yes, but situations may not allow it. It depends on man or human themselves. If they pray and there is enough light so that he is revered so much that they want him to come, and that he could come and not be attacked—he would welcome that opportunity. Because it is an energy that is not readily held here on this Earth just at this time. However, (Jalarm whispered to us) I think, in time, he could well show himself. But keep that quiet. (We all giggled like children.) For he is appearing at many places at this time and people know this. Some people have expectations and are disappointed because their expectations are not met, but then what is the difference from Sai Baba coming to them individually or coming to them in a large group?

The presence of God in the place of the angels and the unlimited beings come and go all the time on your planet Earth. Many people brush it away as imagination, or just take it for granted. But if everybody wakes up and becomes aware, they would find that there is a presence of a Holy One always around them. Is this not so?
...
You do not answer?

Jacqui: Oh! Sorry! I was just thinking of when I was a child, and yes, I saw an angel and many things like that since.

Jalarm: Then why would you doubt that they are here all the time? (Everyone laughed ... and he left.)

Jalarm came again.

Jalarm: I have enjoyed my morning with you girls, and I wish to thank you for being so diligent in the work that you do with us. And I would say also that there are many who are witnessing what takes place here. I do not want you to worry about this. But there are classes in many realms, and we share you with some of those classes. Does that worry you at all?

Sai Baba appearing outside an aeroplane ...

Group: *No.*

Jalarm: This is good. It also helps for communication to take place at different levels and dimensions because, as has already been said, some of the information is difficult to communicate at certain levels. It helps to bridge that gap. If that makes sense.

When you are gathered here, you are all very linked in consciousness and it is probably difficult for you to remember what has taken place. Therefore, I am very pleased that you do record, and you do remember to read what has taken place just to remind you. Because that helps to 'earth' that information. There is nothing more I would like to say, except thank you from my heart.

It is a consciousness—it is one of universal love and we share that with you, we embrace that with you. And we do love you. Thank you, my girls. Thank you.

We closed the Oracle joining hands and chanting Om ...

Chanting the OM ...

Fifty-Seven

Pyramids

In The Mystery School, we have important matters to continue with. Many know of rumours of Star People and fear the presence of the Star People here on Earth. It is to be understood that many, many Star People do in fact take birth as humans to have the experience of  family love, to know that warmth of being nurtured, loved, succour and balm, and being loved simply for who you are! The Star People who come live human lives and take those experiences and memories and impulses to love with them when they leave the human form.

The Pyramids are the next topic of discussion. We learn that they have an important role for human consciousness and raising of energy levels, as Jalarm shares.

Valérie: Does Jalarm know about the Zeta Greys?

Jalarm: Yes, indeed I do and as Valérie has been learning, and we are very pleased indeed that she has made a connection with these people. For in some ways, her connection with them is very real also. Because many people who come onto this Earth are multidimensional. In fact, they have travelled with many lives, many races, and in different planets around the cosmos. And so, they have many experiences, and these are the ones that we like to work with—they volunteer, and they come and help people and humanity.

And so, Valérie is one of these multidimensional beings, as you two are as well. I hope you can relate to this. In fact, I would suggest that you might like to read some of the books that Valérie has been writing because the energy goes with it and, of course, it does help give understanding.

It is spelt out in the books that the Zeta Greys are here to help humanity. They work in many ways to help uplift the consciousness of the human. As it has already been explained, the consciousness is not a very high level of wisdom and that has been chosen on purpose so that the Star People who come from the 'cold blooded' races that do not understand about love at all—they needed to be in a 'playing field' where knowledge and experience could be absorbed and for it to be not too difficult for those that are cold-blooded to come into a human body and experience, often for the first time, the warmth of love and family. And a caring and compassion of family, particularly mothers—for this is something new to them.

Then there are others who have come in who have experienced that but not quite to the level of the wiser ones—if you understand. You are all here to help one another; there is a balance in all of you. There is none better than another. They are all here to give love, to share love, to respect one another, to assist one another when they can, and to accept the differences.

For this is the way it was meant to be on this planet. So, I hope I am giving you some understanding here. And I can assure you that the world is heading towards world peace. And this will come in a time that has already been given, within an eight-year period, which is not very long even in your Earth terms.

So, is there another question you would like to ask?

I would like to say, also, that the Zeta Greys have a certain amount of Reptilian in them, but this also helps them, the same as you as a human have a certain amount of Reptilian in you. It helps to help those that are very Reptilian from the cold-blooded races to interact—*to* interrelate—and to accept differences and to find consensus amongst all. Does this make sense? (We all agreed.)

(Note, the books mentioned are by Judy Carroll, *The Zeta Message, Extra Terrestrial on Earth* and more...)

Jalarm: The free will exists also, so even though you come with a soul and an agreement to play out a life story (a play if you like), as I have said, there are certain times along the way a soul can make choices. And this is for the learning also. But there are certain times in their lives that certain things with some people will take place. And nothing will change that. And after the event, you will know yourself, in your heart, that it was all meant to happen, and you will grow from that.

Your physical body will grow from that. Because there is not enough love given to the physical body, which is allowing you to progress on Earth and share with others. Share your knowledge if you are a lightworker and assist others who are 'open' to learning. For all have come by choice. None are forced, although some, when they get here, feel they do not want to be here. They also feel they have never made a choice to come here, but I can assure you that nobody is forced to come here. They are given counselling, yes, but that is different.

So, are there any more questions?

Valérie asked about the said-to-exist ten pyramids on the Earth and where they are.

Jalarm: This is something I would like you to ask the Oracle. And yes, there are pyramids on the Earth, and they are not just the ones in Egypt on the sands where they can be easily seen. There are others. And these, of course, have been there for a long time and were placed there by the Star People in the first place. So, would you like to ask the Oracle about this?

Jacqui: Er, what was the original purpose of the pyramids?

Jalarm: They are placed with interaction with various planetary systems from the galaxy, and this galaxy that you are in, and they hold the energy. And from that energy that comes through onto your planet—the atmosphere—and it also allows transaction of consciousness from other planets to take place. It also allows a kind of 'doorway' for visitors to come (and there are many already coming), but you cannot see them with your physical human eye. But you can see them clairvoyantly because the 3rd and the 4th dimension is the same, in the Star People's eyes.

It is only the human that does not readily see it, and sometimes do not believe it. But I can assure you, it is. And those two dimensions are melding now, and you are on your way to the 5th dimension, which is where the wisdom and the love of the universe will permeate the whole of this planet. Then World Peace will exist. Because thoughts of war do not operate at that level of knowledge and consciousness.

Jacqui: Do those gateways or dimensional doorways change? I know you say there is, like, a gateway between the pyramid and the star system. I just think of wormholes and wonder if they can change or are they always constant?

Jalarm: I could say they change, but they are also constant. It is to do with the consciousness of each being upon this Earth—and remember the consciousness is in everything upon this Earth. So, does that make sense?

Nothing stands still, so change is happening all the time. You can see it as a ladder, if you like, and the gentle moving up a ladder into a frequency, which is what a dimension is, and that vibration in frequency operates at a certain speed, if measured. This is what changes. This is what changes the consciousness and raises into a point of light that holds consciousness of love and the Creative Source of All that you can relate to. *Does that make sense?*

Group: (Agreed.) Thank you for that.

An Earth-covered pyramid in Bosnia

Fifty-Eight

The Journey of the Foetus

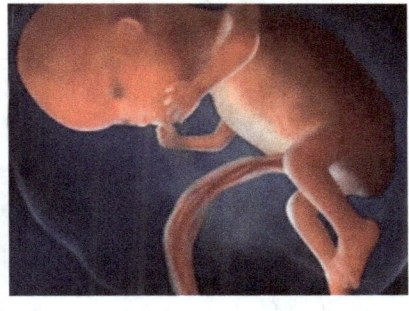

The ladies that make up the Mystery School often share that it is nearly impossible to think or to delve within themselves to find questions to ask during sessions. This is attributed to the high levels of energy present in the Oracle itself and the extraordinary high levels of energy that Jalarm gives out with his presence. We may vouch for this phenomenon ourselves.

Yet, this phenomenon aside, a most important part of the Mystery School is the *discussions* the ladies have once the session has commenced; with the raised levels of energy present, many spirit beings from other worlds attend (we have been told several times—and we have their gratitude for these sessions) and thoughts are floated around them by members of the Hierarchy in order that the ladies pick them up, make them their own, and then begin to develop the material presented.

Collaboration and teamwork—in harmony, cooperation, and understanding—is a most valuable component of the workings of the Mystery School. Often, common-sense is blended with spiritual sense as the participants delve deeper into the work of the school. This provides a most important foundation as we do this day explore about reincarnation, the Zeta Greys, and the journey of the human foetus.

Jacqui wanted to ask about reincarnation. She shared that she had been recommended to read a book written by Dr. Ian Stevenson available only online (he has done a huge amount of work on past lives—there was a group of people in Lebanon who believe you can only be reincarnated as the same sex as you are now). Jacqui went on to share her observations.

Jacqui: But I think from reading his book, and all the research of past lives that he (Stevenson) does, is that your belief structure in whichever group you are in determines what you believe on the other side. That is according to his research.

There were 33% of cases from all around the world of children of where they had been murdered in another life—so they reincarnated quickly, and they usually have birthmarks of where they were shot or stabbed in another life

It is fascinating. Some people believe you don't even reincarnate. So, my question is, *is it your belief structure that decides whether you go to the other side or not*?

After speaking among ourselves, we felt that it was important to know at what level of consciousness we were receiving information. Souls moving to the next world do still hold onto their beliefs from the Earth world—some do not always realise they have died.

Souls who have moved to the World of Light can still hold onto their old belief patterns from Earth—but with further understanding and knowledge of their Soul History, they realise that yes, they do reincarnate back into a different human body, and sometimes into a different race altogether within the Cosmos.

I spoke again, of a book I had just read, written by Judy Carroll and the Zeta Greys, the race who were said to be conducting 'abductions of humans' but goes on to explain how they are really here to assist the human race to evolve and that none are taken without already agreeing to the procedures from our God-Self.

They speak about the 'Guardian Consciousness,' operating at many levels in a fascinating book, *Human by Day and Zeta by Night*. Also, in another book, *The Zeta Message*, they explain the different levels of consciousness as climbing a ladder until finally coming to the angelic realms where they have no abode at all and have no limitations at all.

Just like Sai Baba was on Earth—he could manifest anything, he could shape-shift, he could distant view what was happening around Earth, and he could change things, such as the weather, and heal people and sometimes return them from death.

Valérie: Who is the race organising the coming and going of the souls onto this Earth. Is it one race specifically?

The Oracle: ... (Not a clear response.)

Valérie: Is it different races with one consciousness, such as the Guardian Consciousness?

Jalarm sent the wine glass around in circles, indicating he wished to speak through me again.

Jalarm: I am here, my dear, and you are asking if it is one race that handles the interaction of souls coming and going from the planet Earth—and I would say, no, it is not one race. In fact, there are many races assisting the humans upon this planet. You are also asking if it is the one consciousness you referred to as the 'Guardian Consciousness' and if this is the One influence even though they may have taken on a different body from a cosmic race—and I would say, yes, it is.

And so, my dear, you have vague memories, and in fact you do still operate from the mothership in helping to send souls with the blessing of the Karmic Board ... it is registered and then downloaded into a new little one (human baby) that is ready to be born eventually. A soul can come in quite soon, in the early stages of the embryo, or later. It influences the foetus that is growing and then it comes in permanently, if not before, just after the baby is born. *So, does this answer your question?*

Jacqui: Am I to understand that a foetus can just be growing and not have a soul with it?

Jalarm: The foetus is still growing, yes, as I have said, it is downloaded with a soul—that is an influence that I could describe as a little like a CD, if you like. A very tiny one, but it does have information and consciousness and that is downloaded and then grows with the DNA of the little foetus as it is forming. Does this answer your question?

Jacqui: Yes. Thank you—very interesting.

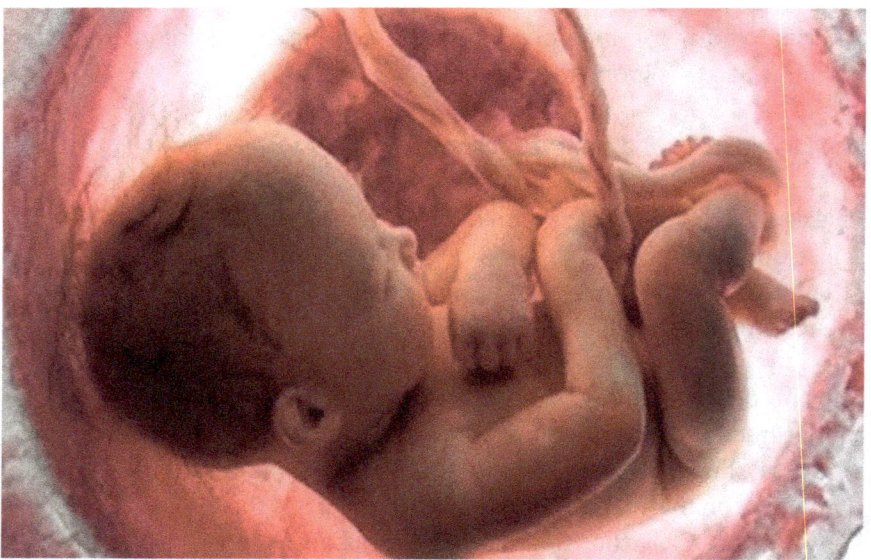

A soul comes to the foetus during pregnancy, often later, and a small CD-like record is 'downloaded' into the soul, which has information and consciousness— this grows with the DNA of the little foetus.

Narayana Oracle has many more articles. I was asked by Alcheringa to stop for a while to do other work. I was to write this book with updated information.

I then returned to work with Jacqui and Jill on 8 August 2021 for more work. Another 'Lion's Gate' opening. We are all in service to the Hierarchy at Andromeda M31.

We have been initiated into the White Sisterhood.

www.narayanaoracle.com mystery school.

PART THREE

Leading to a new world ... and the Star People who want to help us

I was with John, my husband, living in France for six months in 2015. That opened a door where my husband and I were asked to write about past-life memories we had experienced in this life. They are recorded in the book, *Starlady: The True Story of Valérie and Mr Dickens and Other Lifetimes Spent with John Barrow*, Part One. Part Two is the recording of the diary I was asked to write by Alcheringa, *The Book of Love*, while holding the sacred Alcheringa Stone belonging to the Indigenous people who say it came from the stars. It has been safely returned to its proper place in the centre of Australia. In Part Three of the *Starlady* book is the experience channelled from the wife of Alcheringa (Egarina) when she was with him on the mighty mothership 'Rexegena.' Alcheringa, at that time, was the commander-in-chief who supervised the journey and mission to bring the Pleiadeans to Earth 9,000 years ago to establish a strong point of Light in this Dark corner of the Orion Arm of our Milky Way galaxy. Egarina remembered losing her husband and four children, and being one of only ninety of the Star People who survived that attack of the mighty mothership.

The work done by the girls, Jacqui, Jill, and sometimes I, continued for another five years, until October 2020. It continues to be recorded on The Mystery School at www.narayanaoracle.com.

After that, a major lift in consciousness happened on the solstice, 21 December 2020, as experienced at Uluru.

After the major lift in consciousness on 21 December 2020 at Uluru, I was asked by Alcheringa to write yet another book. At eighty-eight years old, I was unsure if I could possibly do it at first, but I was awakened one morning and given the 'outline bones of the book' and advised I had already written most of the work, but it hadn't been published in a book. I was asked to focus on the book and then return to work with the Oracle, Jacqui, and Jill once the manuscript was ready to go to the publishing editor.

So now we are focusing on what happened on 21 December 2020, and how everyone on Earth is being lifted to yet another major cycle of 'Consciousness upliftment', leading us all to the prophesied Golden Age...

Fifty-Nine

Summary

From 21 December 1994 to 21 December 2020

John and I were looking forward to attending our fourth Cosmic Consciousness Conference being held 20–22 December 2020 at Uluru Conference Centre. I had been invited to present as a speaker each year and this year, in particular, there was a big expectation and hope that maybe the Star People would show themselves en masse at Uluru.

When I had been writing the diary, holding the sacred Alcheringa Stone that belonged to the Australian Indigenous people who said it had come from the stars, it was in 1994 and it was when Alcheringa had introduced himself to me. He asked if he could borrow my voice box and began practicing talking and taking over my Earth body's voice box to do so. I agreed, of course. I had already been initiated into working with the Wise ones from other worlds since 1982. He sometimes said to me we were closer than I think. I never asked about that; when you are limited in an Earth body it is sometimes just too much detail when you hear about who you really are in the Star Worlds, and I just felt I would stick to what was happening to me on Earth, and it hasn't always been easy.

In the *Book of Love by a Medium*, in the Summary, dated 21 December 1994, a message was given from Alcheringa, and while he was speaking the energy changed to Sanat Kumara—coming from the highest order. This is now published in Part Two, Summary of the *Starlady* book.

Summary

I have come to understand that Uluru, as an asteroid, came to this Earth at another time before man was on this planet. The action upon this Earth helped to stir up and create and then manifest. The outer Earth itself at that time was going through many changes—time as we understand it does not really matter. The energies that came with Uluru came from another galaxy, from a time immemorial. (Twenty-six years later, we now know that to be Andromeda M31.)

There have been, over the millenia of time that this Earth was taking form, many comets or asteroids that have hit the Earth. They have virtually stirred up the mixing pot, so to speak, and helped Earth to develop. At the time that the rock known as Uluru hit the Earth, a great crater was formed in the land now known as Australia. At that time, I see a different climate existed.

In more recent times, after Earth was inhabited, another massive asteroid hit Earth. This was known as the time of the fall of Atlantis and was almost directly opposite Uluru, on the other side of the planet. The impact sent a wave of energy through the Earth, and I see it cushioning or substantially lifting the rock (known as Uluru). It is interesting that the area known as the Bermuda Triangle and its associated mystery and unstable weather patterns is so close to where that later asteroid was said to have gone down into the sea.

There has been much talk down through the ages about the existence of an advanced civilization on this Earth, that the Star People once inhabited this planet and that a race of peoples evolved on Earth from them. The so-called Ancient Atlantis seemed to hold many keys, but it was destroyed and the Earth and the peoples that survived from that time had to undergo a rebuilding and evolvement with new understanding and allegiance with the Universal Law of God. This is still happening.

A medium known as Azena leaves her body for a short period, allowing a Light Being from the Universal Council of Light to present himself as St Germain taking over her body and speaking through it with much clarity. With permission of Triad Publishing Pty Ltd, who published the book, *Earth Birth Changes*, Peter and Carolyn Erbe have very kindly allowed me to quote St Germain's graphic description of 'The Fall of Atlantis':

'There was a celestial body—an asteroid, and it came into an orbital alignment which was in the evening of time, at dusk when the heavenly bodies that you call Earth, Moon and Venus were aligned. This asteroid was deflected into the orbital pattern of this Earth. It was indeed enhanced through the gravitational fields of Venus and the Moon, towards the deflection in the Earth's orbital pattern.

Now, these scientists upon Atlantis, the technologists, they were aware of this uncommon phenomenon, and they were desirous of establishing their crystalline technology on this asteroid and therefore intended to capture it with, what you term, tractor beams. Allowing it to be brought forth into alignment, to hold still, as it were, and be captured into an orbit of the Earth, likened unto another moon. That was the desire of the Atlantean scientists. They felt their laser power was powerful enough to capture this asteroid body to encircle the Earth and place their instruments of war upon it so the entire planet would be at their submission, would indeed be their kingdom. This was their hearts' desire in that moment. It was a grand one.

There were many who were aware of what their desires were, shrouded as they were. And they counselled them and laboured to bring forth wisdom and love of their brothers, to exist without interference, without dominion. But yet, these entities voiced power, lust and their desire to rule the empire of the world, and, indeed, it was at the threshold of their fingertips, so they felt.

So, they set up their grand instrumentation, which was experimental. It was not, shall we say, a laboratory in nature. Therefore, there was no trial. They felt, therefore, that this was to be a great maiden journey for their new laser technology. The dolphin in that period was embodied in a different fashion, but it was the same sort of consciousness. They came forth and counselled and pleaded with the entities to give forbearance unto this asteroid and allow it to continue its journey in the celestial heavens. They said nay to this and went forth with much confidence and strength of conviction that they were now the new rulers and masters of the Earth plane.

Your brothers, the Pleiadeans of the mountain of Atlas—the Atlantis of your new era to be born yet again—they held counsel among themselves. They understood what was to occur. They also understood beyond the understanding of these scientists that there was to be a deflection of the laser ray, that, when encountering the asteroid, it would be deflected and collide with Atlantis itself in addition to the asteroid. They counselled whether to alert the Atlanteans about this oncoming disaster.

However, they decided to allow the scientists to understand the wisdom about interference and they went forth and brought many of the records of wisdom into the temples of Egypt. The wisdom of the ages encoded in hieroglyphic form, a terminology not understood of your day, not understood of the language of that time, in that era, because they desired not the same occurrence until the wisdom was captured. This counsel was allowed and aligned and so they extended this understanding unto the entity called Noah, to go forth and craft himself a grand ship, a grand ark, as it were, and to go forth in the shining light of his own essence and be patriarch of the new land, to bring the genealogy of the Atlanteans and the Lemurians into the new continents to be dispersed.

This was done and the casting forth of the laser rays, it also was done. It deflected the light of the laser ray and indeed, the asteroid was damaged, it captured the blast, and it brought forth its essence into the atmosphere of the Earth plane in grand fashion.

The asteroid was about six miles in diameter and it was travelling at a rate of about eight miles per second (8 miles = 28,800 miles/h or 46,080 km/h). When it encountered the atmosphere, it lit into a grand blaze. The blaze was blinding. The energy coefficient of it was 18,000 degrees Fahrenheit. The Sun's surface is about 10,000 degrees Fahrenheit. That will give you an idea of how blazing the light came to be upon the plane.

It was a flash that existed for about two minutes of your time, and its explosion into two pieces lasted about the same time. It came down over the Atlantic Ocean and embedded itself in the ocean floor near the Puerto Rico plateau. There are two grand holes there now—about 23,000 feet in depth. This is the impact.

The continent of Atlantis was quite in shock. There was much disarray. They frenzied, panicked, and there was some fleeing. Indeed, there was some flight by ship. The impact brought forth the rubble of the smaller structures travelling behind the asteroid.

Because the impact was loaded with so much heat, so much tremendous potential power, everything it touched immediately vaporized and therefore there was an enormous vapour of gas emission in that area beneath the surface of the Earth. Tremendous subterrestrial power was released throughout the Earth plane.

The Earth's crust was brittle and fractured and all this power created rumblings beneath the surface of the Earth throughout the globe and there were risings and lowering's of the crust in this fashion all over the planet. That is why there were many Atlantises—the submersion of many continents in some fashion or other, in this timing, until the platform of the islands and the continents gave way, and indeed brought forth a grand volcano, which spewed forth fire into the air.

The impact caused a tidal wave of grand fashion—2,000 feet (610 m) in height were the waves. But before they could reach the coastal areas, there was the emission of the volcanoes in that area. There was a torrent of magma spewing forth into the heavens. A tower of light, a pillar of fire, going forth beyond the Troposphere into the Ionosphere. It was of such impact that about 480,000 cubic miles (480,000 miles = 1,966,080 km) of magma were emitted from the volcano of this area called Atlantis. As it spewed forth there was the crashing of the waves and the hissing of the steam quenching the fire and this occurred all over the Earth plane, but in Atlantis.

The magma that spewed into the atmosphere was carried by storms and torrential tornadoes as they enshrouded themselves in mushroom clouds of steam and ash and dust emitted from the volcanoes. What was of volcanic action was set off in a chain reaction. Every volcano on Earth became active to release the pressure from the gases beneath your subterranean understanding.

As this came forth into the air, it was swept into massive clouds that became black as night with amber glow because of the ash and the dust. Massive indeed, and they accumulated their size in tremendous speed. They became the size of continents and hovered low across the continent. It was overcast. It was dark as night. Your land, the Earth plane, your beloved Terra, was shrouded in fog for 5,000 years after this. There was no sun to bring warmth into the land.

The tidal waves crashed into all areas of the Earth plane and funnelled into the glens and valleys and flooded the forests; and then came the cold.

The asphyxiating gases travelled across the Bering Strait and were followed by arctic cold. This continued for 5,000 of your years, until the warming occurred due to the dispersion of the mists, the shroud of gases, dust, and ash. The ash of Atlantis was funnelled through these clouds to all areas of the Earth, so if you, in this day of your time, pick up a clod of clay, it could have been touched by the dust of Atlantis.

The platform of the island of Atlantis sunk 10,000 feet (3 km); not only the land itself but the bottom of the Earth floor that supported the island sunk 10,000 feet. It was a gradual disappearance. This occurrence lasted about one and a half of your days and this translates into about one inch per second of your time.

Now, through the impact of this asteroid body, the Earth's axis experienced a rotational polar shift of about two degrees, and this is still so in your understanding of this day. So, the temperate primordial forests were brought forth in the south, and the pole of north came northward. The cold was of the northern hemisphere.

The pulse and blast, they were two different ones. The first one caused the jarring and rending of the continents from one another. Until this time they were all connected, they were all unified, harmoniously joined within their essence. The impact brought about their severance. They were ripped and torn from one another, and they went eastward and westward, separate. That is where the separate Eastern and Western philosophies came from. That also began the polarities in this fashion, of Alter Ego and Divine Ego, in the manner they are represented upon this plane in your now.

Now, the separation of continents, the continental drift, as it is called, originated from the Atlantean destruction. The second blast went in the opposite direction. It was an echo of sorts and indeed the shock of this created many fragmented islands around the nations because the Earth was brittle in the crust and therefore created a fragmented appearance. The second blast caused the widening of the Atlantic Ocean, for it was much narrower in that day of your time. The wailing and mourning on the Earth plane could be heard many, many dimensions from this one. It was the mourning of humanity for a lost civilization of God.

Then there were the storms, the rains, the heavens breaking open their hearts and allowing their tears to run from the breast of the Earth and allowing Mother/Father principle to mourn for Mother Earth. And indeed, she did. The tidal waves and the torrential rains, in their union, they brought forth much flooding and destruction and damage upon the plane. The sea level around the Earth plane rose approximately an average of about 300 feet (approx. 100 m) worldwide.

Also, the glaciers shifted and broke apart. This was caused in part by the polar shift. However, they did not melt right away in your time, not immediately. It was about 5,000 of your years before they dissipated, when the breaking of the dawn came, and the warming of the temperature. The Ice Age was really the Atlantean age. The present era is the birth of a new land of golden warmth in the understanding of God Divine Essence within the Ice Age of your now.

The ice is not apparent upon the plane now. The ice is within your hearts, and it can be melted and merged with, very much like the snow and the fire melt into one another. The fire within your breast can merge with and melt the ice of another's heart, and that is how you become unified. That is how the manipulators become one with God Divine Essence. Their ice is melting.

Now, many of you remember, but you do not remember. This event of cataclysmic proportions has been engraved upon the hearts and memories and souls of all humanity. But they have forgotten. It haunts them. They have dreams about it. There are relics and echoes and shadows within their experience whispering about it. But they do not understand these whisperings of wisdom. This is brought forth before you this day in your time for you to understand, for you to embrace it, for you to capture what it is that you have experienced, and indeed, enlighten, inflame the world with your new-found knowingness, with your new understanding of what be you and what be your Earth plane, and what be this new Atlantis.

Indeed, to bring the fire of the mountain of Atlantis (Mt. Atlas), and the golden glow of it, to bring it forth for all to see and understand for your own divine example. Burnish yourself with this wisdom and you shall be indeed the refined gold of God.'

End of quotation.

NB: When John and I travelled to France, we felt strongly to visit Notre Dame Cathedral. Just as I sat down on a pew I saw and recognised the spirit of St. Germaine. He walked through the pews and sat beside me, and we talked. He was very happy that I had worked with him and his message about the fall of Atlantis.

I see a Great Crater existing where Uluru stands, but before the fall of Atlantis there was civilization, and this seems to account for the existence of Ancient Hieroglyphics and man made (or Starman made) structures that were later buried by silt and water at the time of the Great Flood. Scientists know it to be an Artesian basin and an inland sea, which is what it was. Because of the climate changes due to the shift in the Earth's axis, it became extremely hot. Water evaporated and left just the sand, or silt, although that table of water is still there, and bores can be put down into it.

It is interesting also that the Australian Aborigines say that the weather patterns go around in circles in the Red Centre of Australia and that has been confirmed by pictures of the land now received by satellite. This information was shown in a museum at Alice Springs.

Since writing the above I have been prompted to sit one morning, realising only afterwards, that the day, month, and year added up to thirty-three, which has always been used by 'upstairs' as a signpost for me—like, 'Take note, we want you to remember this.' Alcheringa wanted to speak more about the new energy that is coming through a gateway on to this Earth, which is lifting consciousness of not only every being on this Earth but every form of life and the Earth itself. He spoke of the gateway coming through the Central Sun and the 'line' of energy and influence known as the energy of the 'Lion'. (I realize now that it was the first opening of the Lion's Gate, since celebrated on the 8th day of the 8th month 1988 and thereafter.)

This graphic quotation above, given to us by St Germaine, ties in with the work that is described below. With the information given to us about Uluru coming from the stars and destroying the dinosaurs and the war that followed…..this also relates to the same information given to us by the Star People about other asteroid bombs being dropped around the earth during the Star War.

It also ties in with the information given to us about the asteroid crashing into the earth, causing the Fall of Atlantis millions of years later in 10,500 BC.

Scientists record that there has been two major upliftments in the area surrounding Uluru at different times.

Is this also what has happened on the other side of the earth?

https://www.sciencemag.org/news/2016/11/updated-drilling-dinosaur-killing-impact-crater-explains-buried-circular-hills St Germaine refers to Puerto Plateau—page 133 'The Book of Love by a Medium'.

Sixty

Visiting Sai Baba

I have visited Sai Baba in India four times over the last three years. When I first went to see him, I felt called and knew it was time to go. My husband was making a business trip to southeast Asia and suddenly said would I like to go to see Sai Baba. I said, well that was strange because I had just heard that day that there was a group going to see him from this area. So, he immediately wanted me to find out the dates they were travelling into India, and it fitted exactly with the times he was proposing for me to be in India and to later join him in Malaysia. So, the day, the month, and the year that I was to meet with the group added up to thirty-three, which has always been an important sign for me and when I did go to see Sai Baba at that time, I was only able to stay for five days.

The day before I was to leave the Ashram, I had been prompted to dress in a white sari for the last blessing and I had received a message from White Eagle that he would send me flowers, and much to my surprise that last morning a young girl did give me some flowers for my hair. Jasmine flowers, which was lovely.

At that last morning I was there for Darshan, which is when Sai Baba walks amongst the people giving of his Light and Blessing. He stopped, then looked directly at me. My eyes were locked, and I stared straight back at him. It was as if time stood still. I later realised he was working on my skin. For no other reason other than he just looked at me, within hours my skin began to itch and react, and as the days passed, my skin became quite visibly inflamed and painfully itchy. The lesions increased and it was as if the disease was being thrown off. It was quite painful actually and it did cover a good part of the body. After a period, it calmed down and although it didn't go away totally, it certainly improved.

Also, on that same trip, on the way out of India and due to plane delays, I missed the plane connection to Malaysia and had to spend the night at Madras on my own. Where I stayed was an Indian-owned hotel, which I later discovered was run by a Sai devotee, although I did not know that at the time. I felt Baba was with me in his subtle form and was looking after me, so I wasn't nervous at all; in fact, I felt I was being prepared to travel in and out of India on my own, which did happen on following trips.

The next day the flight to Kuala Lumpur, Malaysia, where I was to meet my husband was Flight MH 33, which I rather enjoyed as I saw that as a good sign.

Also, just before I left Puttaparthi, where the Ashram is, I had been given a leaf, which the Seva Dals had said was a gift from Sai Baba symbolizing Shivarathri. I thought *how lovely*, but knowing I could not take a live leaf back into Australia, I pressed it between some tissue paper and put it inside a book, and pressed it as a keepsake. However, when I finally arrived home, I found it was still alive even though it was about five or six days later, and I was prompted to put it in a pot of earth. It grew, which surprised me no end. Then another leaf sprouted so that I had two leaves looking at me. All year I watered it and talked to it, but it didn't die, and it didn't grow, it just looked back at me.

Then around a year later my husband, again making a trip into southeast Asia, said would I like to go and see Sai Baba?

I found that the day, the month, and the year of the dates he had allotted added up to thirty-three, and the day I was to leave India also added up to thirty-three. So, I saw that as a sign and that Baba was calling me and so I said, 'Yes, I would like to go,' and overnight I found a new leaf had grown in the little pot. The plant was now three leaves looking at me, which I thought was quite extraordinary.

On my way into India, I stopped off at Singapore and was given by a friend a small photo of Shiva, which showed three small leaves above the forehead, along with three lines and a red dot, which I now know to be the symbol of Shiva. One way and another, I found myself being given a deeper understanding about Shiva and the Shiva Energy.

It was the second trip that I was blessed with an interview with Sai Baba at Brindavan, another Ashram just outside Bangalore. On the very first morning I went to Darshan he gave me the green ring.

It was then that I became very sick, but I understood what was happening. Baba soon let me know he was present in his subtle form by rapping on the table if I didn't follow his instructions. I ran the gamut of the sickness, refusing all medication, for Sai Baba had, in the interview, told me not to take any medicine. I only realised later what he had meant. I had asked him would he heal my skin, but I felt I was being healed on many levels.

Sixteen days later when it was time to go, I was still very weak. I had to return home in a wheelchair and even though I was alone, I felt and knew Baba in his subtle form was with me, for events happened and fell into place so I knew I was being taken care of.

The second year, or third visit, although my husband had said that was the last time I was ever going to India, because he did get an awful fright after seeing me so sick, he said would I like to go to see Sai Baba?

I said to him later I was surprised because I thought he had said there was no way I was going again, and in fact he agreed. He said he couldn't believe he was saying it either. It was like Sai Baba was talking through him.

For the third time I looked again for the signs, and the date I was to go into India added up to thirty-three, and the date I was to come back out again also added up to thirty-three. So, I saw that as a sign, and I very joyously returned to India.

I was not sick this time, but I was fascinated about the leaves, and I seemed to be searching for them everywhere. I couldn't find them. I tried to talk to the Indian people about it and they did have sacred leaves, which they showed me, but they were not the same. As it turned out, this time (although not planned) I was at Puttaparthi for the Mahashivarathri Festival. I started to get the feeling Baba was playing a 'Leela' (cosmic joke) with me and that it was a little like the story of Hanuman (the Monkey God) being sent by Rama's physician to go to the Himalayas where there is a hill between Mt. Kailasa and Mt. Rishabha and bring back a special herb that was the only leaf that would heal the injury Rama had sustained from an arrow. When Hanuman arrived at the Himalayas, he could not remember which was the herb or leaf, so he brought back the whole hill to Rama and Lakshmana. Symbolically, that was the message Baba was giving me. The leaf was a 'soma' leaf, which is not of this dimension. Does he want me to bring back the whole mountain? Somehow it seemed to be connected with the water. I found the leaf was happier growing in the water.

A discourse was given by Sai Baba in the Poonachundra on the day of the Shivarathri Festival. I was there alone, remember, although there were over 30,000 people present for the festival. t could have been more. While I was watching him dressed in yellow, moving about among thousands of people, in the far distance, I suddenly felt his presence embrace me and I was being swirled around in circles, very fast in a dance of Light and Life. Then everything settled...

Baba was sitting on a tall, narrow-backed white chair, which was marked with the Shiva symbol. The symbol was just like the photo I was given in Singapore the year before. Behind him was like a mini Ferris wheel of lights going around and around, which I felt symbolized a star system or maybe the internal movement of an atom.

In front of him was a very simple and clean-cut, huge white desk, which seemed to be made from a strange material that I couldn't help feeling was as if he was sitting on a starship. I was surprised. I expected a desk in wood, heavily carved, and a carved wooden chair as you would expect to find in India.

It was only the following year that I discovered that I might have been the only one seeing the above scene.

The fourth time I wanted to see Sai Baba, I had a deep need to take this manuscript to India in the fervent hope he would call me for an interview and acknowledge the work. I felt it would be like Earthing the information into the 3rd dimension, the information that had been received from another dimension.

Strangely, a group from the area where I live were again going to India, led by Sue, and this time my husband encouraged me to go with them as he was nervous about me travelling in India alone.

There were seventeen of us and I must commend Sue on making it quite clear what she expected from each person, which led to a willingness by all to adhere and become a very unified group. It was obvious Baba was very pleased; he said so. We all dressed in white and wore green scarfs that captured much attention. They were metallic looking, I suppose you could say, but I see them looking really like Light, the same colour of the ring that Baba gave me. That colour, I was led to understand, symbolized the Shakti energy (the gentle aspect of the Shiva energy) that is coming onto this Earth from the central sun and ringing the changes that will lead us into the Golden Age.

Somehow, we all had a presence about us, especially when we stood up to go for the interview in front of 10,500 people. The men said remarks had been made that the 'metal'-looking scarves suggested a spaceship, or space age.

On the morning of 7.2.1995, which adds up to thirty-three, Baba invited us to the interview. There was much laughter. What a wonderful meeting we had with him. There was another Indian couple also called, and the man, enthusiastically telling us about his experiences with Baba, kept cutting across Baba's words. Baba sat back in his chair, looking like God, with his eyes rolled up (playfully) towards the heavens and feigning exclusion, but his eyes looked like bright lights under the partially closed eye lids. Amazing. When he was speaking with us, his eyes sparkled like bright diamonds. It was easy to see he is a Light Being.

There were a few in our group who were quite new to the understanding of Sai Baba, and I think for their benefit he played with manifesting a ring for that same Indian gentleman I have already mentioned. It had an Om symbol on it and then taking it back between his forefinger and thumb, he said maybe he would like a diamond. He just blew on it and before our eyes it became a diamond. He encouraged the ring to be passed around so that everybody could see its authenticity and then he took it back and blew on it again while we were watching and it changed back to the Om symbol; he then gave it away.

He finally put me out of my misery as to whether he would acknowledge the book or not. He said, 'Where is my green ring?' I laughed and he took my hand. I hoped he didn't want to take it back. But he laughed and then put out his hand in a gesture for me to hand him the manuscript. He put it on his lap and opened it. 'The Book of Love,' he said. 'God is Love, walk with God.' Then he said it is not finished, teasing me, of course, because he knew what I was hoping to write about on the last page. I said,

'Baba will you help me?' and he said, 'Yes,' acknowledging that he knew all about its contents and that he would continue to help me. My cup runneth over. I was full of joy.

The changes one experiences in oneself in the presence of Sai Baba are just that—an experience. It is very hard to explain an experience. It is a feeling and a change in perception, it is a change forever.

Twice when sitting in lines waiting to enter the Mandir before sunrise, I saw starships in the outer atmosphere. The first time I thought it was a satellite, but as I was watching, the ship suddenly veered off at right angles, and I know satellites don't do that.

The second time I noticed I had lost a charm in the shape of a 'V' from a bracelet my husband had given me and then I kept noticing 'V's on the ground made from grass or straw. The following morning, I was looking up at the starry sky and there was a 'V' formation of five starships moving quickly across the sky. It was so perfect and as we watched they rolled over into a different formation and went back the way they had come, disappearing out of sight. I felt like a Star lady.

As for my skin, I knew Baba was healing me, the problem is a genetic inheritance like a bothersome virus that exists in a computer—the DNA. It's a chain that has existed from both my mother's genetic history and my father's genetic history. My mother suffered with psoriasis until I was born; it left her after that.

Baba again 'set me up' one day, not long before we were to leave, where he was observing some building extension work near the Mandir. There were 10,500 people behind him and as I hurried to join them, I found myself facing him with nothing between us but a space of thirty feet or so. I stopped in my tracks and wondered if I should fall to my knees, but he just stood looking at me and it was if time stood still. I could not move. Telepathically, he asked me to note the signs around him. He was standing next to a large bell.

This bell cut into the walls at Kariong Tomb always reminds me of the sound of the bell ringing urgently when we had to abandon the mighty Rexegena mothership coming from Pleiades.

1. If I speak in the tongues of men and of angels, but have not love, I am only a resounding gong or a clanging symbol.
2. If I have the gift of prophecy and can fathom all mysteries and all knowledge, and if I have a faith that can move mountains, but have not love, I am nothing.
3. If I give all I possess to the poor and surrender my body to the flames, but have not love, I gain nothing.
4. Love is patient, love is kind. It does not envy, it does not boast, it is not proud.
5. It is not rude, it is not self-seeking, it is not easily angered, it keeps no record of wrongs.
6. Love does not delight in evil but rejoices with the truth.
7. It always protects, always trusts, always hopes, always perseveres.

The First Epistle of Paul the Apostle to the Corinthians, Chapter 13v.1–7

Sixty-One

The Event

(Continued from Summary 21.12.1994.)

What I wanted to share with you was a prophecy we were given by Alcheringa at the same time I was holding the sacred Alcheringa Stone that came from the stars. We were shortly to travel as a group to Uluru to take the paintings of symbols, after writing to the elders for permission to do so at the National Park.

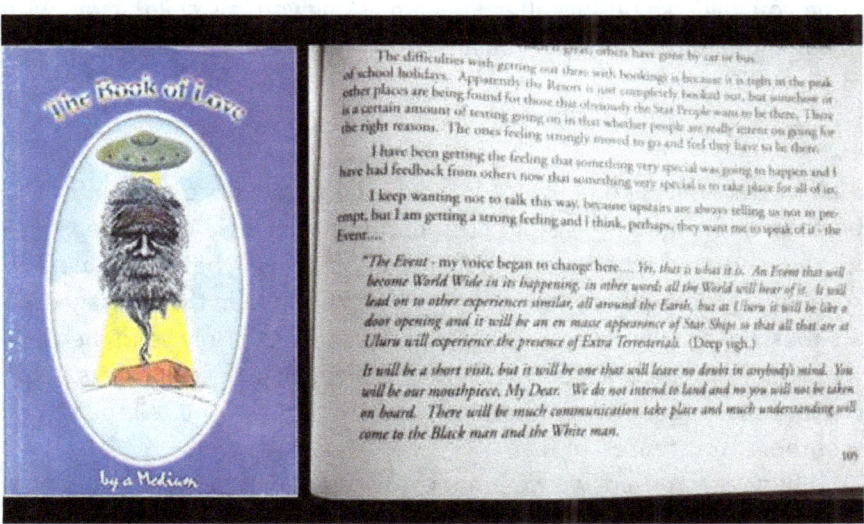

Alcheringa: This information will be shared between you. This will help to bond the two races. It is Alcheringa speaking.

Valérie: I had a feeling, Alcheringa, that some of us may be taken onboard the starship, is that right?

Alcheringa: For some, such as yourself, you will be taken onto the starship in the astral body. You will be given memory so that you will remember all that takes place. (Deep sigh.) You are not imagining this, my child. I am here, and I am speaking to you. Do you not feel the presence?

Valérie: Yes, I do, thank you.

Alcheringa: It would help you, I think, if you do not speak but rather communicate with me telepathically. I will repeat the question, so that it will go on your transcript. You may tell the others if you like. It is up to you.

You feel that you have been misled at times by us, even though we have not exactly deceived you, this is so. But we are always testing to make sure that the choice is the one that you have really made at a deeper level. So, if you wish to wholeheartedly come upon the starship, you are very welcome and we would welcome you with our arms open. I hope you will take up this offer. So, I am asking you, my child, if you wish to come onboard the ship if you are ready to see all as it really is?

Valérie: Yes.

Alcheringa: That is good, my child, that is good. We were hoping for this because this is how we wish to present ourselves, as we really are.

You and the other members of the group will be forerunners in speaking of the experience and to, shall we say, pass on the message. You are messengers. You are messengers of the spirit, the Holy Spirit, because we come from the voice of God. Do you believe this, my child? (Yes.) That is good, that is good. Then there is no reason to fear. And tell the others that there is no reason to fear.

When we returned, we were not conscious of what exactly happened, but it didn't seem to be what Alcheringa had said. We certainly did receive great insight and that is recorded in the *Starlady* book, Part Two. The event did not happen then. There had been no date given and so we still wondered when it would happen.

The Event

---oOo---

Time moved forward and it was finally the fourth visit we made to Uluru, for the 20–22 December 2020 Cosmic Consciousness Conference that THE EVENT FINALLY OCCURRED.

It was a magical time and yet there was a pandemic scare, with some people not being able to come, even taken off the plane when about to leave from Sydney. The organizers adjusted professionally for the pandemic, for which we were all grateful. On the night of 21 December, the Summer Solstice, the National Park was locked, so again, the organizers coped professionally and arranged for buses to take all the guests to a local park at the tiny village of Yulara. It looked a little like rain—but no. Below are some photos of what happened in the sky above Uluru.

The photos show how the colours began to appear. It was breathtaking. Many were convinced the 'turquoise porthole in the sky' was not normal and that it was a Star Gate. Many felt the presence of Star People and it was later reported from around the world that experiences had taken place at the same time. Evan and Steven Strong have collected many reports here: https://forgottenorigin.com

This photo shows the international camera recording so the event could be live screened around the world—just like Alcheringa said, 'All the world will hear of it.'

Camera man on the right... Streaming the Event around the World.

*I briefly saw many indigenous spirits in the distant background, as if wanting to be part of the ceremony.
Then just as we were all watching, two cockatoos flew over the top of us, squawking as if announcing the beginning of something…*

And the Light began to change...

….with the grey sky changing colour, and showing that turquoise Star Gate in the sky.

The colour changed again, feeling so different as if we were on a different planet, and that turquoise Star Gate still showing on the left (the grey sky completely gone).

Thank you, Rufus, for this photo. People began to sing quietly and in total harmony. The sky was now purple.

There was also the conjunction of Jupiter and Saturn, an important time for change.

The Origine elders had their own ceremony, naming Uluru as a Magic Box.
Within the coloured clouds, John and I could see a quarter moon in the late afternoon. When I closed my eyes, I saw an *eye* looking back at me. When I opened my eyes there was the quarter moon, when I closed them it was a full circle. And it kept repeatedly showing that to me.

What was going on? I thought. After the ceremony finished, the moon was seen in the evening sky surrounded by a huge circle. And it looked like a full moon.

Strangely, I had recently read an article that described a full moon being surrounded with a large circle overseeing and blessing the small village where Jesus was born at Christmas time.

Later, when I placed the moon photo—still looking full (even though it was a quarter moon) on my computer—it looked full. It was spinning and moving forward.

So, it was magic. It was dark night by this time.

The circle above was supposed to be the quarter moon—it was spinning and moving forward on my computer.

Then it was reported by Seven Strong that a flash of Light had been captured on camera over Uluru and the surrounding area, which was *not* lightning. It had been predicted by the elders, I think.

Five months later, Dino (the scientist) sent me a photo of Uluru and the surrounding area that had appeared on his computer. When you look at it, begin to look from the sky down and you can clearly see the energy and pattern overlaying the whole environ of Uluru.

Alcheringa advises that on 21 December 2020, Uluru had been 'charged' by the Star People and that it worked its way through the whole of the Earth and was now showing back on the surface where it began. It is known to us as 'Scala' energy, which will assist the raising of consciousness everywhere.

And on the same day—21 December 2020, which was the Winter Solstice in the Northern Hemisphere—the then president, Mr Donald Trump, had signed a bill that was passed in the Senate of U.S.A. for NASA and SETI to release all that was known about UFOs (now referred to as UAPs: Unidentified Aerial Phenomena) within six months of the passed bill. It has been announced with images that there are UAPs that cannot be explained, and the technology used is far in advance of anything available on Earth.

Alcheringa advises that the Star People did not show themselves en masse because of the fear that existed among many people already from the pandemic, and not knowing the future. They thought it was possible that they may cause people to have a nervous breakdown. However, the Star People were there at Uluru. They could see us, but we could not see them. So, this *was* the predicted Event given to us in 1994—and it was streamed around the world, also as predicted.

With regard to the U.S.A. reporting the existence of what is referred to as U.A.Ps, President Obama has confirmed that they exist. And so does President Clinton. It seems Russia is announcing a similar scenario. Also, these YouTube videos are interesting:

About the Soviet Union: https://www.youtube.com/watch?v=DVq7gBH70WE

'Pentagon's long-awaited UFO report to Congress due this month of June 2021' by Mindy Weiberger: https://www.livescience.com/pentagon-ufo-report-coming.html

Well, there are many humans who know the Star People exist—they can see us, but we cannot see them unless they want us to. In this book, they have invited leaders to contact them, and they will show themselves in a Hologram of Light and communicate 'mind to mind.' They will organize human transcribes who allow them to borrow their voice box. They have the technology that can do this. They reside in Andromeda M31 galaxy 6,000 years into our future. They are from the Adonis Race, a hybrid race that has been created looking like humans so that there shall be no fear.

Please see:

YouTube, August 2021, https://www.valeriebarrow.com/?p=5417

YouTube, September 2021, https://www.valeriebarrow.com/?p=5421

Sixty-Two

Personal News for Me from Alcheringa

We were on the plane returning home from Uluru towards Sydney. It was 24 December 2020, only a few days after the Summer Solstice, and I thought I would like to take a photo with my mobile, of the now half-size moon. The window was concave, and I couldn't get a proper view of the moon. So disappointed, I put the mobile away. I was looking at the vast area of flat red/brown land that just went on and on and on and thinking of the story the land must have to tell.

Out of the Blue, Alcheringa began speaking to me, as if he was sitting next to me and asked if I would take a message from him. So, without thinking I recovered my computer, opened the lid, and typed as he began to speak.

Message from Alcheringa 24 December 2020 on flight from Uluru to Sydney

Alcheringa: We are very pleased to be able to work with you, Valérie. You have trained well over the years, and it is now playback time.

It is my pleasure to announce to you that you have entered the local diocese of religion within the outback of Australia. I say this because the original people have looked at all the information they have received from 'upstairs,' or Star People, as sacred.

It is truly your androgenous partner, Alcheringa, who speaks with you now, and I would like you to share this knowledge with everyone—because everyone with a soul has come from an androgenous beginning. There has been separation from that, but the influence is still there in many obvious ways. It will become more obvious to people of Earth as they grow into the layer of consciousness that this knowledge is readily available. There are those on Earth who have already been influenced by that state of being.

The reason the Star People are wanting women to speak up and stand squarely on their feet is meaning they are asked to be firm and not allow men to push them around. We are not asking for women to take over. We are asking for women to demand to be treated equally and respectfully in all the customs and cultures of different races that exist on your planet Earth.

You are all from the same human race. There seem to be differences caused from different beliefs and customs, but the truth is they have all come from the same place in the stars in the beginning.

What man has done to Earth in the first place, man is expected to undo. That 'thinking' and truth done with ceremony, song, and dance for the good of all will heal the Earth and its people. This has begun with the saying, 'As above so below'.

This has begun this past solstice on Earth 2020. Two by two, that is who you truly are.

This is the message I wish to convey—the Star People from the United planetary Worlds from the Milky Way Galaxy and the Angelic Realms from Andromeda Galaxy M31 send universal love and wish to help always. All the humans need to remember is to ask for assistance.

---oOo---

Suggestion given by Alcheringa, the Ancient, Creator Ancestor: Look up the true meaning of diocese and religion.

Diocese (synonym): official seat centre of authority in the beginning.

Religion: the belief in and worship of a Superhuman controlling power, especially a personal God or Gods.

---oOo---

Alcheringa has promised to advise how people can become 'Dreaming' people in a conscious way. It is what scientists call 'Theta' state of sleep, but it can be experienced while awake.

Alcheringa: It is I, Alcheringa, who wishes to talk and share the ancient indigenous knowledge held in their Dreaming state of mind, which scientists refer to as Theta level of consciousness. The Dreaming is the same contact that is made though your soul consciousness, which opens the door to your oversoul, or Godself, and your ancestors. Your Godself exists as sacred geometry—a pattern of design and colour with angle points within the electromagnetic field of creation that encompasses all that is.

Some people on Earth have not yet come to realize their brain is not the only consciousness that exists within them. The brain grows along with the little embryo that is forming in your mother's tummy. The light from the soul is also a consciousness that grows as the soul, that carries the story agreed to in the world of light before it comes as an aspect of the Godself into the human race.

Everyone on Earth has a soul and a story that is meant to be played out from its birth into the Earth race, while the soul is on the Earth planet, and when it is time to leave. In death, the Earth body, along with the brain, returns to the earth, and the soul along with its developed physical being of Light returns to the World of Light. It is never destroyed. Once it returns to its source, it is the Godself—and that is eternal.

The oversoul has many stories. It has lived in many worlds. There are worlds upon worlds upon worlds. There are layers of consciousness that operate at different vibrations and frequencies of Light. You could see it as a ladder. At the beginning, everything is much heavier or slower and divided...and as the vibrations and frequencies increase, the layer of consciousness becomes easier and tighter, or closer together, until the core of suns align and the point of creation is reached. The Centre of all Creation is, as I have said, an electric magnetic forcefield and the consciousness is pure love and compassion.

All living things upon this Earth are raising into this new age, known as the Golden Age.

Valérie is a messenger from the stars who works with Alcheringa, the Creator spirit Ancestor; well known to many of the Australian Indigenous First People.

John is also from the stars. He came as Valérie's soul mate to assist in their mission.

WE HAVE BEEN ADVISED THAT 'ANDROMEDA VAL' AND 'ALCHERINGA' ARE FROM OUR FUTURE AND THEY WANT TO COME AND SPEAK TO OUR LEADERS HERE ON EARTH.

This is the later part of the transcript of what they said, on 6 July 2021, at our monthly meeting. It was recorded on YouTube, along with the full transcript of the meeting:

https://www.valeriebarrow.com/?p=5415

Alcheringa: And when they raise and connect to the raised consciousness, raised frequency, raised energy, and vibration, thoughts of raising a weapon to sort out a problem would never enter their head. And so there would be others waiting to sort out difficulties in, or misunderstandings between, races upon your planet. But there is a great need; there is pollution upon your planet. This has been proved by your scientists. And so, to disagree about whether there's climate change or not, it is not necessary to think that way. It is necessary to fix the pollution. And we are willing to help you with that, and we would like to come and introduce ourselves. We, Andromeda Val, and I, come from the Adonis race that has been created in the past, and we reside at the galaxy Andromeda M31. And we can come. We can appear. We can appear like Andromeda Val appeared beside Valérie's bed, one night, in a stream of light—which is the way we can do it; we can just present ourselves and communicate.

We communicate thought, mind to mind. That is how most of the Star People communicate. So, I'd like you to let your leaders know, because we are not willing to come unless we are invited. It is part of the universal law. We cannot take over and make everything right upon this planet even though the Angelic Realms did create the planet in the first place, from Andromeda and other star beings that assisted in that process.

And there was a Great Plan. The Great Plan, of course, was to hold the divine energy of love and light in this very dark corner of your Milky Way where your Earth is, your planet Earth. It has evolved; it hasn't quite gone the way it was planned when made. And there were interruptions and illegal beings that came and tried to take over the planet. So, there were wars upon this planet also. And so, we have asked Valérie to write about this and we are giving her the information. With that knowledge, we hope that you will come to understand who you truly are and why you are here, and where you are going.

There is no death. The Earth body does return to the Earth. It has a beginning, a middle, and an end, but your soul and your light body continues. You are an eternal being. You are angelic beings from the source of all creation.

So, I leave you with that thought and my love goes out to you. Andromeda Val has already said her love goes to you. And of course, Cosmic Sai Baba, who is organising this, not just this mystery school, shall we say, but also others around the planet. And it will all come together, and all the information will interweave, and it will be like a tapestry of truth for the whole of life upon this planet.

Thank you, thank you, thank you, for allowing me to come. Thank you, God bless you.

This is what our monthly meetings look like on YouTube (and the same with a transcript on my website:

www.valeriebarrow.com

https://youtu.be/pFFIIROgQi8

Other websites are www.narayanaoracle.com and www.cosmicsaibaba.com.

Thank you for your patience in reading our story. We send universal love, and blessings be with you all.

Clairvoyant reading for Valérie Barrow

The Creation of the Adonis Race in Andromeda M31
18 February 2022
Adonis race

(This is the story from the Star People's point of view.)
Calling upon Cosmic Sai Baba and Alcheringa
8 February 2022
From ANDROMEDA

Cosmic Sai Baba and Alcheringa: We are here, my dear, and we are pleased you are willing to write about what happened to the little embryo, which was rescued by us when you experienced a birth miscarriage not long after you were married on 18th June, 1978 to your 2nd husband John Wynford Grey Barrow.

Alcheringa pointed out he has been here since the creation of our planet. He also pointed out that he was speaking from Andromeda and that his eternal self has always been connected to Andromeda, even though he had been working as an Ancestor known to the First Peoples of Indigenous Australia. He asked me to remember that.

Alcheringa and Cosmic Sai Baba both wanted me to write about the creation of the Adonis Race from Andromeda at the bequest of the Angelic Hierarchy from there. Alcheringa confirmed that I was Andromeda Val (his twin soul) and that there had been a separation that had taken place a long time ago. From the Source of Creation where all are Androgynous.

Addressing the story of Andromeda Val, who exists 6,000 years ahead in our time of now (or this era), he announced that as a walk-in, I was her ancestor.

Remember the original Soul/baby was Valérie Judith and was the daughter of Beatrice and Keith born 17 December 1932 ... she lived in that human body until the time of the agreement that there would be a 'soul exchange' (a walk-in, after a near death experience), when Valérie had lived in the body until 1969.

This was the same year my future British husband had come to Australia from Hong Kong. He was unknown to me at this time—and it was a difficult time for me to adjust to the soul exchange at first, not realising exactly why I felt so different.

A walk-in is referred to as a Soul/Light body who has an agreement with a Human in the World of Earth consciousness to exchange souls at a suitable time and take on the healing of that Earth body. It was not the full soul that was leaving. The body, only, was to be healed; this is the effect of previous owner's actions as well as the actions themselves.

Seven years later, John and Valérie met and two years after that, they married in 1978. This is where Cosmic Sai Baba and Alcheringa say they are happy I am willing to write about what happened to the little embryo, which was rescued by them when I experienced a birth miscarriage; not long after, I was married.

The little soul that had been rescued by the Andromedans had to be cleared of all former ancestral emotions and the DNA history had to be eliminated from that particular embryo formed with the loving birth from Valérie and her new husband John.

That earth child, which had her beginnings in the Earth human race, was now free to become part of the Adonis race that was planned to be created for the future, some 6,000 years ahead. That race is now back from the future. This happened to the 144,000 Star People in the beginning and has grown ever since. They have advanced knowledge and skills that are not yet fully known to the earth human race. There are volunteer Star People, who have come to assist the little Earthlings to understand who they really are, why they are here, and where they are going.

The Adonis race is free from the effects of human karma and DNA history, and readily link to the wisdom of those chosen 6,000 years ago. These are now back from the future.

That little embryo then became free and able to become part of the consciousness of Andromeda M31 and free of all past ancestral consciousness in the human race, although she still maintained the image of an Earth human. That was the plan—to create the Adonis race that looked similar to the earthlings—so they could meet and appear as brothers and sisters, and there would be no fear between the different worlds.

In the Universal Law, nothing can just be taken and because this body was allowed to develop on this earth on account of its relationship to the Earthlings and the DNA and RNA of that human race. When my little embryo was taken, it was only taken from all the DNA, etc. needed to develop another race on Andromeda that could survive upon that new world.

Going back to the little one that was rescued ... this happened in quite a number of different places on Earth at that time. Valérie was among the first ... it was a time when the human race experienced what they believe were 'abductions', but at another layer of their oversoul consciousness they had agreed for a full transplantation to take place.

As I have said, in the Universal Law, nothing can just be taken and because this embryo was allowed to develop on this earth because of its relationship to the Earthlings and the DNA and RNA of that race ... when my little embryo was taken, it was only taken for all the DNA/resemblance/image needed to develop another race on Andromeda that could survive upon the world Andromeda. No karma was taken with the embryo. (There is no judgement in all of this.)

This, I understand now, was the meaning of the reading given to me by my friend Helen, under the sign of the Dove, when I was holding the Sacred Alcheringa Stone, belonging to the Indigenous Australians in August 1994.

READING FOR VALERIE BARROW  AUGUST 1994

As I tune in I see you in a state of spiritual enlightenment and illumination. You have been released from the cycle of birth, suffering and death and other forms of worldly bondage.

Your destiny called for the surrender of the personal for the impersonal. This destiny is being fulfilled because of your preparedness to substitute self-centeredness for the welfare of humanity as a whole. It is a difficult destiny to follow. Much self-adjustment was necessary, through suffering and disappointment. You have accepted the worthiness of this humanitarian life path by following your inner guidance.

You are stirred up by an emotional core, high ideals and visions. You are an ambassador for the spirit world. Your refined vibrations enable you to express your fine sensitivity into high minded thoughts. There is a strong urge within you to become a universal sister.

I see you being in communication with many light beings. Because of this you have the need to impact this knowledge while on earth.

You appear to me now, as you are on the Other Side. Tall, slim glowing with beauty, and an immaculate skin. I am now being given to understand that you have taken on Psoriasis, to ease the burden of three other people. Two have already returned to the Other Side. You will not be free of this disease while this person is still on earth. Your higher Self is actually very proud to have taken on this task because much pain and suffering was held away from those 3 persons.

I am being transported now to the Other Side. I see the Hall of Memories - I see you communicating by thoughts alone. I see you "nursing" so to speak those who have recently arrived from the earthly realm. I see several astral worlds. Things are as real as on earth, actually they appear to me to be more substantial because of the extra senses, extra abilities, extra colours and extra sounds. I am being given to understand that there are as many astral worlds as there are vibrations. Astral worlds are different planes of existence, having different frequencies. I am being given an explanation. There are many radio stations all over the world. If those stations tried to share a common wavelength or frequency, everyone would interfere with everyone else. I am being shown that the lower astral is the meeting place for people of different races and creeds and different worlds! It is very similar to life on earth.

As you progressed on the Other Side your frequencies became purer and purer. You are doing a kind of voluntary work by helping those who pass over. You are a kind of midwife awaiting the birth of a new baby. With tender loving care you help them to adjust, you show them the Hall of Memories and you care for them. You also counsel people who have to return to earth. You question them about where would they like to go, what parents do they want and what sort of conditions would enable them to do the task which they plan to do.

Personal News for Me from Alcheringa

- 2 -

I see you working alone - and yet, you are part of a group of 6. By this I am referring to the Other Side. You as a Light Being are a kind of collective Being. There are about 3 more people on earth who come from the same group as you. Three are already on the Other Side. If you feel that you have a deep affinity with a certain person on earth, then it is likely that the person is a member of that group. Although I asked for names to be given - they were not provided. From this the understanding was given that all six incarnated lives contributed to the welfare of one. (Oversoul is given to me). The circle is not complete until the last one returns to the source.

When I asked for your name as a Light Being, I was being given to understand that names are vibrations, and you are known by various vibrations, depending on the various vibrational levels you find yourself in. There is no earthly sound which can even come close to expressing it. I experienced a very beautiful sound but it is like explaining music to a deaf person. However I was given to understand that the "V" has significance: Valda, Vania, Velda, Victoria and Vita were names chosen while incarnated on earth. They each brought a certain quality into your lives.

I am now being shown, that yours husband John works with you on the Other Side. There is a kind of opposition and a kind of total unity present which is hard to put into words. With this brief glimpse - I returned.

With much Love and Light

Alcheringa: I understand this sounds quite complicated, but it is not really; it is just in and out of different layers of consciousness, different worlds, all real; that is why it is said that it is all One—and indeed it is.

Of course, any stories of walk-ins and experiences and understanding of souls is not always who you really think you are. (Smiling.) And so, this is why it is all being shared.

And so, we hope that you can gain something from this information. If not, then just delete it out of your mind. It is not necessary that you know, really. It is just an understanding how the Andromedans were asked to create a new race, the Adonis race, so that they could intercommunicate and present themselves as Earthlings and there would be no fear.

Karma is a word meaning the result of a person's actions, as well as the actions themselves. It is a term about the cycle of cause and effect. ... It makes a person responsible for their own life, and how they treat other people. The theory of karma is a major belief in Hinduism, Ayyavazhi (a branch of Hinduism), Sikhism, Buddhism, and Jainism.

You can read a description of Adonis race on the Narayana Oracle website: https://narayanaoracle.com/?p=1629

About Valérie Barrow (the Medium)

Valérie Barrow's story of the origin of Uluru (an asteroid), and its importance on the evolution of the Australian landscape and animals, is like something out of science fiction movie.

Valérie is a psychic medium and eighty-nine years of age. She has published three books and is an international presenter at metaphysical conferences. She has been initiated many times in her life, enabling an understanding of important creation stories of the Australian Indigenous people and their Dreaming.

Valérie Barrow's life changed at age thirty-seven when she had a near death experience (NDE) during a hospital admission related to a severe skin condition. Since the NDE, she has been receiving spirit messages for forty-two years. Valérie has a genuine interest in passing on her knowledge of Uluru and the rock that has come from the stars.

Valérie's knowledge of Uluru comes from the 'Alcheringa Sacred Stone' (wrapped in paperbark and tied with string, belonging to the Indigenous people). The stone was found inside a cave known as the 'Cave of the Seven Sisters from the Pleiades ' located some 100kms from Uluru. An Afghan cameleer found the stone while travelling in the Red Centre and selling goods from his camel in the early days of European settlement. Another long story...but the stone found its way to Valérie, who lived on a property at Canyonleigh, Southern Highlands, in the late 1980s. She

has since visited the origin of the Alcheringa Stone (Cave Hill), which has a geological composition similar to Uluru, and is a part of the Uluru meteorite trail.

Valérie shared her sacred stone work with her Aboriginal friend, Gerry Bostock, who helped her, over many years, to understand the Indigenous customs and cultures. He confirmed their Ancient Dreaming Story of Uluru coming from the stars. Gerry was an elder, healer, film maker, storyteller/writer, and gave lectures at university.

John and Valérie also recall past lives. These experiences are collected in their second book, *Starlady*.

They received further validation of these past lives via a reader named Diane who lives in Canada, who contacted them, and asked if they had read the book, *Secret Places of the Lion* by George Hunt Williamson written in 1958. They hadn't.

Apparently, it was from a document from a mystery school in the high mountains of Peru—from a people from another world that came here about 18 million years ago.

Diane said, 'Reading about your past lives in the *Starlady* book validates this book for me and will for you." She added, 'It documents all the past lives from the beginning on. Your past lives are confirmed in this book. It confirms your past lives and your husband and more than perhaps you don't know. It's incredible.'

We bought and read the book. And yes, it is incredible and mentioned more that we had been told about, by Alcheringa, but never investigated. It also talks about the *Secret Places of the Lion,* which is the story of *Uluru and the Star People*...and the Lion's Gate.

Mr. George Hunt Williamson is a very clever medium, and reader of the Akashic Records. He is no longer with us, but his legacy is still with us. Thank you, Mr. Williamson.

Personal News for Me from Alcheringa

My husband had past-life memories that are written about in our *Starlady* book. Here is what is recorded in the *Secret Places of the Lion*.

John Wynford Grey Barrow
Amunhotep111. Etc.

Valérie Judith Barrow
Queen Tiyi etc.

Amunhotep III, 1412–1370 B.C. (died 1370 B.C.), father of Akhnaton, Smenkhkare, Tutankhamun, Meriten, Sinuhe; *Zoser, ca.* 3000 B.C., Third Dynasty; *Apepa Aauserra* or *Apofis*, 177 B.C., Pharaoh of Joseph; *Jonathan*, friend of David; *Ramses II*, 1300–1233 B.C., Pharaoh of the "Greater Exodus"; *Plato*, 427–347 B.C., Greek philosopher; *Philip* of Galilee, one of the Twelve Apostles; *King Arthur, ca.* A.D. 500, of the Round Table, of England; *Emanuel Swedenborg*, A.D. 1688–1772, Swedish scientist, philosopher, and mystic.

Tiyi, Queen, ca. 1412–1370 B.C., favourite wife of Amunhotep III and mother of Akhnaton; *Hatshepsut* or *Queen of Sheba, ca.* 1514–1480 B.C., wife of Thutmose II and III and co-regent with both; *Nefretari, ca.* 1300 B.C., wife of Ramses II; *Guinevere, ca.* A.D. 500, wife of King Arthut; *Joan of Arc*, A.D. 1412–1431, French patriot—"Maid of Orleans."

www.ingramcontent.com/pod-product-compliance
Lightning Source LLC
Chambersburg PA
CBHW051834230426
43671CB00008B/954